Special Education and School Reform in the United States and Britain

Edited by
Margaret J. McLaughlin
and Martyn Rouse

London and New York

First published 2000 by Routledge
11 New Fetter Lane, London EC4P 4EE

Simultaneously published in the USA and Canada
by Routledge
29 West 35th Street, New York, NY 10001

Routledge is an imprint of the Taylor & Francis Group

© 2000 selection and editorial matter Martyn Rouse and Margaret J.
McLaughlin, individual chapters the contributors

Typeset in Sabon by Graphicraft Limited, Hong Kong
Printed and bound in Great Britain by MPG Books Ltd, Bodmin

British Library Cataloguing in Publication Data
A catalogue record for this book is available from the British Library

Library of Congress Cataloguing in Publication Data
A catalogue record for this book has been requested

ISBN 0-415-19757-0

Contents

List of illustrations

Tables

Figure

List of contributors

Tony Bowers University of Cambridge, UK

Lou Danielson United States Department of Education, USA

Jennifer Evans National Foundation for Educational Research, UK

Lani Florian University of Cambridge, UK

Michael M. Gerber University of California, Santa Barbara, USA

Margaret Goertz University of Pennsylvania, USA

Cheryl Lange University of Minnesota, USA

Margaret J. McLaughlin University of Maryland, USA

Tom Parrish American Institutes for Research, USA

Diana Pullin Boston College, USA

Sheila Riddell Strathclyde Centre for Disability Research, University of Glasgow, UK

Martyn Rouse University of Cambridge, UK

Judy Sebba University of Cambridge (currently seconded to the Standards and Effectiveness Unit, Department for Education and Employment), UK

James G. Shriner University of Illinois, USA

Martha L.Thurlow National Center on Educational Outcomes, University of Minnesota, USA

Christina Tilstone University of Birmingham, UK

Preface

Governments around the world have become increasingly involved in education during the past decade. Education has been seen as both the cause of and the potential cure for many of society's ills. In many countries, the process of reforming schools to make them more accountable and to raise academic standards began in the 1980s and has continued without pause since. It is an international phenomenon, the United States and the United Kingdom being two of the countries that have continued to experience a series of major changes to the structure, organisation and content of their educational systems.

The agenda of these reforms is primarily about raising academic standards. It is not surprising therefore that students who find learning difficult are not the central focus of many of these initiatives. Indeed, it could be argued that in the first phase of the reforms such students were, at best, seen as irrelevant to policy-makers as they pursued their agendas. Consequently, there are many people on both sides of the Atlantic who are concerned that the reforms may be having a negative impact on the education of students with disabilities and special educational needs.

The major reforms that are affecting education in both the United Kingdom and the United States make for fascinating comparisons because interesting parallels may be drawn between the two systems. Furthermore, there has been a long history of ideas developed in one system being 'borrowed' by the other. In both countries the pace of change is remarkable, but the chronology of the changes is different. Thus, there are opportunities for the study of the impact of change in one country before it is implemented elsewhere (Firestone, 1997).[1]

Many of these issues were raised at the first Anglo American Symposium on School Reform and Special Educational Needs, held at Magdalene

1 Firestone, W. (1997) 'Standards Reform Run Amok: What the British experience can teach us'. *Education Week* 8 October, pp. 30–32.

College, Cambridge University in July 1994 (Florian and Rouse, 1996).[2] The symposium was planned to provide a forum in which issues crucial to the education of students with special educational needs could be discussed in the light of recent changes brought about by reforms at the national, local or school level. This meeting provided the basis for subsequent research that was carried out at the Universities of Cambridge and of Maryland.

As part of this work, another invited symposium was held in Washington DC in October 1997. Again a number of commentators from the United States and the United Kingdom came together to share their experiences and the findings of research in their respective countries that considers the impact of recent school reform initiatives on the education of students with disabilities and special educational needs. Subsequently, the papers presented at the Washington meeting were revised by pairs of authors, one from each country. This volume contains the results of those collaborations. Authors have been listed alphabetically to imply equal contributions to each chapter.

Support for this project has been provided in part by the University of Cambridge School of Education, the University of Maryland and the United States Department of Education.

Margaret J. McLaughlin
University of Maryland
College Park

Martyn Rouse
University of Cambridge
School of Education

2 Florian, L. and Rouse, M. (1996) *School Reform and Special Educational Needs: Anglo American Perspectives*. Cambridge: University of Cambridge Institute of Education.

Acknowledgements

The editors are grateful for the help, support and advice that they have received from family, friends and colleagues. In particular, we would like to express our sincere thanks to all the contributors to this volume. They have been prepared to share their thoughts and professional expertise with colleagues from across the Atlantic and have responded superbly to the challenges of working in this way. We would also like to thank Lynne Tilley and Christine Goad at the School of Education University of Cambridge and Valerie Foster and Lauren Morando Rhim at the University of Maryland for all their support and help.

Special thanks are due to two people who have made this project possible. First to Lani Florian who first suggested such a study. Her experience of policy development, from when she worked in the United States Senate, together with her work in American and British universities, gives her particular insights into what has been happening in the two countries. This book benefits from her enthusiasm, perspicacity and common sense. Second, to Lou Danielson at the United States Department for Education who saw the value in learning from such a comparative analysis. His wisdom is much appreciated.

Finally, we would like to thank Nina Stibbe and Jude Bowen together with their colleagues at Routledge for their guidance, support and patience.

Chapter 1

Introduction

The struggles for reform

Margaret J. McLaughlin and Martyn Rouse

This book is about the journey of two countries and their attempts to improve educational opportunity and outcomes for all children. Each chapter provides an overview and comparative analysis of the origins and evolution of specific educational reforms in the United States of America and the United Kingdom.[1] However, unlike other scholarly endeavours that have chronicled the successes and pitfalls of reform in these two nations, this collection of chapters views these reform initiatives through the lens of education for students with disabilities and special educational needs. This population of students is a particularly interesting and challenging group to consider, given the diversity of their characteristics and educational needs, in light of the call for educational reform that emphasises higher standards and a common curriculum. While the characteristics and legal entitlements of these students often require individualised educational decision making, teachers and families are struggling with how to reconcile the goals and demands of the reforms that include higher standards and more rigorous accountability, while maintaining effective and meaningful practices.

A comparison between the United States and the United Kingdom is useful because the two countries have influenced each other's reforms, and yet their individual policies and practices vary enough to provide interesting contrasts and comparison. Such comparisons are important, not so that we can import ideas from elsewhere, but because they help us to have new insights by providing a different perspective from which we can view ourselves. Comparative analysis can help us to avoid thinking that our way is the only way. More importantly, it can help us to understand who we are, what we believe, what we do and perhaps, what we might do differently (Artiles and Larsen, 1998).

There are many difficulties in carrying out such comparative work between the United Kingdom and the United States. Although the two countries share a common vocabulary, they often place different meanings on these shared terms. Equally, different terms are used in each country to convey a shared concept. Thus, there is considerable potential for misunderstanding. Florian and Pullin explore many of these differences in context, law and language between the two countries in Chapter 2 and the reader is encouraged to consider these issues carefully.

This book is about how special education policy and practice is being negotiated within the context of educational reform in the two countries. There are a number of common themes that emerge throughout the chapters. There are also some very stark as well as subtle differences. For example, both countries can trace their current reform initiatives to the concerns about global competitiveness, curricular equity, and the widespread belief that academic and behaviour standards in schools were too low. These concerns coincided with the contemporary political and economic ideologies of former British Prime Minister Margaret Thatcher and former US President Ronald Reagan which supported deregulation and privatisation in many aspects of the economy and public service. In the education system these philosophies led to demands for enhanced accountability and market-driven policies that would place more power and choice in the hands of the consumer.

In both countries, concerns were voiced by policy-makers from both the left and the right about economic competitiveness and the need for closer ties between schools and the world of business. Similar concerns were reported throughout many English-speaking countries (Kennedy, 1995; Mitchell, 1996). According to O'Neill (1995), government interventions in many countries have been driven by a range of motives including:

- improving national economies by tightening a connection between schooling, employment, productivity and trade;
- enhancing student outcomes in employment related skills and competencies;
- attaining more direct control over curriculum content and assessment;
- reducing the costs to government of education; and
- increasing community input to education by more direct involvement in school decision-making and the pressure of market choice (Ibid., p. 9).

Although the pace and details of the reforms vary between countries, a 'new orthodoxy' has emerged based on the motives listed above. Mitchell (1996) suggests that the reforms are characterised by a common set of features which include:

- choice – providing parents with greater choice of school for their children;
- competition – between schools for students and resources;
- privatisation – reducing public monopolies by contracting out services to private sector suppliers;
- decentralisation – of decision-making through local and site-based management;
- prescription – of curriculum content and assessment systems;
- surveillance – through rigorous quality control procedures using quantifiable outcome indicators.

An obvious difference between the two countries is the role of central government in the defining and shaping of reform. Within the United States, the predominant model of current reform is referred to as 'standards-based'. Despite broad consensus about the issues and acceptance of the 'new orthodoxy', there is not always agreement about specific solutions as the United States is marked by its fierce protection of local control in education which results in the 50 separate states, as well as individual local school districts, crafting similar yet separate reforms. For the purpose of education policy in the United Kingdom, England and Wales share (broadly) the same framework, while Scotland and Northern Ireland have their own systems. Often, similar reforms are apparent throughout the United Kingdom. With respect to students with disabilities, the United States has a decidedly legalistic and uniform set of policy expectations, shaped by the powerful federal legislation, whereas in the United Kingdom the legal protection offered to children with special educational needs is less prescriptive than in the United States.

The problem facing those who wanted to reform education in England and Wales before the late 1980s was that decision-making and policy-making was largely located with the local education authorities (LEAs), the schools and teachers, with very little power being held centrally. If change was to occur, then legislation was required which relocated control of education by taking it away from the producers (teachers, schools and LEAs), retaining considerable powers centrally (in government or government-appointed agencies) and handing the remainder to the consumers (parents) by giving them greater choice and influence over their children's schools. This relocation of power was one of the central aims of the Education Reform Act 1988. This legislation was the most important and far-reaching piece of educational law in England and Wales since the Education Act of 1944 (which ensured universal access to secondary education), because it altered the basic power structure of the education system (Maclure, 1988). It was designed to raise standards by introducing a national curriculum closely linked to national assessment and testing. In addition, control of the education service would pass from the providers (LEAs and teachers) to the consumers (parents) through a series of measures designed to impose the rigours of the market-place on schools. Table 1.1 summarises the major reforms introduced by the Education Reform Act 1988:

Table 1.1 Major elements of the Education Reform Act 1988

- National Curriculum
- national testing and assessment
- publication of test results
- local management of schools
- competition between schools for students
- open enrolment and parental choice
- grant-maintained schools
- city technology colleges

To understand how students with disabilities may participate in the reforms requires an understanding of the context of the reforms in the United States and the United Kingdom, their common origins and intents. Perhaps as noted above, among the most significant is the fact that the principal force driving educational change in both countries was a desire to improve the educational outcomes of students. That is, both countries were driven by political as well as professional concerns about declining academic performances of students as well as perceptions about the lack of relevance or lack of 'authenticity' of much of the curriculum. Evident throughout the chapters is the relative paucity of research related to the efficacy of reforms as well as how students with disabilities are faring within the reforms. One might argue that many of the reforms currently being promulgated in both countries are based more on political ideals than empirical evidence and that concerns about special populations of students may be more subverted to larger national goals. However, as each chapter makes clear, the issues are far more complex and challenge some of the long-held assumptions about students with disabilities and the roles and functions of special educators. These chapters provide the first attempt to document the comparative experiences, perceptions, and evidence of how current educational reforms are affecting one important sector of the population in publicly funded schools in the United States and the United Kingdom. The book documents the lessons learned and explores some of the common as well as particular dilemmas in each country.

The chapters in this book address each of the following major educational reform initiatives in the context of educating students with disabilities and special educational needs: rigorous curriculum and content standards; increased performance expectations through assessment; high stakes accountability for student performance; increasing school and community autonomy in decision making and educational choice. In addition, a final chapter on educational finance has been included because funding special education has become a critical issue in implementing reform. Each chapter is coauthored by a US and UK authority who describes the development and current status of specific initiatives within their respective countries and provides a summary of common challenges and issues. Generally, British spellings have been adopted, except where a particular American term is used. We have tried to define the meaning of terms and/or specific conventions to the extent that they may not make sense to readers from one or the other country, but we have not tried to meld the information into a common statement on reform. As a result, the book provides both rich comparative descriptions of the various educational reforms and a rare opportunity to view the reforms through the different cultural lenses of the United States and the United Kingdom.

The Florian and Pullin chapter presents an overview of the current policy base supporting special education for students with disabilities in the United

States and in England and Wales. It also provides the context for understanding some of the key developments in educational reform with respect to these students. Important developments, such as the recent changes in US federal special education policy as defined within the Individuals with Disabilities Education Act and current developments in England and Wales are briefly considered. The chapter highlights some of the important differences between the two countries, such as the lack of a national (i.e. federal) education policy in the United States and the strict adherence to local control of education. Further differences are reflected in the important role of the courts in shaping US special education policy versus the United Kingdom where the courts play a small, albeit growing, part in policy development.

McLaughlin and Tilstone present the core of the reform agenda in both countries. In England and Wales, the National Curriculum was central to this agenda, while in the United States it was the development and implementation of state content standards. These efforts are illustrative of how the body politic defines 'education'. It is through defining curriculum and content standards, that various political ideals are made concrete. Deciding what are the most important knowledge, skills and competencies that all students must acquire is fraught with debate and uncertainty but, as the chapter demonstrates, is at the heart of reforming education. The National Curriculum and the various state content standards have been fiercely debated and revised as a result of public and professional opinion about the purpose and nature of schooling. In the United States they also reflect changing intergovernmental roles, while in England and Wales, the impact on teachers' professionalism has been great. The chapter also considers how teachers in special and mainstream settings in both countries are attempting to teach a common body of knowledge to the most diverse students within schools. The challenges of meeting individual needs within a common curriculum are discussed, as are the assumptions that underpin such work.

The assessment chapter authored by Rouse, Shriner and Danielson scrutinises the nature and purpose of student assessment in the United States and in England and Wales in light of demands for higher standards for all students and greater accountability for schools. The chapter considers how the methods of assessment that are favoured in a particular time and place, not only result from the prevailing perspectives on disability and the nature of special educational needs, but are also influenced by the legacy of the assessment traditions of each country. In addition, assessment policies and practices are moulded by contemporary social and political pressures. Assessment is increasingly used as a means to influence the curriculum, to motivate teachers and students, and to ensure the accountability of the education system. The chapter considers how pre-existing assessment policies and practice in the field of special education have been affected by recent developments and it examines some of the difficulties involved in creating systems of assessment that include all students.

Sebba, Thurlow and Goertz discuss the complicated and controversial issues surrounding enhanced educational accountability. The drive to make systems, schools, teachers and students accountable for the attainment of certain performance goals is creating high levels of anxiety on both sides of the Atlantic. It could be argued that special education has no history of providing a public account of the outcomes it achieves for the students who participate in its programmes. Yet, public accountability for results could be seen as a crucial aspect of any reconsideration of the policy goals of educational 'equity' and 'excellence'. In order to ensure that curriculum reforms become more than rhetoric, there must be mechanisms that promote and ensure that the performance of all students is made public and has consequences attached. In England and Wales, this means not only the elaborate system of school inspections but also the publication of assessment results as noted in the Rouse, Shriner and Danielson chapter. The primary accountability mechanisms used within the fifty US states consist of public (i.e. state) school report cards of student test scores. Some states and local districts have been requiring that students demonstrate mastery of specific curriculum in order to graduate from high school or be promoted to the next grade. When the stakes are raised, the realities as well as assumptions about how much or how well students with disabilities can learn become starkly obvious. In both countries such public accountability for student performance represents a major shift in how special educators consider students with special educational needs. The focus on an individualised or specialised education often separated from the mainstream created the assumption that a universal accountability system would be impossible. However, as is evident in the Sebba, Thurlow and Goertz chapter, current public policies, as well as emerging data, suggest that, when schools and students are expected to perform better, and given the opportunity to do so, performance improves.

Evans and Gerber discuss what US reformers Smith and O'Day (1991) refer to as the 'third-prong' of reform. That is, increasing autonomy and flexibility in school governance. Within the United States, this has primarily been evidenced through site-based management and increasing the flexibility within public schools to use resources and make decisions about operations, management, and curricular organisation. In England and Wales a similar process, local management of schools (LMS), has been a major aspect of the reforms. It is part of a series of proposals which when taken together are intended to create a market-like system in which schools compete against each other to attract students and resources.

According to Thomas and Bullock (1994), LMS has the following components:

- financial delegation, in which schools are given day-to-day control over their budget and are required to live within this allocation;

- formula funding, in which most of the money delegated is based on the number and age of students on roll, thus creating what is effectively a 'pupil-as-voucher' system;
- staffing delegation, which makes schools take responsibility for the appointment and dismissal of staff;
- performance indicators, intended to provide parents with information about schools in this 'market' (Ibid., p. 41).

The reform of how schools are governed represents an interesting difference between the United States and the United Kingdom. While the embrace of market-driven reforms in the United States is more recent and primarily evident in choice and charter options (see Chapter 6), the notion of increasing flexibility within existing public (state) schools is a key theme in current federal legislation as well as a number of state level reforms. This type of governance reform does not endorse choice or opting out of a public education system but believes that existing structures and power relationships can and should be changed to permit greater community input and the creation of schools that are tailored to a community's needs.

Lange and Riddell approach the topic of choice from two different perspectives. The chapter presents the current and relatively new dimensions of choice that are emerging within the United States: intra-district choice and charter schools. The Scottish perspective views choice in the context of publicly funded schools and considers how students with special educational needs are denied freedom to choose to attend certain schools. In the deregulated educational market-place some children are more attractive to schools than other children, because they bring more resources than they consume. This reluctance of some schools to accept 'difficult' or low-achieving children is one of the unintended and negative consequence of the reforms in some parts of the United Kingdom. Perhaps it is not surprising that some children are more attractive to schools than others, when schools are being held accountable for the results they achieve, and this is linked to high stakes consequences. What has emerged in some instances is that schools are choosing students, rather than parents choosing schools.

The central conflicts surrounding the issue of choice are educational, social and legal. From a social perspective, the desire to create heterogeneous and inclusive schools as part of preparing students to live in a democratic society conflicts with a notion of choosing to be educated with one type of student or in one type of curriculum. From the United States perspective, legal guarantees, particularly for students with disabilities, ensure that students have equal access to schools and curriculum. But these guarantees can conflict with the 'educational right' of a school to define its curriculum and instructional models. When there is not a good fit, who must change – the school or the student? Underpinning this question is the notion of what best serves the public or common good – choice, options, competition or ensuring inclusion?

As Bowers and Parrish so clearly explain, funding special education services is equally problematic in both countries. Issues surrounding adequate funding as well as equity, ensuring that no one group of students lays claim to more than their 'fair' share of resources, are forcing reconsideration of traditional funding structures. But, defining what is enough or adequate to provide education to students with special needs, including in the United States low-income and other at-risk students, is rapidly emerging as a major issue. While acknowledging that students with additional educational needs may require more resources, the notion that the resources should be linked to some performance expectations is, in the United States, a relatively new concept. Further, within the United States, choosing funding options that favour certain social objectives, such as inclusion or a reduction in the identification of at-risk students as 'disabled' in order to receive services, figures prominently within current finance reform. However, most significant are the concerns in both countries about the encroachment of special education funding on general education budgets. This issue is central to many of the reforms discussed in other chapters. For example, a clear issue within the choice and charter school movement, as well as those designed to increase inclusion, is the cost of providing the necessary services and supports to students with special needs. Within small budgets, the impact of special needs students can be great.

Conclusion

The past decade and a half has been a period of uncertainty and turbulence within both the United States and England and Wales as the two governments have grappled with implementing ambitious reform agendas. Neither the predictions of dire consequences nor greatly enhanced student performance have been entirely realised. The reforms have produced outcomes that have been positive for some students and negative for others, not all of which were predictable. As in any competition, there have been losers as well as winners as a result of the market-place reforms.

Perhaps one of the most significant outcomes is that the critical importance of education has been firmly placed within the public eye and has remained a conspicuous issue for politicians. The dialogue and open concerns about education have laid open the competing ideologies as well as the public's hopes for education, and a set of tensions or even competing priorities have become apparent. Some of these include the tensions between equity and excellence; inclusion and exclusion; producers and consumers; individual entitlement and the common good; and altruism and self-interest.

What these chapters make evident is that there are as yet no answers, no simple solutions. There are professionals and community members endeavouring to reduce confusion and negotiate the various reform mandates and mitigate negative consequences of some of the hard-edged market-place reforms. This is an important task, because the competitive nature of some of the reforms has the potential to create losers as well as winners. It seems likely that the losers will be those who are already the most disenfranchised members of society. It is therefore vital that the reforms are not allowed to reinforce existing inequalities in education by producing an educational under-class. If this were to be allowed to happen, it would further exacerbate the problems of social exclusion faced by both countries. This, at a time when there is a growing awareness among politicians and educators of the long-term costs associated with the creation of a social underclass.

On a more optimistic note, there is also a sense of hope and belief among many that the reforms may indeed have focused debate, and that the policy goal of excellence for all can be realised. It is clear that higher student achievement is now a central policy goal in both countries and the needs of students who find learning difficult are now more likely to be considered in policy mandates. But perhaps the most immediate and far-reaching benefits to date are that through the open debates and discussions about the pur-pose and nature of schooling comes both an awareness and openness to explore change and to acknowledge that education is central to a democratic society and that all members of that society must fully participate in the benefits of education and be party to defining or shaping that education. Within that spirit and commitment to educating all students successfully, we offer this book.

Note

1 The United Kingdom consists of four separate but linked countries: England, Northern Ireland, Scotland and Wales. Northern Ireland and Scotland have their own education and legal systems which, although reflecting many of the features of the rest of the United Kingdom, are distinct. England and Wales share a (largely) common system and are governed by the same laws. The chapters in this book refer to reforms in England and Wales, with the exception of the Lange and Riddell chapter which is about Scotland.

References

Artiles, A.J. and Larsen, L.A. (1998) 'Learning from special education reform movements in four continents', *European Journal of Special Needs Education*, 13,1: 5–9.

Kennedy, K. (1995) 'An analysis of policy contexts of recent curriculum reform efforts in Australia, Great Britain and the United States', in D. Carter and M. O'Neill (eds) *International Perspectives on Educational Reform and Policy Implementa-tion*, London: Falmer Press.

Maclure, S. (1988) *Education Reformed*, London: Hodder & Stoughton.

Mitchell, D. (1996) 'The rules keep changing: special education in a reforming edu-cation system', *International Journal of Disability and Education*, 43,1: 55–74.

O'Neill, M. (1995) 'Introduction', in D. Carter and M. O'Neill (eds) *International Perspectives on Educational Reform and Policy Implementation*, London: Falmer Press.

Smith, M. and O'Day, J. (1991) 'Systemic school reform', in S. Fuhrman and B. Malen (eds) *The Politics of Curriculum and Testing*, New York: Falmer Press.

Thomas, H. and Bullock, A. (1994) 'The political economy of school management', in S. Tomlinson (ed.) *Educational Reform and its Consequences*, London: IPPR/Rivers Oram Press.

Chapter 2

Defining difference

A comparative perspective on legal and policy issues in education reform and special educational needs

Lani Florian and Diana Pullin

Introduction

Among the English-speaking nations there is a long history of sharing and exchanging social, political, and scientific information. The political and legal structure of the early United States was both a reflection of, and a reaction to, the English system. Educational practices and theories have been shared frequently between the two nations (Cole, 1989). In fact, the current waves of educational reform of the 1980s and 1990s designed to foster improved student achievement proceeded almost simultaneously in the United States and the United Kingdom, as did efforts begun in the mid-1970s to improve the quality of educational services to students with disabilities. However, while these two sets of educational initiatives occurred almost simultaneously, variations have arisen because of fundamental differences in context, particularly with respect to the underlying perceptions of the nature of education and the role of schools in society. This chapter explores these differences. Comparative study of educational reforms in the United States and England and Wales (as opposed to the United Kingdom, as Scotland and Northern Ireland have their own systems) presents an opportunity to contrast two very similar, yet distinct approaches to the concomitant tasks of providing special education for some pupils while enhancing educational achievement for all. Because the two systems share many common social and public policy goals, a study of the variations between them addresses some fundamental questions concerning the nature of schooling and the relationship between schools, communities and individuals, especially when it comes to who receives special education and how this is provided.

This chapter will look at significant differences in the public policy and the role of law in education in the United States and England and Wales. In particular, it will address various conceptions of the nature of a child's entitlement to educational opportunities; control of education; the obligations of educators in responding to individual difference; and procedural protections for participants in the educational process. The chapter will focus particularly upon the legal and public policy issues in promoting high content and performance standards for all pupils and in enhancing educational attainment and accountability for students with special educational needs in the United States and England and Wales.

In the course of this analysis, there will also be consideration of the differences in language and meaning in the two systems, as these variations not only reflect an opportunity for real miscommunication in any comparison, but also an opportunity to assess how language represents different cultural understandings about children and about schooling. For example, in the United States the term 'specific learning disability' refers to 'a disorder in one or more of the basic psychological processes involved in understanding or using language, spoken or written, which may manifest itself in an imperfect ability to listen, think, speak, read, write, spell, or do mathematical calculations' (20 USC. 1402, 1997). In the United Kingdom such pupils are often referred to as having specific learning difficulties. The term 'learning disabilities' is more likely to be used within the health and social services systems in the United Kingdom to describe individuals with cognitive impairments who have difficulties in adaptive skill areas such as communication, self-care, home living, social skills, community use, self-direction, health and safety, functional academic skills, leisure and work. These difficulties in adaptive skill areas are at the heart of the United States definition of mental retardation. In the United Kingdom, the term mental retardation is considered offensive and would never be used to describe such people.

Policy goals and the law of special educational needs

Both the United States and the United Kingdom share a commitment to the value of education and the importance of governmental support for education; however, the two systems differ both in the manner in which they articulate their commitments to the education of all students and their particular commitments to the education of students with special educational needs.

Rights to education in the United States

In the United States, since the colonial period, there has been an articulated commitment to educational opportunity. Universal access to elementary and secondary educational opportunity became a widespread goal for the nation beginning in the 1950s. In conjunction with the goal of universal educational opportunity, educational issues in the United States are heavily influenced by a set of legal requirements ensuring access to education. Most of these provisions, however, have traditionally been made at the state and local levels rather than by the federal government. The United States Constitution includes no provision about education; however, each state's constitution addresses access to education. Under this system of education, local school districts are responsible for delivering services to children. These services are provided with financial assistance from the state and federal governments in accordance with the requirements set forth in state and federal laws about the way education is to be provided. These requirements govern the qualifications of education personnel, the resources available for educating students, the processes and procedures for educating, and general requirements for the curricular offerings of schools.

Some state constitutions contain provisions setting forth a guarantee to what is, in essence, an adequate level of education. For example, in a case involving a challenge to the state system of funding local school districts, the Supreme Court of Kentucky interpreted the Kentucky Constitution as providing a fundamental right to education which requires the state's legislature to provide for an efficient system of common schools throughout the state (*Rose v. Council for Better Education,* 790 S.W. 2d 186 (Ky. 1989)). The Court interpreted this to mean that each and every child in Kentucky must be provided with an equal opportunity to have an adequate education (Underwood, 1995). The Court defined 'adequate education' by reference to seven desired outcomes of education:

1   sufficient oral and written communication skills to enable students to function in a complex and rapidly changing civilisation;
2   sufficient knowledge of economic, social and political systems to enable the student to make informed choices;
3   sufficient understanding of governmental processes to enable the student to understand the issues that affect his or her community, state, and nation;
4   sufficient self-knowledge and knowledge of his or her mental and physical wellness;
5   sufficient grounding in the arts to enable each student to appreciate his or her cultural and historical heritage;
6   sufficient training or preparation for advanced training in either academic or vocational fields so as to enable each child to choose and pursue life work intelligently; and
7   sufficient levels of academic or vocational skills to enable public school students to compete favourably with their counterparts in surrounding states, in academics, or in the job market.

These seven desired outcomes of a public elementary and secondary education were later embraced fully in similar school finance cases decided by courts in other states, including Massachusetts, New Hampshire, Ohio and Vermont.

Despite the silence in the federal Constitution on issues of education, there are other provisions of that document which have been widely used to compel schools to provide certain types of educational services. For example, the due process and equal protection guarantees of the United States Constitution have been found to require that any testing programme used to determine the award of a high school diploma must be a reasonable means for achieving a legitimate governmental objective and must be fair in its implementation. A Florida statute requiring students to pass a minimum competency test to receive their high school diploma was found to violate the Due Process and Equal Protection Clauses where the state's compulsory attendance law and state-wide education programme granted students a constitutionally protected expectation that they would receive the diploma if they successfully completed high school (*Debra P. v. Turlington*, 644 F.2d 397, 404; (5th Cir. 1981); 730 F. 2d. 1405 (11th Cir. 1983)). Further, students must receive adequate notice that passing an examination is a requirement for receiving a diploma. Such notice is necessary for students to have adequate opportunity to prepare for test, for school districts to develop and implement remedial programmes, and for the state to correct any deficiencies in the test and to set a proper cut-off score (Pullin and Zirkel, 1988).

A test or assessment may deny constitutionally guaranteed due process and equal protection rights if it is found to be fundamentally unfair in that it *may* have covered matters not taught in the schools (McDonnell, McLaughlin and Morison, 1997; Pullin, 1994). The due process guarantees of the United States Constitution have also been found to incorporate requirements of 'curricular validity', e.g. that test items adequately correspond to the required curriculum in which students should have been instructed before taking the test, and the test must correspond to material that was actually taught in schools. The courts determined that the fundamental fairness guarantees granted by the United States Constitution require that a state prove that students subjected to a testing requirement for award of a high school diploma were taught the materials covered on the test (McDonnell, McLaughlin and Morison, 1997; Pullin, 1994).

The protections found in the United States Constitution and in many state constitutions ensure that the educational services provided to students must be sufficient to afford them a fair opportunity to be taught the information and skills required to succeed in a system of high educational standards.

Rights to education in the United Kingdom

Universal access to education is also the public policy goal of the British education system, although there is no written constitution to govern the provision of any services provided by any level of government. The education system has been governed by an increasingly complex series of laws, beginning in the 1830s when the government first began making grants to build and maintain schools historically operated by churches. As a result, state education, or that which is 'maintained from public funds and free to its users' (Sallis, 1994, p. 5) evolved around the dual systems of church and state, where public money has been used to fund what are known in the United States as 'parochial' schools.

The Elementary Education Act 1870 marked the beginning of compulsory state education with the establishment of school boards in areas where there were insufficient church schools. Over the course of the next hundred years, subsequent laws improved and expanded the system of state education in pursuit of universal access. In 1880 school attendance became compulsory and by 1890 elementary schooling was free of cost. In 1944, the Butler Act established three stages of state education – primary, secondary and further, with rules for the transfer from one stage to the next. The 1944 Act served as the foundation upon which subsequent education laws were based. Until 1980, state education was widely understood as a national system of education locally administered and publicly funded (Sallis, 1994). A spate of legislation from 1980 to 1993 introduced the market-place reforms detailed in the introduction to this book. Although some of the early education laws remain on the statute books today, consolidating legislation in 1996 has streamlined much education law, greatly improving its accessibility (Poole, Coleman and Liell, 1997).

Under the British system of state education, local education authorities (LEAs), parents and pupils have certain duties and powers which constitute a 'right to education'. Local education authorities also have a duty to make certain educational provisions and the power to provide others. They have a duty to provide suitable and sufficient education to all children aged 5–19, and an additional duty to provide to children under 5 who have been identified as having special educational needs. Parents have a duty to ensure pupil attendance until age 16, at which age pupils may leave school if they so choose. However, the LEA must provide suitable full-time education until age 19 if the parent or pupil wishes for the pupil to stay. Unlike the United States there is no equivalent to the high school diploma. Instead, there is a public examination, the General Certificate of Secondary Education (GCSE), which is taken at the end of the 11th year at the age of 16+. The GCSE is a national examination that is externally administered, set and graded by independent examination boards. The grades achieved by students determine their future educational pathways such as whether or not they are eligible to attend university. Thus, the process of examination is one of sorting. It does not deny, as much as determine, educational opportunity.

Rights to special education

Both the United Kingdom and the United States can trace the development of a separate system of special education in part to the enforcement of compulsory school attendance laws, enacted first in Britain in the 1870s, and then in America around the turn of the century. Though intended to implement a policy of universal education, the policies of both countries contained

exceptions resulting in the legal exclusion of certain groups of children, particularly individuals with disabilities (Cole, 1989; Sarason and Doris, 1979;
Meyer, 1961). The idea of extending public education to all was revolution-
ary at the time compulsory attendance requirements were initiated. As the
importance of addressing the special educational needs of some students
was slowly recognised, England and Wales preceded the United States in
making specific provisions in law for these students.

Special education law in England and Wales

By 1921, in England and Wales, five categories of children with 'handicaps'
received educational services, though by law, until 1934, these services could
only be provided in special schools or classes (Cole, 1989). In Britain, the
1944 Education Act established a model of primary, secondary and further
(i.e. post-16) education for all except the 'ineducable', according to their age,
aptitude and ability. Classification and 'scientific' selection based on testing
characterised a tripartite system of school organisation so that after age 11,
the brightest pupils were offered places at grammar schools, while others
attended either technical or secondary modern schools. Eleven categories of
pupils with 'handicaps' were established. These pupils were educated under
separate provision, often in special schools. So-called ineducable children
with I.Q.s of 50 or less, were provided for by local health authorities.

   The 1970 [Handicapped Children] Education Act transferred responsibility for these children from local health to education authorities and in
so doing, finally extended to all the concept of education *for all*. Typically
LEAs discharged this new responsibility by adding to their existing system
of special schools which were organised by disability type. Thus, the Junior
Training Centres previously administered by the health authorities became
schools for children who were then called educationally subnormal (severe),
a new addition to the network of special schools. Special schools, organised
by category of handicap offered school places to an estimated 2 per cent
of all children. On average such special schools served between fifty and a
hundred pupils. They were often 'all-age' schools, serving children between
the ages of 2 and 19. Children with learning problems, not educated in
special schools, were considered slow learners. They attended mainstream
schools, perhaps receiving support either in remedial classes or withdrawal
groups. What was available varied within and between LEAs as there was
no particular statutory provision for such students.

   In 1973, a government-funded enquiry was established to review the
education of children with disabilities (DES, 1978). Chaired by Baroness Mary
Warnock, its report was published in 1978, three years after the enactment
of P.L. 94-142 in the United States. Undoubtedly, the Warnock Committee
was aware of and was influenced by developments across the Atlantic. In
fact the 1976 Education Act required the integration of all 'handicapped

children'; however, there was no fixed start date for integration and this section of the Act was never implemented.

The Warnock Report embraced many concepts similar to those enshrined in US law, such as the education of children with disabilities in mainstream schools to the maximum extent appropriate, given the child's needs. It also elaborated on this concept by differentiating forms of integration as locational, social or functional. Warnock also took on the conceptually more sophisticated idea that a special educational need was not necessarily fixed, but something that up to 20 per cent of children might experience at some time during their school years. Thus, Warnock introduced the idea that special educational need (SEN) was about the child's education, as opposed to his or her 'handicap'. Though it embraced the notion of a continuum of individual need from the least to the most acute, necessitating more or less restrictive placements, the Report emphasised education in the mainstream whenever possible, although the law articulates three qualifications to this. The Report was extremely well received by professionals and policy-makers, as evidenced by the incorporation of many of its ideas into the subsequent 1981 Education Act.

The 1981 Act also required local education authorities to make and maintain Statements of special educational need, a legally binding document specifying the additional resources required to meet a child's need. The circularity of the definition of SEN led to many subsequent problems about eligibility. No new money was made available by the government to implement any of the recommendations of the 1981 Act. The government argued that the requirements in the law were merely an extension of existing good practice (Tomlinson, 1982). Unfortunately, the vagueness of the definition made it possible for well organised and articulate pressure groups to commandeer large portions of available resources resulting in big differences in eligibility criteria between LEAs.

Current special education policy in England and Wales embraces a broader conception of special educational needs than is the case in the United States. Unlike the system of special education in the United States, such pupils may or may not have disabilities. The idea of a broad definition of special educational need has characterised special education policy in England and Wales since the Warnock Report was issued in 1978. The 1981 Education Act abolished the eleven categorical definitions of handicapped children. It defined a child as having a 'special educational need' if he or she had a learning difficulty which calls for special educational provision. Such a child is one who:

(a) has significantly greater difficulty in learning than the majority of children of the same age;
(b) has a disability which either prevents or hinders the child from making use of the educational facilities of a kind provided for children of the same age in schools within the area of the local education authority;

(c) is under 5 and falls within the definition of (a) or (b) above or would do if special education provision was not made for him or her.

In the United Kingdom, a child may have a disability or a difficulty or both. He or she may have a disability that gives rise to a learning difficulty resulting in the identification of special educational need requiring special educational provision. Furthermore, just as it is possible in the United States for a child to have a disability that does not require special education (e.g. epilepsy), an English child may have a disability but not a learning difficulty. However, unlike the United States, in England a child may have a learning difficulty though he or she does not have a disability. Inherent in UK policy is the idea that some learning difficulties which may lead to the identification of special educational need may not be the result of within-child factors. Thus, it is legally possible for a child to have special educational needs in one school but not in another. In addition, only pupils with Statements of special educational need are entitled to the type of legal protection available to all students with disabilities in the United States. The statutory assessment and Statement are in many respects legally similar to the assessment, identification and IEP (individual education plan) requirements under US law. However, unlike the United States, many children in Britain with special educational needs receive special educational services without the need for statutory assessment or Statement.

Since Warnock, it has been assumed that about 20 per cent of school-aged children will have special educational needs requiring additional help at some point in their school careers. Approximately 2 per cent of children will have severe physical, sensory, intellectual or emotional difficulties, some of which will remain with them throughout their lives. When a pupil is thought or known to have a disability or a special educational need, he or she is referred to a staged assessment process as outlined in the Code of Practice on the Identification and Assessment of Special Educational Needs (DfE, 1994), and may receive special education services. Pupils with complex needs may go on to receive a statutory assessment resulting in a Statement of special educational need. The actual number of pupils who receive special educational support is not known, as national statistics are only compiled on pupils who have Statements of special educational need and/or attend special schools. As of January 1996, 8.12 million pupils were enrolled in 26,369 maintained and independent schools in England. The Department for Education and Employment (1997d) reported that 41 per cent of the 227,000 pupils who had Statements of special educational need attended special schools. An independent statistical analysis for the same period reported that 1.4 per cent of English pupils aged 5–15 were placed in special schools, while 58.8 per cent of pupils with Statements were being educated in mainstream schools (Norwich, 1997).

Special education law in the United States

In the United States for the past twenty-five years, federal and state statutes, regulations, and court and administrative hearing officer decisions have played a dominant role in the education of students with disabilities (Benveniste, 1986; Chambers, and Hartman, 1983; Hehir and Latus, 1992; Huefner, 1991; Ordover, Boundy and Pullin, 1996). These legal mandates resulted from a civil rights movement in the early and mid-1970s on behalf of persons with disabilities, who had previously been excluded from many of the educational, economic, and social benefits of society (Butts and Cremin, 1953; Cremin, 1951; Meyer, 1961; Sarason and Doris, 1979). In the United States in 1969, only seven of the fifty states were serving the needs of more than half of their students with disabilities (Weintraub, Abeson and Braddock, 1971). To address these deprivations, the United States Congress passed a federal law providing financial assistance to the states and requiring that states and local school districts provide all children with disabilities in need of special education an appropriate education at public expense.

The categories of students covered by federal law are those meeting both of two criteria: a defined disability, and a need for special education because the disability has an adverse educational impact. Unlike the British social model of disability which recognises that individual need arises from a complex interaction of factors, rather than a deficit within the child, the categories of disabilities covered under the United States law were derived from a largely medical model (Minow, 1990). Since the federal laws were first passed in the mid-1970s, the categories of disability have been refined and expanded slightly in accordance with developments in the fields of medicine and psychology. The categories of disability now covered by the federal law, according to its most recent amendment in 1997, are: mental retardation; hearing impairments (including deafness); speech or language impairments; visual impairments (including blindness); serious emotional disturbance; orthopedic impairments; autism; traumatic brain injury; specific learning disabilities; and health impairments (20 USC. 1402, 1997). The law also covers pre-school children who have developmental delays and need special education. There is great diversity among the students covered by the law, both within and across the types of disabilities covered (McDonnell, McLaughlin and Morison, 1997).

The appropriate education required by federal law must be designed on an individual basis to meet the unique needs of the child and be provided in the least restrictive environment. At around the same time as the enactment of the federal law in 1975, each state passed a similar set of requirements. The federal law also set forth detailed procedural protections for children and their families to ensure compliance with the law, including the right to use the federal court system to obtain enforcement of these legal rights, if necessary. The law has been reviewed and amended several times by the

Congress and is now known as the Individuals with Disabilities Education Act (IDEA). Its original provisions are still essentially intact and it continues to provide not only these legal guarantees to over 10 per cent of the school-aged population, but also federal financial support of over two billion dollars a year, which covers about 7 per cent of the total costs of educating these children (McDonnell, McLaughlin and Morison, 1997; Underwood and Mead, 1995; Turnbull, 1993; Rothstein, 1990). By 1995, almost 4.76 million students, or 10.45 per cent of the entire elementary and secondary school population in the United States were being provided special education. Almost 2.4 million of these were students with specific learning disabilities.

As a condition of receiving federal aid for special education, state and local educational agencies are required to provide all children with disabilities free appropriate public education (FAPE) in least restrictive educational environment (LRE), with each child afforded procedural due process protections to ensure that the IDEA's goals were met. The cornerstone of the IDEA protections is the FAPE requirement. The law defines 'the term "free appropriate public education" [to] mean special education and related services that – (A) have been provided at public expense, under public supervision and direction, and without charge; (B) meet the standards of the State educational agency; (C) include an appropriate pre-school, elementary, or secondary education in the State involved; and (D) are provided in conformity with the individualised education program required under [IDEA]' (20 USC. § 1401(a)(18)). The landmark US Supreme Court case interpreting the meaning of the FAPE requirement holds that in order to be 'appropriate', the package of special education and related services provided to a child with disabilities must be designed in conformity with IDEA's procedural requirements, and be reasonably calculated to enable him or her to receive educational benefits. The Court concluded, 'if personalized instruction is being provided with sufficient support services to permit the child to benefit from the instruction, and the other items on the definitional checklist are satisfied, the child is receiving a "free appropriate public education" as defined by the Act' (*Board of Hendrick Hudson Cent. Sch. Dist. v. Rowley*, 458 US 176, 189 (1982)).

Academic progress alone does not in all cases signify that free appropriate public education has been provided. Later court decisions and the federal government's implementing regulations for the law have held that the definition of the 'education' that must be provided under IDEA has broad meaning. FAPE includes special education and related services necessary to allow students to attain desired outcomes, as well as any programming needed to address their supplemental individualised educational needs (Underwood and Mead, 1995; Turnbull, 1993; Rothstein, 1990). Protections under the federal Constitution must also be considered here. In a case concerning the federal constitutional rights of students with disabilities built upon these same sets of federal constitutional claims, a federal appellate court found that students with disabilities could not be denied diplomas for having failed the state's competency test, because their programmes of instruction (IEPs) were not developed to meet the goal of passing the state's minimum competency test required to receive a high school diploma (*Brookhart v. Illinois State Bd. of Educ.*, 697 F.2d 179, 187 (7th Cir. 1983); Pullin, 1994; Pullin and Zirkel, 1988).

Disability rights laws in the United States

In addition to the provisions of the IDEA, there are two broad federal civil rights statutes that bar discrimination against persons with disabilities. The first, Section 504 of the Rehabilitation Act of 1973, provides the following protection: 'No otherwise qualified individual with a disability . . . shall, solely by reason of his or her disability, be excluded from the participation in, be denied the benefits of, or be subjected to discrimination under any program or activity receiving federal financial assistance' (29 USC. § 794(a)).

The second federal civil rights law, the Americans with Disabilities Act (ADA), expressly prohibits public entities from '[p]rovid[ing] different or separate aids, benefits or services [to persons with disabilities] that are not as effective as those provided to others' (28 USC. § 35.130(d)). Title II of the ADA prohibits any state, school district or school from excluding from participation, denying benefits, aids, or services, or otherwise discriminating against a qualified individual with a disability, on the basis of his or her disability (42 USC. § 12131). The Act would, therefore, protect qualified students with disabilities who are expected to master skills expected of all students, but who require alternative or different assessment or method of assessing particular competency.

Provisions of Section 504 and ADA are designed to ensure equal opportunities for persons with disabilities to 'benefit' from educational programmes and activities. These statutes and their implementing regulations provide additional legal protections to students with disabilities covered under the IDEA and also cover students who are not eligible for IDEA programmes. Section 504 and the ADA are designed to cover individuals who have a disability and need some special services but do not need special education and related services. So, for example, students with mild disabilities who only need limited accommodations such as physical access or extended time to complete tasks, would not be covered by IDEA, but would be covered by ADA and Section 504. However, because of the increased state and federal aid available under IDEA, there may be an incentive for some local schools to place ADA or Section 504 students into the IDEA-funded system. There are no data readily available on the students who fall under only Section 504 and ADA, nor on those who might have been placed into the IDEA-funded system when they really were not in need of full special education services.

Under the ADA and Section 504, it is a prohibited discriminatory practice for public school systems, on the basis of disability, to '(i) [d]eny a qualified handicapped person the opportunity to participate in or benefit from . . . [an] aid, benefit or service; (ii) [a]fford a qualified handicapped person an opportunity to participate in or benefit from . . . [an] aid, benefit, or service that is not equal to that afforded others; (iii) [p]rovide a qualified handicapped person with an aid, benefit or service that is not as effective as that provided to others; [or] (iv) [p]rovide different or separate aid, benefits or services to any handicapped person or to any class of handicapped person unless such action is necessary to provide qualified handicapped persons with aid, benefits, or services that are as effective as those provided to others' (34 C.F.R. § 104.4(b)(1)).

To be 'equally effective', an aid, benefit or service 'must . . . afford [disabled] persons equal opportunity to obtain the same result, to gain the same benefit, or to reach the same level of achievement' (34 C.F.R. § 104.4(b)(2)). Routinely excluding students with disabilities from state and local programmes designed to promote increased educational achievement would violate the rights of students with disabilities to equal educational opportunities guaranteed to them by federal law.

Disability rights law in England and Wales

In 1995 Parliament passed legislation intended to protect individuals with disabilities from discrimination, and in so doing, combined the concepts of special educational needs and equal opportunities in law for the first time (Gerschel, 1998). The implications of the Disability Discrimination Act (DDA) for schools and LEAs were described by the Department for Education and Employment (1997) as follows:

- To enable a disabled person to do their job, governing bodies and LEAs must make reasonable adjustments to their employment arrangements or premises, if these substantially disadvantage a disabled person compared to a non-disabled person.
- Governing bodies and LEAs must not unjustifiably discriminate against disabled people when providing non-educational services (e.g. when they let rooms in school for community use).
- Governing bodies, in their annual report to parents, must explain their admission arrangements for disabled pupils, how they will help such pupils gain access and what they will do to make sure they are treated fairly (DfEE, 1997a, p. 1).

Standards-based reform initiatives

Both the United States and England and Wales have made recent commitments to requiring education of all students to high standards of achievement with high levels of public accountability. Again, the two systems are very similar and yet also quite different.

Education reform in the United States

Efforts to enhance student achievement through legally mandated education reform initiatives have often marked the United States landscape in the second half of the twentieth century. Indeed, as one set of prominent commentators has noted, in the United States education reform is 'steady work' (McLaughlin and Elmore, 1988). These reform efforts have most often been 'top down' initiatives from the state or federal level which are usually politically motivated, are rarely based upon scientific or professional evidence on effective educational practice, and are designed to compel particular approaches or outcomes from educators in local schools. Most often these approaches have resulted, for various reasons, in little or no measurable impact in terms of increased student achievement (Wise, 1979). Beginning in the late 1980s and early 1990s, however, the education and policy analysis literature began to reflect a growing view that effective education reform to enhance student achievement would require a 'systemic approach' in which all aspects and all levels of the educational enterprise were jointly engaged in system-wide and co-ordinated efforts at reform (Smith and O'Day, 1991). These approaches were coupled with a growing sentiment within the education professions and among many business and political leaders that effective education reform required the articulation of clear content and performance standards for expected educational outcomes and mechanisms for assessing whether the desired standards were being met. Yet, because of the legal presumption in favour of local control of schools, federal mandates do not exist, although federal financial incentives to reform are in place. States, however, have all imposed 'standards-based' education reform initiatives, in one form or another, upon local educators. Often, in an effort to encourage or even compel reforms, these reforms involve student assessments, usually attached to high-stakes consequences, such as the award of diplomas to individuals or the allocation of financial resources to schools or educators (McDonnell, McLaughlin and Morison, 1997).

The nature of the role of the federal government in the standards-based education reform movement has evolved quickly in the past decade. In 1994, the passage of the Goals 2000: Educate America Act was designed as a voluntary programme of grants to states to achieve the national education goals. The programme encouraged the use of tests or assessments of achievement in the educational standards, with the hope that the tests would play a key role in encouraging states and local school districts to promote achievement on the education standards embedded in the test. The law also required that states ensure that students had a fair opportunity to learn the material in the national content standards (defined in what came to be known as the OTL, or opportunity to learn, standards). However, with the Republican take-over of the Congress in 1994 immediately after the implementation of the Act, the perceived national mood of resistance against federal intervention in state and local affairs quickly led to a revision of the federal law. The now significantly diluted requirements of Goals 2000 enacted in 1996 are designed to encourage state and local voluntary initiatives to use educational standards and assessment to promote education reform, with many of the requirements of the earlier act removed. As a result, deference to state autonomy was increased, the OTL standards were removed from the law, and it is now increasingly clear that there probably will be neither a national curriculum nor national tests in the United States.

However, a federal government role in promoting education reform does exist. At the same time that the federal Goals 2000 initiative was being revised, Chapter I/Title I, a law designed to promote opportunities for under-achieving students and the largest programme for federal financial aid to the states, was under periodic review by the Congress. In its re-authorisation of that law, the Improving America's Schools Act (IASA), Congress required that states wishing to receive federal funding must have challenging state content and performance standards and state assessments of success in meeting the standards. In addition, IASA requires that students with disabilities must be included in the state initiatives in teaching and assessment. Goals 2000 and the Improving America's Schools Act embody the principles that all children can learn and achieve to high standards and that all students are entitled to participate in a broad and challenging curriculum. These principles of high standards and achievement for all have clear implications for the education of students with disabilities, who have often not been well served by the nation's schools.

Shortly after these federal law changes, the United States Congress also rewrote the provisions of the IDEA to pursue the same types of goals. The IDEA now includes a clear and strong affirmation that state education reform initiatives must fully include students with disabilities (P.L. 105-17). The nature and extent of each student's participation in these initiatives must be determined on an individual basis by the team of educators and parents formulating a student's IEP. The IEP must specify the nature of the student's participation and must state the modifications/accommodations that should be made for the student to participate in state or district-wide assessment programmes (20 USC. 1414(d) (1997), P.L. 105-17, s. 101). The recent amendments to the IDEA also clearly articulate each state's responsibility to include students with disabilities in performance goals, in assessments, and in the reporting of test or assessment results with the inclusion of students with disabilities in the reported data (P.L. 105-17, s. 101).

Over the past five years, the United States Congress has moved increasingly towards providing more flexibility to the states and local school districts. States and local schools have been given more latitude to work outside the boundaries of many legal requirements concerning education. In addition, most states have empowered a number of publicly funded alternative 'charter schools' which are also allowed to operate outside most of the legal conditions governing the traditional system of public schools. However, the Congress has maintained a strong commitment to the goal of full inclusion of students with disabilities in education and this social policy goal resulted, in 1997, in a clear and strong affirmation that, whatever choices states make about standards-based or other education reforms, those initiatives must fully include students with disabilities (P.L. 105-17, 1997).

The recent wave of education reform initiatives in the United States have been focused at the state and local school system levels. Federal government guides and supports many of these reform initiatives, and while Congress in 1996 gave the states and localities greater flexibility in determining their own routes toward educational reform, those paths, once taken, are now clearly required to include full participation for students with disabilities. Under the 1997 amendments to the IDEA, the federal law explicitly requires that students with disabilities participate in state and local school reform efforts. Students with disabilities must be included in state and local assessment or alternate assessments must be developed for students with disabilities who are legitimately exempted from regular assessments. These exemptions would only be allowed for compelling reasons and would be limited to situations in which a student with a disability could not participate because the disability bars effective participation or would result in invalid or unreliable test results. The nature and extent of each student's participation in these initiatives must be determined on an individual basis by the team of educators and parents formulating a student's IEP. The IEP must specify the nature of the student's participation and must state the appropriate modifications/accommodations to be made for the student to participate in state or district-wide assessment programmes. The clear presumption behind the most recent statutory changes is a presumption that students with disabilities should have access to the general curriculum, including its assessment and accountability components (20 USC. 1414(d) (1997), P.L. 105-17, s. 614). The recent amendments to the IDEA also clearly articulate each state's responsibility to include students with disabilities in performance goals, in assessments, and in the reporting of test or assessment results with the inclusion of students with disabilities in the reported data (P.L. 105-17, 1997).

Prior to the passage of these most recent revisions of the federal laws, while there were few court decisions regarding the applicability of the federal special education laws to standards-based reform, there were determinations that the denial of diplomas to students with disabilities who had been receiving the special education and related services required by IDEA but were unable to pass a state competency test did not constitute a denial of free appropriate education required under the Act. Denial of high school diplomas where students complete IEPs but did not pass the state competency test does not violate federal special education statutes. However, once a standards-based system is implemented, students with disabilities are entitled to IEPs designed to prepare them to succeed in the system (McDonnell, McLaughlin and Morison, 1997; Pullin and Zirkel, 1988).

Education reform in England and Wales

Until the 1988 Education Reform Act, English and Welsh LEAs had considerable power to decide on the form and structure of schools and their curriculum. This tradition involved a national system of education determined locally and delivered by LEAs, much like the relationship between most of the 50 American states and their LEAs. However, unlike the United States, the system of publicly funded education in England and Wales includes many types of schools which may or may not be within the jurisdiction of the LEA. These include church schools (Catholic, Anglican, or Jewish, but for the most part, not Muslim schools) and voluntary schools which are like the quasi-independent schools sometimes found in New England. Since the 1988 Education Act it also includes city technology colleges, which are a type of secondary school, and grant maintained schools. Grant maintained schools used to be LEA schools until they opted out of the LEA in favour of receiving government funding directly. Schools are funded by various mixtures of central government block grant, private fund-raising and local taxes. Finally, just to complicate the picture completely, English public schools are, of course, private.

The Education Reform Act 1988 (ERA) altered the education landscape. Until this time, education legislation was viewed as enabling rather than prescriptive. The ERA introduced a National Curriculum, national testing and assessment procedures. Though the needs of pupils with SEN were not considered in the development of the ERA, it established in law an entitlement to a National Curriculum for all pupils.

The ERA increased competition between schools by adopting market-place policies such as local management of schools, open enrolment and parental choice. As Rouse and Florian (1997) noted, special education policies which had been developed based on different principles were about to feel the consequences of a shift from legislation and policies based on principles of equity, social progress and benign professionalism to new legislation underpinned by the principles of academic excellence, choice, competition and parental self-interest. Indeed it was not long before the incompatibility between the ERA and the 1981 Act was apparent.

Lunt and Evans (1994) found that the pressure of the reforms led to an increase in the identification of students with SEN to secure additional resources. Lewis, Neill and Campbell (1996) reported that this increase, coupled with greater parental demand for high-quality special educational provision, created additional pressures for local education authorities.

Government commissioned studies identified a number of implementation problems associated with the 1981 Act, including a lack of fiscal account-ability in resource allocation, long delays in the statutory assessment process, vagueness in the statementing process and an increase in the number of appeals brought to the Secretary of State for Education and Employment (Audit Commission, 1992a, 1992b).

In 1993, Parliament passed another Education Act which contained many technical amendments to existing law. The 1993 Act amended the 1981 Act to address some of the identified incompatibilities and problems includ-ing the existing appeals process. It also required the government to issue a Code of Practice on the identification and assessment of special educational needs (DfE, 1994), intended to provide practical guidance about what spe-cial educational needs provision should be made available, when and how. The provisions of the 1993 Act were incorporated unchanged in the 1996 Education Act.

The Code of Practice has a unique status. It is not law, although it is pro-vided for in law. It is not a part of the statutory regulations, though it is related to them. The Code is not legally binding but, by law, responsible agencies must 'have regard' to it. In other words, it is up to the LEAs, schools, health and social services to decided how to meet the statutory requirements of the law, but they are required to do so 'in light of the guidance of the Code' (Foreword to the Code, paragraph 5). Just as the requirements of the 1981 Act were considered an extension of good practice, the Code of Practice was intended to promote good practice by providing a detailed frame-work within which decisions about how special education provision could be best provided for individual children, particularly those in mainstream schools. Thus, the Code sets out a five-stage assessment process, which is similar to the pre-referral, referral assessment, identification, and placement process established by the regulations which accompany P.L. 94-142. The main difference is that in the Code of Practice, 'special educational needs are defined by reference to the quality and nature of support in the school and do not arise solely from within-child characteristics' (Lewis, Neill and Campbell, 1996). Noteworthy here is the idea that special educational needs can be met without a statutory assessment or statement of special educational need, and that education itself is about access not to schooling, but to a national curriculum. The educational entitlement to a broad, balanced and relevant national curriculum has brought about many changes in provision to children with special educational needs.

Many of the practices incorporated into the Code were already in operation in various places around the country. For example, the Code calls upon main-stream schools to name a special educational needs co-ordinator, or SENCO as they are commonly known; however, the idea of a SENCO is not new. Many schools had a tradition of identifying someone to co-ordinate SEN provision from among the school staff. What the Code did was elevate the role by creating a job description for the SENCO which outlined seven key areas of responsibility. These are:

1   the day-to-day operation of the school's SEN policy;
2   liaising with and advising fellow teachers;
3   co-ordinating provision for children with special educational needs;
4   maintaining the school's SEN register and overseeing the records on all pupils with special educational needs;
5   liaising with parents of children with special educational needs;
6   contributing to the in-service training of staff;
7   liaising with external agencies including the educational psychology service and other support agencies, medical and social services, and voluntary bodies.

It is important to point out that schools are not obliged to employ teachers with a qualification in special education to carry out this task, as there is no mandatory qualification for teachers of pupils with special educational needs except for the teachers of the visually impaired, hearing impaired or both. Specialist initial teacher training in special education was abolished in the early 1980s. Although all teachers in training are now supposed to receive preparation in dealing with pupils with special educational needs, the extent to which this occurs is variable. Recent years have also seen the progressive reduction in funding for continuing professional development for teachers. Thus the job description for SENCO in the Code ensures that at least one person in the school will have some responsibility for, if not qualifications in, teaching pupils with SEN. As a result of the Code, schools have had to pay much closer attention to their special education policies. Every school is now required to produce a policy which addresses a series of pre-specified areas.

As noted above, the 1996 Education Act reaffirmed the policies in the 1981 and 1993 Education Acts. In this way the influence of the Warnock Report reverberates in current policy. Today the conditions which qualified the provision of special education in mainstream schools twenty years ago still stand. National data on placement rates show that LEAs with the highest rates of placement in special schools are eight times more likely to place pupils in such schools than those with the lowest rates (Norwich, 1997). Such variability suggests a great deal of LEA discretion is exercised when decisions about the efficient use of resources and the education of other children are being made.

In October 1997, the Department for Education and Employment released a Green Paper, *Excellence for all children: meeting special educational needs* (DfEE, 1997b) on special educational needs. Green Papers are widely circulated consultation documents which precede White Papers, which in turn

outline an action plan for legislative change. The proposals are then considered by Parliamentary Committees before a Bill is introduced. In this case,
the Green Paper on special educational needs was called for in the recently
published White Paper on education, *Excellence in Schools* (DfEE, 1997c).

Excellence in Schools was the first White Paper of the new Labour
Government and highlights many of its priorities for raising standards. Pupils
with special educational needs were not ignored in the White Paper. In the
discussion on standards, accountability and school structures, the Paper
envisions a reconfigured role for special schools as community special
schools which support their mainstream counterparts. The Paper states that:
'Where pupils do have special educational needs there are strong educational,
social and moral grounds for their education in mainstream schools' (p. 34).
Consistent with the proposals in the White Paper which call for expanding
the examples of excellence that have emerged in some schools and LEAs,
the Green Paper on special educational needs addresses some of the policy
implementation problems that have emerged as schools struggle to meet the
requirements of the Code of Practice.

Excellence in Schools is underpinned by six principles and sets out what
the government hopes to achieve over the next five years. The principles
are that:

1   Education will be at the heart of government.
2   Policies will be designed to benefit the many, not just the few.
3   The focus will be on standards, not structures.
4   Intervention will be in inverse proportion to success.
5   There will be zero tolerance of underperformance.
6   Government will work in partnership with all those committed to raising
    standards (p. 5).

The White Paper argues that raising standards requires a balance of pressure
and support to schools and teachers. It acknowledges that support requires
investment and growth will be dependent on the availability of resources
(p. 13). *Excellence in Schools* established a National Advisory Group on
SEN to develop the recently issued Green Paper outlining how commitments
on special educational needs can be achieved against the background of the
principles set out above. The Green Paper, *Excellence for all children*,
affirms the government's promise that its policies for raising standards
are for all children, including those with SEN. The Green Paper calls for
revisions to the Code of Practice, a renewed emphasis on early identification, intervention, and prevention of learning difficulties, and a clear structure for teachers' professional development. The proposals are intended
to reduce the number of pupils who need statements of SEN, as well as increase
school capacity to educate increasing proportions of such pupils in mainstream schools.

The extent to which this dual consultative process will help to ensure that pupils with special educational needs are included in the new reform proposals is unclear. The acknowledgement of special educational need within a call for high standards which benefit all pupils is a promising beginning. The Green Paper adopts a policy of increased inclusion but within a framework of special education. It clearly advocates a continuation of the highly individualised approach for children with complex needs. However, other policy revisions aim to 'develop an education system in which specialist provision is seen as an integral part of overall provision' (p. 44). Whether the actual policies which evolve from the Green and White Papers will be complementary or create new tensions remains to be seen.

Policy differences between the United States and England and Wales

By adopting the terminology and procedures of US policies such as Individual Education Plan, Transition Plan, and a system of appeal (a due process hearing in the United States is similar to the SEN Tribunal established in the Code), both the 1993 Education Act and the Code appear to move UK policy closer towards that which exists in the United States. Yet important differences among these policies are obscured by this use of common terms. Two examples are explored in detail below.

First, the English IEP contains elements that are similar to the American IEP, such as identifying the child's current level of attainment and setting realistic, measurable and achievable goals and objectives within a specified timescale. In England, a child's 'current level of attainment' is not the same as what would be called his or her 'current level of functioning' in the United States. The level of attainment is a specific reference to the child's progression in the National Curriculum. Moreover, the English IEP does not replace the Statement of SEN, which also contains elements of the American IEP. Statements include information about the levels and duration of additional support, or related services, as the Americans call them. Also, it is the Statement and not the IEP that is legally binding in England in the way that the American IEP is legally binding. The English IEP may be binding once produced, but there is no requirement that all pupils with SEN have an IEP. Parents cannot appeal the contents of an IEP; however, inspection bodies such as OFSTED (Office for Standards in Education) may check the IEP against actual provision as part of their review. This is in direct contrast to the situation in the United States where every student who is identified as being in need of special education will always have an IEP and a right to enforce its terms through administrative hearings and court review. In Britain a pupil will have an IEP if he or she has a Statement of SEN; but many pupils who have IEPs will not have Statements. This is because in Britain an IEP can be developed when the pupil is at Stage 2 of the Code, after an expression of concern about the child has been registered but before external specialist support such as that provided by a special education support teacher, social worker or educational psychologist is needed.

Clearly, use of the term IEP obscures important differences between the British and American systems which is further complicated by the volume of US research on the subject. Writing recently in the widely circulated *British Journal of Special Education,* Cooper (1996) noted the legal distinction between the IEPs in the United States and England and, in the absence of literature on British IEPs, went on to identify issues of quality and problems of implementation that were drawn largely from the United States literature. By reporting the problems identified by American researchers, Cooper anticipates problems that may or may not be relevant in the United Kingdom. Perhaps British IEPs by virtue of their status as non-legally binding documents will be more flexible and useful to classroom teachers than the American IEP.

The system of appeal set out in the 1993 Education Act will be familiar yet different to the professional American audience. The 1993 Act established an independent judicial body known as a Tribunal, with authority to resolve disputes about how and where to meet SEN. Appeals against decisions made by LEAs are heard by a panel of three people chaired by an attorney. Tribunal members meet the same standard of impartiality required of a hearing officer in the United States. Any appeal to the Tribunal is expected to be resolved within five months, and there are specific timelines for various notifications and responses. The main difference between the due process procedures in P.L. 94-142 and the 1993 Education Act is that there are limitations on the issues which can be brought to the Tribunal. Unlike the United States where the parent or the LEA can request a hearing to address a dispute arising from any aspect of the provision of an appropriate education, only six decisions made by LEAs give parents a right of appeal. These are:

1   a decision not to make a formal assessment,
2   a decision not to make a Statement of SEN,
3   the contents of a Statement in so far as they relate to the child's needs and the provision to be made to meet those needs, including the school named in the Statement or the failure to name a school,
4   a decision not to reassess a child's needs,
5   a decision not to change the name of a school at which the child is placed, and
6   a decision to cease to maintain a Statement (Special Educational Needs Tribunal Annual Report, 1994–95, p. 6).

A parent cannot appeal to the Tribunal if he or she is unhappy about other decisions. The Department for Education booklet which outlines the appeal procedures for parents makes this quite clear. It states that one 'cannot appeal to the tribunal against the way the LEA conducted an assessment, or the length of time it took; the way the LEA are arranging to provide the help set out in [the] child's Statement; the way the school is meeting [the] child's needs; or the description in the Statement of [the] child's non-educational needs or how the LEA plan to meet those needs' (p. 4). Moreover, the parental right of appeal, when it does exist, exists only for a two-month period from the time of the LEA decision which gave rise to the right of appeal. Although LEAs are required to notify parents of the right to appeal, they are not required to tell them about the two-month timeline.

The Tribunal will have regard to the Code of Practice when it makes decisions. The Special Needs Tribunal issues an annual report which summarises types of appeal by various variables such as the nature of SEN, outcome, and distribution of appeals by LEA. A *Digest of Decisions* which reviews selected representative cases is published quarterly. In recent years, the largest percentage of appeals has been against the contents of a Statement, followed by a refusal to assess. The available data on appeal outcomes suggest that appeals are likely to be upheld when the issue is about issuing a Statement of special educational need, or its contents. When the issue is about placement, appeals are more likely to be dismissed. It is difficult to interpret the extent to which the issues brought to the Tribunal reflect the actual concerns of parents because appeals can only be made on the basis of the six issues outlined above.

While there is no right to schooling in England and Wales, and a right to education in only some states in the United States, the current wave of standards-based reform initiatives has the effect of creating a definition of, if not a right to, an expected education, either the education set forth in the United Kingdom's National Curriculum, in US state content standards or the content measured on a high-stakes test or assessment. For most US students with disabilities, content and performance standards will, in effect, define much of the content of their IEPs. The provisions of state and federal special education law, coupled with the federal constitutional right to an opportunity to learn, will become potentially powerful tools to ensure the delivery of a particular educational content to these students. In the United Kingdom the entitlement to a broad, balanced and relevant national curriculum now drives the curriculum for pupils receiving special education provision. The statutory inspections process ensures a minimum standard is met or schools are closed. Though the United States has no explicit national curriculum, nor testing or assessment procedures, states continue to look to one another and to professional associations for assistance during the rapid implementation of reforms; as a result, many educational and accountability approaches are copied over and over again. Similarly, a relatively small number of testing/assessment contractors are available to assist with implementation and, inevitably, approaches are replicated from locale to locale in the interests of economy and efficiency.

There is a different tradition of individual rights in Britain. This difference between the United Kingdom and the United States in the concept of rights was commented upon by Oliver when, in an interview about the history of the disability movement in the United Kingdom, he noted:

> there has always been a distinction between what we mean by IL [Independent Living] in Britain and what they mean in the States. Independent Living in America is organised around self-empowerment, individual rights and the idea that in the land of the free and the home of the brave (all that crap) individuals, if they are given access under the law and the constitution, can be independent. In Britain IL entails collective responsibilities for each other and a collective organisation. Independent Living is not about self-empowerment; it is about individuals helping one another.
>
> (Campbell and Oliver, 1996, p. 204)

The distinction between concepts of social justice predicated on individual rights versus those which are based on more communitarian values has been explored by Christensen and Dorn (1997). Their review found limitations on both views when applied to special education. Instead they call on the field to adopt a more robust view of social justice to underpin policy.

Within the United Kingdom there is no individual right to schooling as such. There is a statutory duty placed on LEAs to provide sufficient school places, an entitlement to the National Curriculum, and a requirement on parents to ensure attendance. The altered relationship between the LEA and the school which resulted from the enactment of the 1988 Education Reform Act has created a situation where LEAs still have the responsibility for statemented pupils with SEN, without the authority to require schools to enrol them. The relationship between the LEA and the school is further complicated by many schools' status as grant maintained. A grant maintained school is one that has opted out of the LEA and, though it may still be in its jurisdiction, it receives its funding direct from central government, rather than through the LEA.

British systems have traditionally been based on more communitarian views of social justice than have those in America. The changes during the Thatcher years stressed the rights of the individuals over communitarian views about the public good. Education is just one area of public policy that has felt the consequences of these changes and it is now struggling with a series of dilemmas and tensions as a result. But as Lindsay (1977, p. 26) has noted: 'there will always be a tension between lack of resources and aspirations, and between the need to distribute resources to those who need extra to achieve equality of opportunity and those for whom extra resources will have a markedly enhanced effect on producing excellence.' It is not suggested that a return to the old order is necessary, or even desirable. However, a new way of resolving the tensions is required.

Conclusion – lessons learned – a way ahead?

This chapter has examined the legal and public policy frameworks for standards-based education reform initiatives and for the education of students with disabilities and special educational needs in the United States and England and Wales. It has addressed the content and control of education, the role of schools in standards-based education and in the education of students with disabilities, and the public policy and legal issues for students in both systems. The many issues concerning implementation of the current standards-based education reform initiatives in both the United States and in England and Wales reflect shifting, sometimes conflicting, perspectives and policies concerning jurisdictional control and influence over educational decision-making, and the considerable ambiguity over the nature and role of schools.

In the United States, recent efforts have reflected a desire for enhanced accountability for the performance of all students, including students with disabilities. At the same time, there is now an effort to move away from categorising and labelling students with disabilities, to a system of making federal support available for the proportions of students needing extra educational services. This increased recognition of responsibility for the performance of all students, coupled with a de-emphasis on the use of structured systems of labelling disabilities, suggests both a broader perspective on the necessity for successfully educating all students and a willingness to undertake new approaches to pursuing this goal.

From the United Kingdom, Rouse and Florian (1997) have suggested that the tensions produced by the conflicting policies of education for all and standards-based reforms can be addressed by interventions which mediate those tensions. For example, school improvement initiatives have a mediating effect on the tension between excellence and equity. Parent–professional partnerships mediate the tension between producers and consumers of educational services. Recent calls in England for a relational theory of social justice (e.g. Christensen and Dorn, 1997) which acknowledges the complex nature of disability and the history of discrimination faced by people with disabilities could potentially mediate the difference between the individualistic and communitarian philosophies which underpin special education policy in both the United States and the United Kingdom. Such an approach might help to move special education policy in both the United States and the United Kingdom beyond the limitations inherent in their respective views and toward a universal education policy which recognises that we all are at risk of disability. For example, future education policies could be built around the possibility that what appears marginal (i.e. a disability or a learning difficulty) is actually a fundamental aspect of the human condition, in that a disability or disabling condition can be acquired by anyone at any time. Zola (1989) showed how this kind of reorientation in thinking about disability could be applied in the areas of housing, transportation and employ-ment policy. An application of this reorientation of thinking about disabil-ity to education would require policies which acknowledge that the needs and abilities of all pupils are not static but constantly changing. Such an acknowledgement would permit the much-needed flexibility required for the building of human capital in a world where both the incidence and nature of disability are subject to change.

References

Audit Commission (1992a) *Getting in on the Act*, London: HMSO.
—— (1992b) *Getting the Act Together*, London: HMSO.
Benveniste, G. (1986) 'Implementation and intervention strategies: The case of 94–142', in D. Kirp and D. Jensen (eds) *School Days, Rule Days: The Legaliza-tion and Regulation of Education* (pp. 146–163), Philadelphia: Falmer Press.
Butts, R.F. and Cremin, L. (1953) *A History of Education in American Culture*, New York: Holt.
Campbell, J. and Oliver, M. (1996) *Disability Politics: Understanding our Past, Changing our Future*, London: Routledge.
Chambers, J.G. and Hartman, W.T. (eds) (1983) *Special Education Policies: Their History, Implementation and Finance*, Philadelphia: Temple University Press.
Christensen, C.A. and Dorn, S. (1997) 'Competing notions of social justice and contradictions in special education reform', *The Journal of Special Education*, 31,2: 181–198.
Cole, T. (1989) *A Part or Apart? Integration and the Growth of British Special Educa-tion*, Milton Keynes: Open University Press.
Cooper, P. (1996) 'Are individual education plans a waste of paper?', *British Journal of Special Education*, 23,3: 115–119.
Cremin, L. (1951) *The American Common School: An Historic Conception*, New York: Teachers College, Columbia University.
Department for Education (DfE) (1994) *Code of Practice on the Identification and Assessment of Special Educational Needs*, London: The Stationery Office.
Department for Education and Employment (DfEE) (1996) *Education Act 1996*, London: HMSO.
—— (1997a) *Circular 3/97: What the Disability Discrimination Act Means for Schools and LEAs*, London: Her Majesty's Stationery Office.
—— (1997b) *Excellence for all children: Meeting Special Educational Needs*, London: The Stationery Office.
—— (1997c) *Excellence in Schools*, London: The Stationery Office.
—— (1997d) *Statistics of Education: Schools in England, 1996*, London: The Stationery Office.
Department for Education and Science (DES) (1978) *Special educational needs. Report of the committee of enquiry into the education of handicapped children and young people*, London: HMSO.
Gerschel, L. (1998) 'Equal opportunities and special educational needs', in C. Tilstone, L. Florian and R. Rose (eds) *Promoting Inclusive Practice* (pp. 52–67), London: Routledge.

Hehir, T. and Latus, T. (eds) (1992) *Special Education at the Century's End: Evolution of Theory and Practice Since 1970*, Cambridge, MA: Harvard Education Review.

Huefner, D.S. (1991) 'Judicial review of the special education program requirements under the Education for All Handicapped Children Act: Where have we been and where should we be going?', *Harvard Journal Of Law And Public Policy*, 14,2: 483–514.

Lewis, A., Neill, S.R. St. J. and Campbell, R.J. (1996) *The Implementation of the Code of Practice in Primary and Secondary Schools: A National Survey of Perceptions of Special Educational Needs Co-ordinators*, Coventry: The University of Warwick.

Lindsay, G. (1997) 'Values and legislation', in G. Lindsay and D. Thompson (eds) *Values into Practice in Special Education* (pp. 15–26), London: David Fulton.

Lunt, I. and Evans, J. (1994) *Allocating Resources for Special Educational Needs Provision* (Special Educational Needs Policy Option Group), Stafford: NASEN Enterprises.

McDonnell, L., McLaughlin, M. and Morison, P. (eds) (1997) *Educating One and All: Students with Disabilities and Standards-Based Reform*, Washington, DC: National Academy Press.

McLaughlin, M. and Elmore, R. (1988) *Steady Work Policy, Practice and Reform of American Education*, Santa Monica, CA: Rand Corporation.

Meyer, M. (1961) *The Schools*, New York: Harper.

Minow, M. (1990) *Making All The Difference: Inclusion, Exclusion, And American Law*, Ithaca, NY: Cornell University Press.

Norwich, B. (1997) *A Trend Towards Inclusion: Statistics on Special School Placements and Pupils with Statements in Ordinary Schools England 1992–1996*, Bristol: Centre for Studies in Inclusive Education.

Ordover, E., Boundy, K. and Pullin, D. (1996) *Students with disabilities and the implementation of standards-based education reform: Legal issues and implications*, Paper Presented to the National Research Council of the National Academy of Sciences.

Poole, K., Coleman, J. and Liell, P. (1997) *Butterworth's Education Law*, London: Butterworths.

Pullin, D. (1994) 'Learning to work: The impact of curriculum and assessment standards on educational opportunity', *Harvard Educational Review*, 64,1: 31–54.

Pullin, D. and Zirkel, P. (1988) 'Testing students with handicapping conditions', *Education Law Reporter*, 411.

Rothstein, L.F. (1990) *Special Education Law*, White Plains, NY: Longman.

Rouse, M. and Florian, L. (1997) 'Inclusive education in the marketplace', *International Journal of Inclusive Education*, 1,4: 323–336.

Sallis, J. (1994) *Free for All? A Brief History of State Education Including Summaries of all Recent Legislation*, London: The Campaign for State Education.

Sarason, S. and Doris, J. (1979) *Educational Handicap, Public Policy, And Social History*, New York: Free Press.

Smith, M. and O'Day, J. (1991) 'Systemic school reform', in S. Furhman and B. Malen (eds) *The Politics of Curriculum and Testing: The 1990 Yearbook of the Politics of Education Association* (pp. 233–267), London: Falmer Press.

Special Educational Needs Tribunal (1995) *Annual Report 1994–5*, London: SEN Tribunal.

Tomlinson, S. (1982) *A Sociology of Special Education*, London: Routledge and Kegan Paul.

Turnbull, H.R., III (1993) *Free Appropriate Public Education: The Law And Children With Disabilities* (3rd edn), Denver, CO: Love Publishing Co.

Underwood, J. (1995) 'School finance adequacy as vertical equity', *University of Michigan Journal of Law Reform*, 28,3: 493–519.

Underwood, J.K., and Mead, J.F. (1995) *Legal Aspects Of Special Education And Pupil Services*, Needham Heights, MA: Allyn and Bacon.

Wise, A. (1979) *Legislated Learning: The Bureaucratization of the American Classroom*, Berkeley, CA: University of California Press.

Weintraub, F., Abeson, A. and Braddock, D. (1971) *State Law and Education of Handicapped Children: Issues and Recommendations*, Arlington, VA: Council For Exceptional Children.

Zola, I.K. (1989) 'Towards the necessary universalizing of disability policy', *The Milbank Quarterly* 67, (Suppl.2 Pt.2), 401–427.

Chapter 3

Standards and curriculum

The core of educational reform

Margaret J. McLaughlin and Christina Tilstone

Introduction

The core of reforms in both England and Wales and the United States is focused on changing what students are expected to learn, as well as how teachers deliver instruction. In the United Kingdom, the National Curriculum has redefined both core knowledge and skills and is shaping instruction in the classroom. Similarly in the United States, content and instruction are being redefined through the development of state content standards. In both countries the new standards of content and curriculum reflect the desire to enhance student achievement through an increase in the amount of subject matter (e.g. the skills, knowledge, understanding and application) at progressively higher levels.

The National Curriculum in the United Kingdom and the content standards developed by states and professional organisations in the United States have the same purposes. They publicly identify what is important for the staff of schools to teach, and represent statements of beliefs and ideologies about the mission of schools and the expected student outcomes. The United Kingdom and the United States have both experienced intense political debates and activities on the development of standards and the definition of curricula. Politicians, the business community, professional teachers organisations and other professional societies, as well as individual teachers and the public at large have all contributed to the debate.

Standards (US) and the National Curriculum (UK) are designed to help teachers and administrators to identify important instructional strategies and to guide the allocation of resources. As the following sections illustrate, the genesis of the National Curriculum and the various content standards in the United States are similar, as are many of their intended goals. Key differences, however, exist in the degree to which content standards guide, rather than control, teaching and learning. The specific focus of this overview, of the origins and experiences of the two countries in implementing new curriculum and content standards, is on ways in which the changes are impacting on students with disabilities.

The National Curriculum in the United Kingdom

The need to improve standards in schools in the United Kingdom was highlighted in the famous speech delivered by James Callaghan (the then Labour Prime Minister) at Ruskin College, Oxford in 1976, which was regarded as 'a major attack on British schools' (O'Connor, 1987, quoted in Benn and Chitty, 1996). He focused on employability as the main reason for re-organisation, and stressed the need to improve relationships between industry and education. The Conservative Government, elected in 1979, re-emphasised the importance of raising standards and the direct result was the Great Education Reform Bill, which later became the Education Reform Act (DES, 1988), designed to radically reform the education system to ensure that, industrially at least, Britain could compete with the rest of the world. Before 1988, curriculum content, planning and implementation were the responsibility of schools, teachers and the local education authorities, but the Act placed the responsibility for most forms of curriculum development firmly in the hands of central government. Competition and value for money were central and the vocabulary of education resembled that of the manufacturing industry (Warnock, 1996). The Education Reform Act 1988 went beyond a common curriculum and its national testing and assessments, and included competition between schools for student places; open enrol-ment; parental choice; and the setting up of grant maintained schools and city technology colleges.

The structure of the National Curriculum

The National Curriculum had few champions in the academic and teach-ing professions. Its critics emphasised that the legislation which had led to its inception was derived from a contradictory philosophy and value posi-tion (Lawton, 1988; Lindsay, 1997) and were quick to point out that local management of schools and grant maintained schools were designed to introduce 'free market approaches' which force schools to take a measure of control, whilst the National Curriculum itself, with its emphasis on testing, and the four-year cycle of Ofsted (Office for Standards in Educa-tion) inspections were aggressive attempts to manage from the centre. In the opinion of the then Secretary of State, Kenneth Baker, 'only a National Curriculum, centrally imposed, could ensure all-round improvements in standards'. At a major teachers' conference in 1987, he described the Eng-lish system as 'a bit of a muddle, one of those institutionalised muddles that the English have made peculiarly their own' (quoted in Lawton and Chitty, 1988, p. 1).

The National Curriculum applies to pupils of compulsory school age (5–16 years) in maintained schools (including grant maintained) on the basis of four key stages (Table 3.1). Carpenter and Ashdown (1996) claim

Table 3.1 Key stages

Key Stages	Year groups	Pupils' ages
Key Stage 1	1–2	5–7 years
Key Stage 2	3–6	7–11 years
Key Stage 3	7–9	11–14 years
Key Stage 4	10–11	14–16 years

Table 3.2 The National Curriculum subjects

Core subjects
• English
• Maths
• Science

Other foundation subjects
• Technology (design technology and information technology)
• Geography
• History
• Physical education
• Music
• Art
• Modern foreign languages (introduced at 11 years; Key stage 3)

that it has no underpinning philosophy and is basically a syllabus, hastily devised by teams of experts in each of the subject areas (Table 3.2). In each subject, and for each key stage, 'programmes of study' identify what pupils should be taught, and 'attainment targets' indicate expected standards of pupil performance. In the 1995 review of the National Curriculum, 'level descriptions' (and in the case of art, music and PE, 'key stage descriptions') were introduced alongside attainment targets; all designed to test a pupil's knowledge of the programmes of study. The level descriptions (in eight levels of difficulty) allow summary judgements to be made on pupils' achievements (Byers and Rose, 1996). Summative assessment in the National Curriculum combines teacher assessment and national, externally prescribed tests and tasks (Standard Assessment Tasks or Tests: SATs). SATs are administered in the final year of a key stage and methods of assessment vary depending on the subject and the key stage. At Key Stage 4, for example, public examinations are the main means of assessing attainment, whereas at Key Stage 1 teachers have fought for a greater emphasis on teacher assessment. Assessment is dealt with in detail in the next chapter, but the following three important issues apply to children with special educational needs:

- the process of combining data to arrive at a standard test and task level has masked attainments, especially for children with learning difficulties, for whom small gains and/or uneven development need to be emphasised;
- the aggregated results of the SATs published in league tables in the national press emphasise the performance of schools with the highest attainments, implying that other schools are failing. Some schools are reluctant, therefore, either to admit children with special educational needs or to enter them for SATs in case they depress the scores;
- from Key Stage 2 onwards, testing in mainstream and special schools is often undertaken under formal examination conditions which are unfamiliar to children with special educational needs, causing anxiety and contributing to poor performance. (Adapted from Lewis, 1995, 1996.)

The statutory requirements governing the curriculum in maintained schools are that the curriculum should be balanced and broadly based which:

(a) promotes the spiritual, moral, cultural, mental and physical development of schools and of society and
(b) prepares pupils at school for the opportunities, responsibilities and experiences of adult life.

(Education Reform Act 1988, paragraph 1;
Education Act 1996, paragraph 342(b).)

Provision for sex education from the age of 11 and for all pupils to receive religious education and attend religious worship is also statutory.

The National Curriculum and children with special educational needs: the initial concerns

The global term 'special educational needs', adopted by the Warnock Committee (DES, 1978), is diverse and forms part of a continuum of need:

some permanent, some temporary, some easily supplied, once identified, some requiring considerable expertise and expense to supply.

(Ibid., p. 53)

Terms such as 'emotional and behavioural difficulties' and 'severe learning difficulties' have remained as descriptions within this imprecise formulation, but exact estimates of how many children have special educational needs are difficult to make as much depends on individual and local circumstances:

it may be entirely consistent with the law for a child to be said to have special educational needs in one school, but not in another.

(DfEE, 1997a, p. 12)

It is, however, estimated that 18 per cent of pupils (1.5 million of the total school population) have special educational needs. Schools are urged to follow a standard procedure for the assessment of a pupil's special educational needs, prior to asking for a formal, statutory assessment leading to a 'Statement'. Statements are made for those pupils whose needs are such that extra resources are considered necessary to enable them to learn. A Statement is central to securing adequate educational provision for children who will require specialised help for a large part of, or throughout, their school careers. Although the National Curriculum has proved a challenge for all teachers of children with special educational needs, it is the shaping of the curriculum for the Statemented group in particular (recently estimated as 3 per cent) which has been most difficult.

The subject content of the original National Curriculum Orders was heavily overloaded and narrowly focused and did not reflect the special educational needs of any child. Regrettably, the first documents failed even to mention children with special educational needs, and the teaching profession assumed that those who had compiled the documents considered the academic content inappropriate for such children. As an underlying principle of the reform was geared to the growth of industry, teachers were genuinely concerned that those children who may only be able to make a minimal contribution to a technologically advanced and highly skilled workforce would be segregated and marginalised (Baynes and Dyson, 1994; Griffiths, 1994).

For children with 'severe learning difficulties' ('mental retardation' in the United States), whose legal right to education was as recent as 1971 in England and Wales and 1974 in Scotland, there was a real danger that history might repeat itself and that they would be permanently excluded from the education system. Their teachers were in the difficult position of having to fight for entitlement to a curriculum (which did not reflect their pupils' needs) in order to support their human rights. These teachers, along with others of pupils with special educational needs, responded positively and used the changes as an opportunity to review and reconsider their work. The National Curriculum required all teachers to undertake a rigorous examination of their existing practices and the National Curriculum Council (NCC) provided a plethora of guidance documents. Eventually the voices of teachers of children with severe learning difficulties were heard and specific guidance was produced (NCC, 1992a, 1992b). A report on a series of visits by Her Majesty's Inspectors in 1989–90 to twenty-six ordinary and fifty special schools, catering for the whole range of special educational needs, revealed:

> a widespread commitment to planning for possible access to the National Curriculum for all children.
>
> (DES, 1990, p. 9)

Disapplications and modifications to parts of the National Curriculum are permissible in law through a specification in a pupil's Statement of Special Educational Needs. Teachers, however, have been reluctant to use such methods as most believe that full participation in the National Curriculum is desirable and, if such pupils are given help, possible.

Teachers of children with special educational needs as innovators

Their definition of 'help' included the identification of training needs and requirements both in the subject content of the National Curriculum Orders for children with special educational needs and in the teaching approaches required. The resources for in-service training were slow to materialise and the challenges of an alien curriculum resulted in teachers in special education collaborating to ensure that the reforms worked for all pupils. Despite their low morale, brought about not only by their lack of power to determine the curriculum, but also by the amount of documentation and the implication that they were incompetent and the root cause of falling standards, teachers formed their own National Curriculum monitoring, development or cluster groups. Some groups involved mainstream and special school staff working together, and their regular meetings provided a forum for debate and opportunities for the welcome exchange of information (Tilstone, 1991a, 1991b). In one region, 250 teachers of children with special educational needs attended the initial meeting in order to discuss ways of shaping the National Curriculum to meet the needs of their children. This initiative led to monthly meetings (attended by more than 400 teachers) at which each subject of the National Curriculum was discussed. Sub-groups considered specific problems and produced working documents. The enthusiasm and commitment of many teachers was demonstrated by their willingness to attend weekly meetings in their own time, often at a considerable distance from their homes, over a period of two years. Although not research-orientated, in the generally accepted sense, the groups responded creatively and critically to the curriculum on offer. Innovation was in evidence in many schools, where staff produced detailed documentation of their policies and practices, which became more transparent through discussion and debate inside, and outside, the school (Moses, 1996).

The major National Curriculum review

It was recognised that the curriculum was overloaded and, as a direct result of pressure from professional groups, teachers of children with special educational needs were fully involved in consultations on proposed changes. In 1993 the Secretary of State for Education invited Sir Ron Dearing, Chairman of both the NCC and SEAC (National Curriculum Council and School Examination and Assessment Council) and Chairman Designate of the new combined Authority, the School Curriculum and Assessment Authority (SCAA), to review the National Curriculum in England. It was recognised that the National Curriculum had been problematical for all teachers, particularly those of pupils with special educational needs, and that a new slimmer, fitter curriculum was needed. The benefits for all children of the new Orders included: greater clarity and smoother progression within each subject; the heightened profile of information technology; and more time for other aspects of the whole curriculum. Dearing emphasised the importance of further areas of study and the building of a whole curriculum of which the National Curriculum is only part – a message which had been understated at the outset.

Particular attention was given to pupils with special educational needs by introducing access statements in each Order which led to the use of appropriate aids, the adaptation of equipment and communication systems and work on the content of the curriculum at levels relevant to developmental, rather than chronological, age. Teachers found the new Orders more user-friendly, particularly for children with Statements, and welcomed the greater emphasis on the 'whole curriculum'. Personal and social education (so important for the balanced development of pupils with special educational needs) although not recognised as a subject in its own right, regained the status it deserved (Sebba, Byers and Rose, 1993). More explicit recognition of personal and social education is now being planned by the newly formed Qualification and Curriculum Authority (QCA, formerly SCAA) as part of the next curriculum review in the year 2000.

The strengths of the National Curriculum for children with special educational needs

While the introduction of the National Curriculum resulted in some negative reactions from special educators, the positive effects on children with special educational needs were also recognised. Its strengths included:

- an emphasis on breadth and balance;
- rigorous examination of curriculum practices by teachers themselves;
- clear policy statements;
- the opportunity for staff in all settings to exchange ideas;
- experiments in methodology;
- a framework for inclusion.

A major strength of the National Curriculum is that its common curriculum framework has the potential for aiding inclusive practices, and makes it possible for more children to be educated in the mainstream. This potential, however, was not realised in 1991/92 when a rise in special school placements was detected, but a recent report compiled for the Centre for the Study of

Inclusive Education (CSIE) (1997) shows that in 1996 the special school population dropped to the lowest it has ever been (88,849, or 1.4 per cent of all 5 to 16-year-olds), and that 71 out of 107 local education authorities reduced the number of pupils placed in special schools. The findings support Thomas's (1997) arguments that administrators should be, and are, planning for desegregation, rather than 'fighting rearguard actions against it' (Ibid., p. 103). The CSIE figures must, however, be viewed with caution. In 1991/92, 3,833 pupils were permanently excluded from schools in England and Wales (DfE, 1993), rising to 12,476 in 1995/96 (the latest year for which full data are available; DfEE, 1997c). Pupils with Statements are, according to Donovan (1998), seven times more likely to be excluded (0.98 per cent) than children without statements (0.14 per cent). These figures do not take into account the indefinite or unofficial exclusions, of which the highest proportion continue to be those with special educational needs, particularly children with emotional and behavioural difficulties.

Although the Code of Practice (DfE, 1994), with its staged assessment procedures, should allow the early identification of such children, Parsons and Howlett (1996) and Booth (1996) show that this is not so. They highlight the differences in the implementation of the Code across schools and LEAs, and Booth gives examples of schools avoiding the formal assessment routes for pupils with emotional and behavioural difficulties in order to retain a 'fast disposal route' out of education for 'problem' pupils.

There is, therefore, a tension: the National Curriculum has the potential for increasing inclusion, but inadequate testing procedures; league tables of test results; a lack of resources and in-service training for the teaching profession, together with wide variations in the interpretation of policy, have not encouraged schools to accept the most vulnerable or 'difficult to teach' children. Nevertheless, there is a general recognition that a 'curriculum for all' has informed strategic planning towards structures which give meaningful expression to inclusion (Byers and Rose, 1996; Lewis, 1991; Tilstone, 1996). Such structures, however, cannot guarantee quality. Much of the literature on inclusive practices in the United Kingdom is descriptive rather than evaluative, owing to the lack of a consensus on what constitutes effective inclusion. To date, initiatives to decrease the numbers of pupils in special schools have followed two distinct routes. The first is to integrate children into mainstream schools and classes through a range of provision in order that they spend part of the school day with peers of approximately the same chronological age (Lewis, 1995). A more recent approach has focused on improving the capacity of mainstream schools to accommodate pupil diversity (Booth, Ainscow and Dyson, 1998; Hopkins, West and Ainscow, 1996; Sebba with Sachdev, 1997). Whatever the approach, the clear message is that the quality of the educational experience for each child with special educational needs depends on a more accessible programme of in-service education for teachers (Hornby, Atkinson and Howard, 1997).

The Green Paper *Excellence for All Children: Meeting Special Educational Needs* (DfEE, 1997a) states that the Government aims to increase the level and quality of inclusion within mainstream schools, 'whilst protecting and enhancing specialist provision for those who need it' (Ibid., p. 43). Accusations of 'having your cake and eating it' may come from radical inclusionists, but teachers in mainstream classrooms, whilst fully agreeing with the principles of inclusion, recognise that they need the necessary expertise if it is to become a realistic goal.

Raising student performance

The Government's view, that a National Curriculum, centrally imposed, is the only way to ensure an all-round improvement in standards, is not supported by evidence from the classrooms. It became clear in the 1990s that the tightly prescriptive curriculum was having a negative effect on the achievements of some children, especially those with special educational needs. Campbell (1997), at an invitation conference on the development of the primary curriculum, stated that research evidence indicated:

> depressingly little change (in the raising of standards) and, probably, little development in the curriculum.
>
> (Ibid., p. 22)

Further government initiatives are now in place, however, and a consultation document, *Excellence in Schools* (DfEE, 1997b), makes it clear that its top priority of raising standards in schools will continue to be driven from the centre. Task forces have been set up to examine major aspects of the education system, including 'special educational needs', 'numeracy' and 'literacy'. Benchmarking and target-setting are either proposed or in place within the education system. Although their introduction is proving a potential minefield, pilot schemes highlighted the benefits for pupils with special educational needs. Despite reservations about additional centrally driven initiatives, the teaching force has welcomed the possibility that the new steps may provide additional resources and reliable mechanisms for the monitoring of standards. The new Labour Government's Standards and Effectiveness Unit has promised to work with teachers and to equip them with a framework for teaching basic skills.

From September 1998, schools will be required to set aside a formally structured, daily hour for work in literacy. The National Literacy Strategy requires the appointment of literacy consultants at LEA level; the setting of area and school targets; and the identification of literacy consultants in each school. It has also made funds available for a complex training framework and extra books for every school. There should be benefits for most children with special educational needs, although the policy, which applies to mainstream primary schools, is designed to raise average levels of attainment. What help the government has in mind to raise literacy skills at the lower end of the attainment range is not clear and, as literacy is not context-free, the problem goes beyond education and embraces child poverty and social disadvantage (Dyson, 1997; Robinson, 1997).

Target-setting and benchmarking

Central to the improvement cycle for raising standards are the statutory requirements (in place in September 1998) for schools to set targets in the core subjects of the National Curriculum, and to publish them in their annual reports. These should link with the national targets for maths and literacy, and will be based on an analysis of pupil performance, moving to what it is reasonable to expect them to achieve over a three-year period. At the time of writing, discussions were under way on how targets could be most suitably expressed for special schools and units (SCAA, 1997; NFER, 1998). As target-setting has always been an integral part of teaching children with special educational needs, the main issue is one of whether they are best expressed in a standard format or whether the complex needs require a more flexible approach.

'Benchmarking', the process of measuring standards of 'actual performance against other schools', is difficult for teachers of children with special educational needs. The consultation document (SCAA, 1997) states that:

> benchmarks show the standards achieved by the best members of a group and present sound contextual information to assist others in setting their targets.
>
> (Ibid., p. 8)

Comparisons of 'like for like' are difficult, especially if the nearest special school with similar characteristics is many miles away and has a different LEA policy. For schools to have confidence in the benchmarking process the implications for the education of those with special educational needs must be at the forefront of the debate.

A summary of UK efforts

The key to raising standards is with the teachers themselves, as demonstrated by the effectiveness of the networks initiated by teachers of children with learning difficulties in raising awareness that a truly national curriculum could not ignore children with special educational needs (Tilstone, 1991b). The training and the education of the profession at both initial and in-service levels has never been more crucial than at a time of radical changes in the education system itself. Although the training of teachers of children with special educational needs was one of the main concerns of the Warnock Report (DES, 1978), it has never been accorded the care and support it deserves (Tilstone and Upton, 1993). These teachers have constructed platforms for their own narratives and it is essential that they are provided with the tools to raise their own standards through continued professional development. Many children with special educational needs do not have access to properly trained teachers and in a survey carried out in 1996, for example, it was found that 46 per cent of teachers of children with severe learning difficulties had had no specialised training (Porter, 1996). Rapid legislative changes have resulted in a shell-shocked profession; the consequent lack of confidence and self-esteem is a major problem in recruitment, and undoubtedly a shortage of teachers will be a major concern well beyond the millennium. Although debates in the United Kingdom are intense about what constitutes effective training for teachers of children with SEN, and how it can be funded, a lack of resources and changes in funding have forced the closure of some training courses and the disbanding of teams of special educators. The Government has responded to the overall shortage by quick fix measures offering a fast track into the profession and placing the major emphasis on school-based training, with less time for a special needs element. In addition, National Curriculum specialisms have squeezed out much of the training for work with children with special needs in initial teacher education (see Davies and Garner, 1997, for a critical analysis of recent and contemporary trends). Reports prepared for the Department of Education and Employment (SENTC, 1996; TTA, 1997) argue that a more carefully planned and structured approach to initial teacher education and continuing professional development is urgently needed. The Government has recently (through the Teacher Training Agency) detailed national standards (at present out for consultation) for all teachers, including those of children with special educational needs. Nevertheless, there is much to be done if more than lip service is to be paid to the raising of standards.

Content standards in the United States

A central feature of current reform in the United States has been the creation of new content and performance standards. These have been developed to bolster student achievement in traditional subject matter content as well as in new skill areas such as technology. The standards have been built around certain assumptions, such as the need for students to acquire the knowledge and skills that will allow them to become effective workers and participants in an increasingly competitive global society, and politicians and businesses have been influential in promoting higher standards as a critical foundation for more effective schools. In addition, the creation of content standards has also been promoted as a tool for ensuring greater equity across schools and districts. If schools are guided by a core of common content standards, in conjunction with greater accountability, all students should have an opportunity to learn intellectually demanding subject matter. These changes are seen as impacting most those students in high poverty schools as well as non-majority cultures, thus ending what Toch (1991) describes as the United States history of educating the middle classes and training the lower classes.

The 1989 Education Summit of governors is commonly cited as the point at which the movement to create standards and increase student achievement coalesced (McLaughlin and Sheppard, 1995). At the Summit, the then President Bush and the nation's governors agreed on a national vision for education and adopted six broad goals to be achieved by the year 2000. These goals, along with two additional ones, were incorporated into the federal legislation known as Goals 2000: Educate America Act (P.L. 103-227) enacted in 1994 under the Clinton administration. This legislation codified the national education goals and encouraged the adoption of state standards and assessments. In addition, the legislation calls for states to develop increased accountability for student achievement. In return for increased curricular control and accountability for results, schools and local districts were to be granted greater flexibility in how they used federal targeted resources. Direct federal influence is limited under Goals 2000 by the amount of federal funding available to states. However, the three-prong strategy of standards, assessments and accountability, and more flexible governance was integrated into other key federal legislation.

Improving America's Schools Act (P.L. 103-328): Title I

The Improving America's Schools Act (IASA), the reauthorization of the Elementary and Secondary Education Act (1994), contains new requirements for obtaining funds under Title I, the largest federal school aid programme, which serves poor, underachieving students. The purpose of the legislation is 'to enable schools to provide opportunities for children served to acquire the knowledge and skills contained in challenging state content standards and to meet the challenging state performance standards developed for all children' (P.L. No. 103-328, s. 1001(d)). To receive Title I grants, states are required to submit plans that provide for challenging content and performance standards, state assessments, yearly reports on meeting standards, and provisions for teacher support and learning aligned with the new curriculum standards and assessments. Assessment results must be disaggregated by race, gender, English proficiency, migrant status, disability, and economic status (103-328, s. 1111). Because Title I provides well over $7 billion a year in federal funding and includes a detailed set of mandates that local districts must meet as a condition for funding, it is likely that the federal government's influence over the standards and assessments in individual states will be greater through Title I than through Goals 2000.

Standards and federal special education policy

The Individuals with Disabilities Education Act (IDEA) is the federal legislation that defines the special educational policy framework in the United States. Since initial enactment of this legislation, concerns have increased over poor post-school outcomes of students with disabilities (Wagner *et al.*, 1993) and the lowered expectations for those students as evidenced in their Individual Education Program (IEP) (Pugach and Warger, 1993; Sands, Adams and Stout, 1995; Shriner *et al.*, 1993; Smith, 1990). Efforts to improve student outcomes have centred on increasing inclusion of students with disabilities in general education classrooms and, most recently, ensuring access to the general education curriculum and assessments.

The most recent amendments to IDEA preserve the critical civil rights features of the original legislation but add several new requirements designed to specifically align with the model of school improvement in Goals 2000 and other federal legislation. Some of the significant provisions relating to standards and curriculum are discussed below.

Performance goals and indicators

States are required to establish goals for the performance of children and youth with disabilities and to develop indicators to judge the progress of students on these goals. States must expand data collection to examine critical indicators of student progress, including student assessment data and graduation rates.

School-based improvement plans

A state may grant authority to local school districts to select individual schools to design and implement a school-wide improvement plan for students with disabilities and other students. The plans must include full participation of all members of that school community and must be grounded in school-wide goals and indicators and sound assessments of how students with disabilities are meeting those goals.

Participation in assessments

The legislation requires that children with disabilities be included in general education state and district assessments, with accommodations as needed, and to report performance of those students. Exceptions can be made if participation will invalidate the assessments or reporting will result in disclosure of individual students with disabilities. For students with disabilities who cannot participate in state and district assessments, the states and local districts must develop guidelines for their participation in alternate assessments and must develop and conduct these and report performance of students with disabilities starting on 1 July 2000.

New IEP provisions

Several changes to the IEP requirements require specific attention to how an individual student will access the general education curriculum regardless of the setting in which he/she will receive their special education and related services. Among the new IEP requirements are:

- a statement of the child's present levels of educational performance, including how the child's disability affects the child's involvement and progress in the general curriculum; for pre-school children the statements refer to how the disability affects the child's participation in appropriate activities;
- a statement of measurable annual goals, including benchmarks, or short-term objectives, related to meeting the child's needs and to enable the child to be involved in and progress in the general curriculum;
- a statement of the special education and related services and supplementary aids and services to be provided to the child, or on behalf of the child, and any programme modifications or support for school personnel necessary for the child to advance toward attaining the annual goals, to be involved and progress in the general curriculum, and to participate in extra-curricular and other non-academic activities, and to be educated and participate with other children with and without disabilities in activities;
- an explanation of the extent, if any, to which the child will not participate with children without disabilities in the regular class and in activities;
- a statement of any individual modifications in the administration of state or district assessment of student achievement that are needed in order for the child to participate in the assessment or a statement of why that assessment is not appropriate and how the child will be assessed.

Members required to be on an IEP team now include both the special education teacher and, where appropriate, the general education teacher and/or others who are knowledgeable about the general curriculum. These changes are important signals for how special education is expected to become more integrated into general education policies and classroom practice.

The evolution of content standards

Despite strong federal support for 'common' standards and the develop-ment of national content standards by professional organisations, standard development is decidedly a state-level activity. According to a 1996 survey conducted by the American Federation of Teachers (Gandal, 1996), forty-eight states had developed standards in one or more of the following content areas that were ready for implementation: math, science, English/language, arts, history, and social studies.

Shifting the focus of control over standards setting to the states represents a political compromise of sorts. As a nation that has long cherished the right of local boards of education to control curriculum, there was concern that national standards meant a national curriculum. This was politically unpalat-able to many. At the same time, concerns about global competitiveness, sup-ported in part through research such as the Second and Third International Mathematics Study (SIMS and TIMMS) (Schmidt, McKnight and Raizen, 1997) that documented national differences related to curricular focus and student achievement promoted policymakers to seek greater curriculum standardisation. Studies such as the international comparison as well as other large-scale studies of national student performance suggested the need to ensure that all students, regardless of where they went to school, have access to the same challenging curriculum. Yet, despite the desire for 'common' standards, current content standards reflect the variability and political nuances of individual states, particularly the degree to which a state gov-ernment wants to mandate local education policy.

Several national surveys of state standards have been conducted. These and a few small-scale studies describe some of the core features as well as vari-ation among content and performance standards currently being developed by states. For example, in some states content standards are broad, rhetorical goals that local districts are urged to follow, e.g. 'All students should under-stand and apply knowledge about political systems'. Other state standards are considerably more precise, with textbooks and assessments linked directly to the standards. Some standards define what students should be able to do at certain benchmark years, such as 4th grade or at the end of middle school. Others define standards for each grade-level. According to the American Federation of Teachers survey, only fifteen states have developed standards that are specific enough to permit development of a common core curric-ulum (Gandal, 1996). The states also differ in how they use the standards as part of their accountability systems. Some states impose no direct con-sequences on either schools or students for mastery of the standards. Others link standards to mandated assessments, the results of which are used to reward or sanction schools or as a condition of high school graduation.

The various national and state content standards have both political and economic motivations. Emphasis on math and science, technology, and enhanced communication skills are viewed as critical to employees and to ensuring that all students are internationally competitive and have also been influenced by new theories of learning. All of these factors have resulted in certain common features of content standards. Examinations of a number of state and national content standards that have been developed both at the national and state levels (Blank and Pechman, 1995; McDonnell, McLaughlin and Morison, 1997) indicate that most content standards focus on application and 'big' ideas, as opposed to discrete facts. There is also a focus on multi-disciplinary content, particularly evident in the integration of writing across all subject matter areas. Blank and Pechman (1995) note that the majority of math and science standards adopted by states provide pedagogical guidance reflecting 'constructive or active' lessons requiring students to solve problems and demonstrate their understanding of mathematical operations as opposed to emphasising basic computation or getting the right answer.

Students with disabilities and content standards

Students with disabilities were not explicitly considered in the national content standards developed by the various professional organisations (Shriner *et al.*, 1993), although the national science standards minimally reference students with specific disabilities, such as those with physical or learning disabilities (National Research Council, 1996). Individual states have varied in terms of how inclusive their standards setting has been (Goertz and Friedman, 1996). Examples of state efforts in more inclusive standards setting can mean assigning special educators to content standards-setting teams, seeking reviews of content standards from representatives of special populations, and identifying accommodations for specific content standards.

A few states, (e.g. Kentucky and Vermont), have developed content standards within broad learner outcomes that are appropriate for students with disabilities. Michigan has developed separate outcomes for seven types of students with disabilities (Michigan Department of Education, 1995). Maryland has adopted a set of alternate outcomes and content and performance standards for students with severe cognitive disabilities who participate in a functional curriculum. With the recent reauthorization of IDEA, however, more states and local jurisdictions must consider how to include all students in their content standards and assessments.

A recent national survey conducted by the Council of Chief State School Officers (Rhim and McLaughlin, 1996) asked all fifty and six 'extra states' (e.g. District of Columbia and Puerto Rico) whether any of their content standards that were being implemented or developed would apply to students with IEPs. Of the forty-eight states responding to the survey question, thirty-five reported that standards would apply to students with disabilities with IEPs; nine states reported that their content standards would not apply; and four states would allow local school districts to decide. Of the thirty-five states indicating that their content standards would apply to special education students, seventeen reported that all standards would apply to students with a mild disability, only twelve would apply standards to students with both mild and severe disabilities, while seventeen states added the qualifier that participation in standards would be an IEP decision.

Will standards impact the education of students with disabilities?

Relatively little is known about how newly defined state and or local standards are impacting classroom instruction. To understand the potential effects of those standards requires that the concept of 'content' standards, which define what should be taught, be distinguished from 'performance' standards, which set the desired level of knowledge or skill a student should attain. A National Academy of Sciences committee examined the issue of how students with disabilities will be included in standards-based reforms (McDonnell, McLaughlin and Morison, 1997). This included how students with disabilities will access a general education curriculum based on a uniform set of content standards. The committee concluded that while it might be possible to assume that some set of common broad content standards could be defined that encompass the critical or core curriculum for all students, it is not conceivable that every student can meet the same levels of proficiency in common content.

Two recent surveys (Koretz *et al.*, 1996a, 1996b) of teachers in Kentucky and Maryland, both states with strong standards-based reforms, suggest that teachers have doubts about whether 'all students can learn to a high level'. These surveys focused on teachers' perceptions regarding student performance as opposed to appropriateness of content. An overwhelming majority (83 per cent) of Kentucky teachers agreed that, regardless of whether it is possible for all students to learn to that level, it is an appropriate message to send Kentucky students. However, very few (9 per cent) agreed that all students can reach the same high level of performance, with most teachers in the sample (90 per cent) saying that novice, the lowest performance level in the Kentucky system, is a high level for some students. The results from the Maryland sample are essentially similar, except that a slightly higher proportion of teachers (21 per cent) felt that students could learn to the same high level. What the surveys did not ask was whether teachers agreed that the content standards were right for all students.

The issue of appropriateness of the standards as well as the goodness of fit to effective instruction for students with disabilities were closely examined by the National Academy of Sciences committee. The conclusion was that standards that are exclusively academic will not provide the requisite instruction in vocational or other critical 'functional' domains that some students with disabilities require. Further, effective instruction for students with disabilities requires intensive and discrete presentation of specific skills, which may be at odds with the more constructivist pedagogy implicit in some standards.

A small-scale study involving five local school districts (McLaughlin, Henderson and Rhim, 1997) investigated how districts are implementing a variety of new educational reforms, including state and/or local standards. Using interviews and classroom observations, the research revealed several interesting findings regarding how general and special education teachers are responding to standards.

In general, the state and local standards varied across the district in terms of how specifically they define what students should know and be able to do. Locally developed standards tended to be more comprehensive and more explicit, while state standards were more global goals referenced to specific benchmark years. Regardless of the level of specificity, none of the standards were considered to be detailed enough to specify what teachers should be teaching and schools needed to engage in 'aligning' the standards with their current curriculum, textbooks and organisation. This alignment process was very uneven across schools and it infrequently involved special educators.

Teachers also reported that state and local standards expanded the scope of subject matter they had to teach. Math and science teachers tended to be particularly stressed by the new curricular demands. The increased expectations leave little time for reteaching or helping students who did not grasp a concept on the first presentation. Most teachers believed that the pace of learning has dramatically increased in classrooms, and some feel that content coverage, not mastery, is the goal.

The standards are often interdisciplinary and emphasise application rather than rote knowledge, and most teachers interviewed believed that standards are changing the ways that they instruct students. They report more 'hands-on' and more project-based learning and more writing. Teaching basic facts, memorisation, and simple computations or operations were de-emphasised in favour of solving problems or using knowledge to perform 'real-life' tasks.

Impacts on students with disabilities

Most administrators and teachers expect that students with disabilities will participate in and be assessed on new content standards, except for students with severe cognitive disabilities who may require a more functional curriculum. In general, teachers were somewhat uncertain whether policy-makers would move beyond rhetoric to ensure that students with disabilities will meet the new standards.

However, special education teachers believe standards offer students with disabilities exposure to a wider variety of subject matter. This was particularly true for upper elementary and middle school students in areas such as math and science. Instructional changes attributed to standards include increased emphasis on experiments and 'authentic' problem-solving. All of these strategies were perceived to support the participation of students with disabilities in the standards and new curricular frameworks.

Special educators also generally endorsed the common curricular framework that standards provided and were hopeful they would lead to universal expectations for a student. One high school special education teacher commented:

> I think we're hopeful because [the standards] give us some real concrete direction to work towards with the kids, and anything that is more clear and more precise than just covering the content in American history . . . will help us.

Of universal concern to special education teachers was how much teachers varied with respect to expectations for students with disabilities.

Finding sufficient instructional time and opportunity to help students with disabilities learn the new subject matter content and still gain important other skills that might be more functional for them was a common concern. Some teachers were hopeful that certain functional skills and learning strategies could be incorporated into subject matter instruction, but other non-academic areas may not be easy to integrate. Teachers were concerned about the increased instructional demands placed on the students and the lack of adequate time to address all of what a student needs. As one teacher noted:

> I think we're going to have to be real careful that we don't bypass the students' needs because we have become so focused on the standards in our instruction.

A clear effect of the interdisciplinary nature of standards is the need for teacher collaboration across the content areas, which was occurring among general educators, between for example, math and language arts teachers, as well as between special and general educators. The standards provided a common language for teachers and discussions about individual students centred on whether or how to modify a standard, provide assessment accommodations, or design instructional strategies. Not surprisingly, teacher collaboration seemed to be more flexible and routine at the elementary school. However, in districts that required all students to meet certain performance standards for graduation requirements, general and special educators were coming together, sometimes awkwardly, to make instructional accommodations.

There are a number of decisions regarding an individual student's programme that special education teachers must make. Perhaps the most perplexing is determining if a specific standard (the expected knowledge and skills) is appropriate for a given student, or if the teacher needs to modify the standard or provide a different curriculum altogether. One junior high school special education teacher questioned the relevance of some curricular goals and content standards for special education students:

> I always feel a dilemma and I know some of my colleagues do too. For instance . . . math. Well sure, I can give the students an equation and they can just plug it into the calculator, but they wouldn't know what they were doing. So I'm always struggling with, do I do the pre-algebra little simple equations with the calculator or do I really teach them what they need to know when they go out in the world? I mean like money, and other functional things . . . More and more I'm finding a wider discrepancy between what the curriculum says and what they need to know.

Related to the issue of determining whether the standard was relevant for a student, was determining when a standard should be modified and what accommodations might be necessary in instruction. Teachers often confused the two concepts and provided extensive modifications, particularly to performance expectations, believing that they were just accommodating a student's disability. Administrators questioned accommodations that were so extensive that they effectively changed the content and the expected student performance. Lack of guidance and assistance to teachers resulted in lowered expectations and created haphazard performance goals for students under the guise of full participation in standards.

Summary of US efforts

The current focus on developing standards, coupled with enhanced accountability and new forms of assessment, is changing the context of classrooms in many school districts across the United States. Securing the participation of students with disabilities in this process is a challenge to local school districts and will require a systematic and defensible decision-making process that can be applied to individualised educational plans for students with disabilities. The National Academy of Science Committee (McDonnell, McLaughlin and Morison, 1997) suggested that educational planning for any student with a disability begins with the assumption that he or she will fully participate in the common content standards. Decisions to modify standards in one or more domains should consider the following three issues:

- Do the common content standards represent skills critical to the individual's success once he or she leaves school?
- Do the common content standards represent critical skills appropriate for the particular age of the student?

- Can the curriculum of the common content standards be fully taught to the student without jeopardising his or her opportunity to master other critical, functional behaviours?

(Ibid., p. 145)

Decisions should also carefully separate what a student ought to be learning from his or her current level of performance. Exempting a student from a standard because he 'can't read well' is not the same as exempting or altering a standard because it is not important for him to learn the material. The challenges inherent in a standards-based approach to education are enormous. Current teacher practices and approaches to educating students with disabilities will need to be altered. Perhaps, most significantly, long-held constructs about students with disabilities and their legal entitlement will have to be considered within the framework of standards.

General conclusions and implications

Several conclusions can be drawn from the experiences of the United Kingdom and the United States in implementing new standards-based curricula, within both general and special education classrooms. The curricular reforms guided by the content standards that are defining what teachers are to teach are being shaped by similar forces in both countries. Political concerns, such as global economic competitiveness and the desire for schools to better serve the workplace, are also potent forces together with the sort of national pride and competition that drives each country to produce more top academic performers on international assessments. These political realities have created a climate that promotes a more challenging curriculum; one that demands that students learn more and higher levels of subject.

In addition, subject matter content, as defined in standards or the National Curriculum, in both countries tends to stress application and more 'authentic' problem-solving. There appears, however, to be a great deal more controversy and state-by-state variability in the United States regarding these pedagogical reforms, particularly with respect to reading instruction. Debates over whole language versus phonetic-based approaches have escalated to the highest political levels in some states, and one state recently revised its math standards to place more emphasis on computation. Other controversies include what history or literature should be taught.

Fuelling the political controversies is the fact that each country has yet to marshal sufficient empirical support for the curricular reforms. In the United Kingdom, there is scant evidence that student performance has significantly improved as a result of the curriculum reforms. Within the United States, policy-makers point to some increased scores on the National Assessment of Educational Progress (NAEP) in certain content areas and at specific grade levels as evidence that students are being taught more demanding content, although other national as well as state-level assessment data have not been consistently positive across all grade levels or segments of the student population.

Given the current lack of clear evidence linking standards to higher levels of student achievement and the vacillating political support for the content or pedagogical approaches demanded by the standards, it is interesting that both countries maintain a base of support for the concept of centralised national or state standards for the curriculum. The United Kingdom has fine-tuned the existing National Curriculum with the hope that it will result in higher levels of student achievement, and similar adjustments have occurred within some US states. Yet, centralised versus local curricular control varies. Nevertheless, even in states with voluntary standards or curricular frameworks, local districts concerned about the performance of their students, are developing strong and challenging content standards.

A broad and focused curriculum

In both countries, curriculum reforms have sought to increase the amount of knowledge and skills, as well as cognitive demands, within core academic subject areas. All students are encouraged to increase their knowledge in specified subjects (in the United Kingdom, particularly in literacy and numeracy) and must be able to integrate and use it in new and more complex ways. Although both the standards and the National Curriculum are intended to focus the instruction in classrooms and to eliminate extraneous subject matter or content, teachers and local school administrators have expressed dismay over the amount of subject matter they are expected to cover within the same instructional time: a situation acknowledged by the international comparison of math instruction in the United States and Japan (Schmidt, McKnight and Raizen, 1997).

The focus on application in some subjects, as opposed to simply learning facts in others, has also challenged teachers to change from teacher-directed instruction to student-directed learning. Yet, in both countries debates over pedagogy and the use of constructivist approaches have imported more skill-based instruction into the curriculum. The changing content and pedagogical demands are creating enormous pressures for more teacher development. Within the United States capacity-building strategies include increased professional development for teachers, although, to date, far fewer resources have been allocated to these activities as compared to the development of assessments and accountability mechanisms.

In the United Kingdom the National Curriculum has provided the greatest challenge to the professional development of teachers of children with special educational needs. Unlike the United States, increased professional development is only just becoming part of an overall reform strategy. Changes in funding arrangements in the United Kingdom through the introduction of local management of schools (LMS) and local management of special schools (LMSS) (details of which are given in Chapter 7) have had a dramatic effect on the ways in which the professional development for teachers of all children has been financed and delivered. Schools themselves are largely responsible for funding in-service training, although the moneys available are dependent on formula funding which is based ultimately on the number of pupils on roll. The result has been that schools have tended to use their precious resources for one-off days of quick-fix staff training which, although often school-based, frequently employs visiting experts, who may, but often do not, have experience and expertise in special educational needs. Consequently, their contribution to the long-term planning, development and evaluation of the curriculum content of the school may be inadequate.

Students with disabilities and standards

In neither the United States nor the United Kingdom is there evidence, as yet, to suggest that the participation of students with disabilities in the 'standard-based' curriculum results in better achievement, let alone better post-school outcomes. Nonetheless, both countries are ensuring that these students fully participate in the reforms to increase public accountability for teaching and to prevent exclusion from classrooms. Both countries face challenges. For example, the subject matter dictated by the National Curriculum and US state standards is overwhelmingly academic and does not necessarily reflect all those critical domains of knowledge which some students with disabilities need to prepare them for a successful transition to adult life. When and how to modify or expand the standards to include all essential knowledge are critical decisions left to special and general education teachers and families in both the United States and the United Kingdom. Such decisions are complicated within the United States by the extreme heterogeneity of the population of students identified as eligible for special education, a large proportion of whom have learning and other 'mild' disabilities. Most require accommodations and supports, but not a curriculum that is modified or differentiated. Contrast these students with those who have a need for a more functional curriculum that includes vocational and independent living skills and may require extensive modifications of standards, and the complexity of the decision-making becomes evident.

In the United States, decisions on how to allocate scarce instructional time is left to individual teachers without formal guidance; equitable access to curriculum is unlikely. Decision-making is more formalised in the United Kingdom, where teachers from special schools have formed networks to discuss ways of ensuring the participation of all students in the National Curriculum. As a result of their work, the teachers themselves have been able to directly influence changes to the National Curriculum in both content and in the ways in which students with disabilities can now work at their developmental versus chronological levels. Within US states and local districts some special educators are beginning to participate in similar professional networks, most often informally as members of subject matter or grade level teams within a school. Such teacher-driven activities appear to offer the best opportunity to date for achieving true access to standards.

The negative impacts of performance standards

In both countries, special educators fear that when the assessed performances of students with disabilities are compared to those of other students, there will be negative consequences. Indeed, within the United States there has been some evidence that administrators or school-based personnel have used special education referrals as a means to avoid accountability. However, as the recent IDEA amendments require all students with disabilities to participate in the state or district large-scale assessments and/or an alternative assessment, the special education loophole is closing. Nevertheless, in an environment that puts a premium on higher levels of student achievement, special education with its individualised instruction can provide the extra remedial support many students need to help them to meet the new instructional demands. Concerns over performance aside, many special education teachers are legitimately worried about how technically feasible it is to expect every student with a disability to learn the same content as non-disabled peers.

Standards and impact on inclusive practices

In the United Kingdom, the participation of students with disabilities in the National Curriculum is credited in part with promoting more inclusion in general education classrooms. Similarly in the United States, reports of increased general and special educators' collaboration within the curriculum suggest that the dialogue surrounding inclusion may centre on how to help a student with a disability learn important subject matter, as opposed to simply being physically present in the general education classroom.

Further, the scope and sequence provided by a set of standards or a National Curriculum provide a common language and set of expectations across grade and age levels for both special and general educators. The standardisation of content ensures breadth and balance in the curriculum offered to each student with a disability and encourages and supports both teacher innovation and the rigorous examination of curriculum and classroom practice. Finally, when coupled with assessment, achievable performance standards and public accountability for results, the standards can provide a framework for higher achievements.

In summary, experience in both the United Kingdom and the United States suggests that teachers and others directly involved in the education of students with disabilities perceive that establishing access to the same curriculum as students without disabilities is important to the instructional process and enhances instructional decisions. What is not yet evident, however, is whether such access will lead to sustained higher levels of achievement among students with disabilities and whether the knowledge and skills gained through this curriculum are the ones that will prove necessary for successful transitions from school. What we do know is that special education teachers and their colleagues in general education will determine the success of these policy decisions. Their knowledge of specific subject matter and their under-standing of how students learn will be critical. So too will be the need to engage in more meaningful collaboration to improve student performance, and not just student placement. To respond to these needs, teachers will require professional development and organisational support on planning time, and greater flexibility in their organisation of the curriculum.

References

Baynes, A. and Dyson, A. (1994) 'Education towards employment: a project for people with learning difficulties', *British Journal of Special Education*, 21,4: 142–146.

Benn, C. and Chitty, C. (1996) *Thirty Years On: Is Comprehensive Education Alive and Well or Struggling to Survive?*, London: David Fulton Publishers.

Blank, R.K. and Pechman, E.M. (1995) *State Curriculum Frameworks in Mathematics and Science: How Are They Changing Across the States?*, Washington, DC: Council of Chief State School Officers.

Booth, T. (1996) 'Stories of exclusion: natural and unnatural selection', in E. Blythe and J. Milner (eds) *Exclusion from School: Inter-professional Issues for Policy and Practice*, London: Routledge.

Booth, T., Ainscow, M. and Dyson, A. (1998) 'England: inclusion and exclusion in a competitive system', in T. Booth and M. Booth (eds) *From Them to Us: an International Study of Inclusion in Education*, London: Routledge.

Byers, R. and Rose, R. (1996) *Planning the Curriculum for Pupils with Special Educational Needs*, London: David Fulton Publishers.

Campbell, J. (1997) 'Towards curricular subsidiarity?', in *Developing the Primary School Curriculum: the Next Steps* (papers from an invitation conference by the School Curriculum and Assessment Authority on 9/10 June 1997), London: SCAA.

Carpenter, B. and Ashdown, R. (1996) 'Enabling access', in B. Carpenter, R. Ashdown and K. Bovair (eds) *Enabling Access: Effective Teaching and Learning for Pupils with Learning Difficulties*, London: David Fulton Publishers.

Centre for the Study of Inclusive Education (1997) *A Trend Towards Inclusion (Statistics on Special School Placements and Pupils with Statements in Ordinary Schools in England, 1992–1996)*, Bristol: CSIE.

Davies, J.D. and Garner, P. (eds) (1997) *At the Crossroads: Special Educational Needs and Teacher Education*, London: David Fulton Publishers.

Department for Education (DfE) (1993) Press release on the National Exclusions Reporting System. London: DfE.

—— (1994) *Code of Practice on the Identification and Assessment of Special Educational Needs*, London: DfE.

Department for Education and Employment (DfEE) (1996) *Education Act 1996*, London: Stationery Office.

—— (1997a) *Excellence for all Children: Meeting Special Educational Needs*, London: Stationery Office.

—— (1997b) *Excellence in Schools*, London: Stationery Office.

—— (1997c) Press release 342/97.

Department of Education and Science (DES) (1978) *Special Educational Needs: Report of the Committee of Enquiry into the Education of Children and Young People* (the Warnock Report), London: HMSO.

—— (1988) *Education Reform Act*, London: HMSO.

—— (1990) *Special Needs Issues: a Survey by HMI* (Education Observed Series), London: HMSO.

Donovan, N. (ed.) (1998) *Second Chances. Exclusion from School and Equality of Opportunities*, London: New Policy Institute.

Dyson, A. (1997) 'Social and educational disadvantage: reconnecting special needs education', *British Journal of Special Education*, 24,4: 151–156.

Gandal, M. (1996) *Making Standards Matter 1996: An Annual Fifty State Report on Efforts to Raise Academic Standards*, Washington, DC: American Federation of Teachers Educational Issues Department.

Goals 2000: Educate America Act of 1994, Pub.L. 103-227, H.R. 1804, 103rd Congress, 2nd Session.

Goertz, M.E. and Friedman, D.H. (1996, March) 'State education reform and students with disabilities: A preliminary analysis', *Year 1 Technical Report, Center for Policy Research on the Impact of General and Special Education Reform*, Alexandria, VA: National Association of State Boards of Education.

Griffiths, M. (1994) *Transition to Adulthood: the Role of Education for Young People with Learning Difficulties*, London: David Fulton Publishers.

Hopkins, D., West, M. and Ainscow, M. (1996) *Improving the Quality of Education for All*, London: David Fulton Publishers.

Hornby, G., Atkinson, M. and Howard, J. (1997) *Controversial Issues in Special Education*, London: David Fulton Publishers.

Koretz, D., Mitchell, K., Barron, S. and Keith, S. (1996a) 'Perceived effects of the Maryland school performance assessment programme', Los Angeles, CA: UCLA/National Center for Research on Evaluation, Standards, and Student Testing (CRESST).

Koretz, D., Barron, S., Mitchell, K. and Stecher, B.M. (1996b) 'Perceived effects of the Kentucky instructional result information system (KIRIS)', Santa Monica, CA: RAND.

Lawton, D. (1988) 'Ideologies of education', in D. Lawton and C. Chitty (eds) *The National Curriculum* (Bedford Way Papers, 33), London: Institute of Education, University of London.

Lawton, D. and Chitty, C. (eds) (1988) *The National Curriculum* (Bedford Way Papers, 33), London: Institute of Education, University of London.

Lewis, A. (1991) *Primary Special Needs and the National Curriculum*, London: Routledge.

—— (1995) *Primary Special Needs and the National Curriculum* (2nd edn), London: Routledge.

—— (1996) 'Summative National Curriculum assessments of primary-aged children with special educational needs', *British Journal of Special Education*, 23,1: 9–14.

Lindsay, G. (1997) 'Values and legislation', in G. Lindsay and D. Thompson (eds) *Values into Practice in Special Education*, London: David Fulton Publishers.

McDonnell, L., McLaughlin, M. and Morison, P. (eds) (1997) *Educating One and All: Students with Disabilities and Standards-Based Reform*, Washington, DC: National Academy Press.

McLaughlin, M.J., Henderson, K. and Rhim, L.M. (1997, March) 'Reform for all? General and special education reforms in five local school districts', Paper presented at the American Education Research Association Annual Meeting, Chicago, IL.

McLaughlin, M.W. and Sheppard, L.A. with O'Day, J. (1995) *Improving Education Through Standards-Based Reform: A Report by the National Academy of Education Panel on Standards-Based Reform*, Stanford, CA: National Academy of Education.

Michigan Department of Education (1995) *Model Content Standards for Curriculum*, Lansing, MI: Michigan Department of Education.

Moses, D. (1996) 'Special educational needs', in P. Croll and N. Hastings (eds) *Effective Primary Teaching: Research-Based Classroom Strategies*, London: David Fulton Publishers.

National Curriculum Council (1992a) *Curriculum Guidance 9: The National Curriculum and Pupils with Severe Learning Difficulties*, York: NCC.

—— (1992b) *The National Curriculum and Pupils with Severe Learning Difficulties: INSET Resources*, York: NCC.

National Foundation for Educational Research (1998) *Target Setting in Special Schools: Trials*, Slough: NFER.

National Research Council (1996) *National Science Education Standards*, Washington, DC: National Academy Press.

Parsons, C. and Howlett, K. (1996) 'Permanent exclusions from school: a case where society is failing its children', *Support for Learning* 11,3: 109–112.

Porter, J. (1996) 'Issues in teacher training', in B. Carpenter, R. Ashdown and K. Bovair (eds) *Enabling Access: Effective Teaching and Learning for Pupils with Learning Difficulties*, London: David Fulton Publishers.

Pugach, M.C. and Warger, C.L. (1993) 'Curriculum considerations', in J. Goodlad and T. Lovitt (eds) *Integrating General and Special Education*, pp. 125–148, New York: Merrill-Macmillan.

Rhim, L.M. and McLaughlin, M.J. (1996) 'State policies and practices: Where are the students with disabilities?', *Center for Policy Research on the Impact of General and Special Education Reform*, Alexandria, VA: National Association of State Boards of Education.

Robinson, P. (1997) *Literacy, Numeracy and Economic Performance*, London: Centre for Economic Performance.

Sands, D.J., Adams, L. and Stout, D.M. (1995) 'A statewide exploration of the nature and use of curriculum in special education', *Exceptional Children*, 62,1: 68–83.

SCAA (1997) Target setting and benchmarking in schools (Consultation Paper, September 1997), London: SCAA.

Schmidt, W.H., McKnight, C. and Raizen, S.A. (1997) *A Splintered Vision: An Investigation of US Science and Mathematics Education*, Boston, MA: Kluwer Academic Publishers.

Sebba, J., with Sachdev, D. (1997) *What Works in Inclusive Education*, Ilford: Barnardo's.

Sebba, J., Byers, R. and Rose, R. (1993) *Redefining the Whole Curriculum for Pupils with Learning Difficulties*, London: David Fulton Publishers.

SENTC (1996) *Professional Development to Meet Special Educational Needs* (a Report to the Department for Education and Employment), Stafford: SENTC.

Shriner, J.G., Kimm, M.L., Thurlow, M.L. and Ysseldyke, J.E. (1993) 'IEPs and standards: What they say for students with disabilities', Technical Report 5, Minneapolis: National Center on Education Outcomes, University of Minnesota.

Smith, S.W. (1990) 'Individualized education programmes (IEPs) in special education: From intent to acquiescence', *Exceptional Children*, 51,2: 6–14.

Teacher Training Agency (1997) *Survey of Special Educational Needs Training Provided by Higher Education*, London: TTA.

Thomas, G. (1997) 'Inclusive schools for an inclusive society', *British Journal of Special Education*, 24,3: 103–107.

Tilstone, C. (1991a) *Teaching Children with Severe Learning Difficulties*, London: David Fulton Publishers.

—— (1991b) 'Teacher education: the changing focus', in R. Ashdown, B. Carpenter and K. Bovair (eds) *The Curriculum Challenge*, London: Falmer Press.

—— (1996) 'Changing public attitudes', in B. Carpenter, R. Ashdown and K. Bovair (eds) *Enabling Access: Effective Teaching and Learning for Pupils with Learning Difficulties*, London: David Fulton Publishers.

Tilstone, C. and Upton, G. (1993) 'Enhancing the quality of provision', in J. Visser and G. Upton (eds) *Special Education in Britain after Warnock*, London: David Fulton Publishers.

Toch, T. (1991) *In the Name of Excellence: The Struggle to Reform the Nation's Schools, Why It's Failing, and What Should Be Done*, New York: Oxford University Press.

Wagner, M., Blackorby, J., Cameto, R., Hebbler, K. and Newman, L. (1993) *The Transition Experiences of Young People with Disabilities. A Summary of Findings From the National Longitudinal Transition Study of Special Education Students*, Menlo Park, CA: SRI International.

Warnock, M. (1996) 'The work of the Warnock Committee', in P. Mittler and V. Sinason (eds) *Changing Policy and Practice for People with Learning Disabilities*, London: Cassell.

Chapter 4

National assessment and special education in the United States and England and Wales

Towards a common system for all?

Martyn Rouse, James G. Shriner and Lou Danielson

Introduction

Assessment is a process that has become so ubiquitous, so much a part of modern life, that few people question its fundamental principles and techniques. It is a process that supports a multi-million dollar industry. It involves various professionals and agencies in carrying it out and there are multiple audiences for its results. It is surrounded by a scientific aura that promises to provide easily understood answers to complex questions about human abilities, predispositions and attainments. Furthermore, assessment stands at the heart of recent attempts to reform education in many parts of the world.

This chapter considers the complex issues and dilemmas relating to assessment of students with disabilities and special educational needs. It will scrutinise the nature and purpose of the assessment task in the United States and in England and Wales in light of recent reforms that have been driven by demands for higher standards for all students and greater accountability for schools. A comparison between the United States and England and Wales is useful because the two counties have influenced each other in the past, and yet as Firestone and Winter (1998) point out, their approaches to assessment are different enough to permit more variation than is observable in either country alone. The chapter will consider how the methods of assessment that are favoured in a particular time and place not only result from the prevailing perspectives on disability and the nature of special educational needs, but are also influenced by the legacy of the assessment traditions of each country. In addition, assessment policies and practice are moulded by contemporary social and political pressures. Indeed, in many modern societies, the state is increasingly using assessment as a means to influence the curriculum, to motivate and control teachers and students, and to ensure accountability of the education system (Broadfoot, 1996).

A number of questions are addressed. How have pre-existing assessment policies and practice in the field of special education been affected by recent developments? What are the difficulties involved in creating a system of assessment that includes all students? The chapter examines some of the assumptions that underpin assessment policies and practice in the two countries and considers some of the similarities and differences between them. It is beyond the scope of this chapter to consider all aspects of the assessment process, but it is necessary to begin with some consideration of the purposes of assessment in the two countries.

A number of reasons for assessing students could be listed. Such a list of purposes might include:

- helping to make placement/eligibility/selection decisions;
- diagnosing the strengths and weaknesses of individuals;
- providing feedback to teachers and learners;
- providing evidence for decisions about certification/graduation;
- for evaluation and accountability;
- providing information to parents and others about student progress.

Assessment has become a hugely complex task that is surrounded by competing issues and agendas. It is carried out for many purposes, using many different techniques and yet Harlen (1994) reminds us that assessment is simply the process of making judgements about a student's performance on a particular task.

Assessment, disability and special educational needs

Assessment has played a pivotal role in the development of special education in both countries. Historically, this task was directed towards categorising and segregating children with disabilities and learning difficulties in order to identify and label children who would not benefit from mainstream schooling. Various tests and screening procedures, such as I.Q. tests, were developed for this purpose enabling decisions about placement and provision to be made for 'special children'. The purpose of such assessment was to determine eligibility for special education. These approaches were concerned with looking for deficits in children and they emphasised the difference between the so-called special and normal populations. Furthermore, professionals have employed a variety of diagnostic methods of assessment in order to plan appropriate interventions designed to remedy the perceived deficit. Many of these procedures, such as the Illinois Test of Psycholinguistic Abilities (ITPA) which first appeared in 1961 (Kirk, McCarthy and Kirk, 1968), and the approaches based on the work of Marianne Frostig (Frostig and Horne, 1964) originated in the United States and were 'borrowed' by professionals in England and Wales.

Over time, the negative consequences of ability testing (Gould, 1997) and the limitations of certain diagnostic procedures became apparent. This resulted in dissatisfaction with traditional views of assessment and with the consequences of such approaches. It coincided with the growing recognition that contextual factors, such as the quality of teaching and the curriculum, have a major impact on learning. In England and the United States commentators were calling for the assessment of both the characteristics of the child and the child's total environment (Ainscow, 1988; Ysseldyke and Christenson, 1987). This view holds that, since the child's learning takes place in a particular context, assessment must also take into account that context and its influence on the child. It adopts an 'ecological perspective' which recognises that features of the learning context, such as the curriculum, the teaching, the organisation of the classroom and other school variables as essential factors that influence learning. Teachers in both countries were encouraged to be aware of various aspects of classroom life and to account for these factors during assessment.

Such interactive, or ecological, explanations became an essential feature of the concept of special educational needs that emerged from the Warnock enquiry in England and Wales (DES, 1978). As a result, a social rather than a medical model of disability influenced the enactment of the subsequent 1981 Education Act. This was associated with changes in the concept of special education, in which the thinking about categories of handicap began to be replaced by the idea of a continuum of special educational needs (SEN) and the idea that learning difficulties could only be understood in the context in which they occurred.

Analysing the learning environment as an approach to assessment of special needs does not prescribe particular forms for assessment. However, it recognises the importance of teachers in the assessment process and values the information that teachers have about their students (Ainscow and Tweddle, 1988; Rouse, 1991). Proponents of this view of assessment stress the need for students to play an active role in their own assessments (Gersch, 1992), through negotiation and collaboration (James, 1989). They also stress the importance of student involvement for effective instructional planning (Ysseldyke and Christenson, 1987; Cullingford, 1997).

The role of teachers

These developments in assessment theory meant that teachers were required to play a significant role in the assessment of their pupils. In the words of Gipps (1994), 'the teacher has moved centre stage as an actor in assessment rather than being a simple administrator of "better" tests derived elsewhere' (p. 10). In response to the pivotal role accorded teachers, researchers such as Lloyd-Jones (1986) have called on teachers to make assessment-based decisions. To them, such decisions would improve teaching and learning as a whole and in particular provide for the learning needs of children who are experiencing learning difficulties. One way in which teachers can provide for the needs of their pupils is to use assessments to plan their teaching activity. In this respect, it can be argued that assessment has evolved from a separate entity in special education, the main purpose of which was for selection and placement, to recognising the central role of teachers in improving teaching and learning. These developments required new forms of 'authentic' assessment that were directly related to the curriculum and carried out by teachers as part of everyday classroom activities.

This issue is an important one, considering the reconceptualised view of special education which implies that educational assessment should be carried out primarily to guide the planning and implementation of instruction (Rampaul and Freeze, 1992). The argument dwells on the premise that the conceptual change in assessment, from assessing for placement to assessing to meet learning needs, makes even greater demands on teachers to use assessment for planning to accommodate for differences in learning (Bryans, 1994).

Historically, teachers have played a more important role in the assessment process in England than they have in the United States. Broadfoot (1996) argues that the role of teachers is growing in many countries. Meanwhile, Madaus, Clarke and O'Leary (1997) suggest that there is little evidence of such a trend in the United States. In fact one of the motives for mandating 'high-stakes' testing programmes at state and local levels, and behind calls for 'national but not federal' standards in tests, is a deep mistrust of teachers' assessment of student attainment. Different assessment traditions in Europe and the United States have had an impact upon the extent to which teachers are involved in the assessment process and the levels of public confidence in teachers as assessors (Madaus and Kellaghan, 1993). Historically, educational assessment in the United States has been dominated by psychometric assumptions and approaches (Berlak et al., 1992). Various technical advances produced a sophisticated technology of testing and the development of a multi-million dollar industry which was largely detached from teachers and the process of education itself (Madaus and Kellaghan, 1993). Although these approaches were considered to be psychometrically sound, many commentators felt that they reduced learning to a process of memorising simple facts which could be assessed by multiple-choice tests. Because of the limitations of such externally set and administered tests, that do not relate directly to the curriculum, there have been calls in the United States for greater use of classroom-based authentic assessment involving teachers of a type that are more common in England (Baker, O'Neill and Linn, 1993). However, progress in this regard has been difficult because of public expectations and long-standing psychometric concerns for technical adequacy. We shall return to this issue later in the chapter.

While educationalists were attempting to reconceptualise the assessment task as outlined above, a more radical set of changes to education generally were about to be introduced on both sides of the Atlantic.

Towards national systems of assessment

Concerns about standards

During the 1970s and 80s politicians in both countries began to express concerns about the alleged poor performance of students on international comparisons, even though the evidence for such international comparisons is difficult to collect (OECD, 1992). Various reforms were enacted to address these concerns, including the introduction of national standards and systems of assessment. These changes were seen as one way of improving standards in schools with the expectation that there would be benefits for the national economy by tightening a connection between schooling, employment and trade.

In England and Wales, the Education Reform Act 1998 relocated control of education policy from local education authorities to central government. In addition the British parliamentary system permitted reform at a pace and to an extent that would be impossible in the United States, where control of education is more devolved. Thus, the extent to which reform has been imposed on the system has been greater in England than in the United States (Firestone, 1997). This has led some commentators to suggest that as the debate about a national testing system in the United States continues, there is much to be learned from the recent English experience with National Curriculum assessment (Madaus and Kellaghan, 1993). However, one of the difficulties involved in making direct comparisons between two countries is the way in which shared terms do not necessarily have shared meanings. This is particularly the case with terms relating to disability, curriculum and assessment. Florian and Pullin explore this issue elsewhere in this book.

England and Wales

The United Kingdom consists, of course, of four linked but separate countries: England, Northern Ireland, Scotland and Wales. Scotland and Northern Ireland have different educational systems from that of England and Wales and are not directly considered in this chapter.

The Education Reform Act introduced for the first time a National Curriculum, intended to raise standards and improve national competitiveness (see Chapter 3). In addition, there was to be a national framework for assessment and testing at ages 7, 11, 14 and 16, designed to ensure that all state schools complied with the National Curriculum. The concept of national testing and assessment was one of the most controversial aspects of the reforms. Not surprisingly, given that the intent was to raise standards, the involvement of children with special educational needs was not considered when the original proposals were announced, and many commentators foresaw difficulties ahead (Weddell, 1988).

There is a long history in England and Wales of distrusting simple pencil and paper tests set by people outside the classroom. Innovative approaches to assessment including the use of portfolios and performance-based assessment had been under development for many years. Many of these innovations were the result of teachers working together to produce systems of assessment that would motivate students, relate directly to the curriculum and be capable of demonstrating learning. Thus, when the government-appointed Task Group on Assessment and Testing (TGAT) chaired by Black (DES, 1988) suggested a national system that would combine standard assessment tasks and teacher assessment, using the principles of curriculum-based assessment, they were largely welcomed by educators. The TGAT Report described assessment as being at the heart of promoting children's learning. Its proposals were ambitious, including elements of both formative and summative assessment. Formative assessment would occur through systems that were carried out by teachers, criterion referenced, linked to the National Curriculum attainment targets and designed to lead to the improvement of the quality of teaching and learning. To achieve comparability, teacher assessment would be subject to a complex process of group moderation. Summative assessment would use much of the data generated through teacher assessment supplemented by standard assessment tasks. It was expected that this process would provide reliable data that could also be used for certification, accountability and evaluative purposes.

The national assessment system consists of two main methods: first, teacher assessment (TA) based on teachers' informal observations of students' attainment in the National Curriculum, and second, externally set assessment tasks. According to Gipps, Clarke and McCallum (1998), the combination of teacher assessment and test results has been a contentious issue. The rule at first was that when the results of these two methods differed, the test result would take precedence.

The time-scale for implementation of the TGAT proposals proved unrealistic. The first assessment of 7-year-olds in English, mathematics and science took place in 1991 amid considerable political and educational controversy. The right wing of the governing Conservative Party (including Margaret Thatcher herself) thought the proposals were too expensive, too complex and not sufficiently rigorous. Subsequently the three largest teacher unions boycotted national assessment, stating it imposed too much work on teachers and that their members had received insufficient training in how to carry it out.

It was not only the assessment process that caused difficulties for teachers and schools but also the ways in which assessment data were to be used. The primacy of the accountability function of national assessment soon emerged when it became clear that the aggregated results of the national assessment from each school were to be published in newspapers, leading to comparisons between schools and local education authorities. The intention of these so-called 'league tables' was to provide information to parents so that they might make a more informed choice about which school to send their child to, on the basis of comparing schools' past performance. However, the use of raw test results to construct league tables of schools is rendered problematic because schools and local education authorities serve different kinds of communities. Furthermore there was an incentive for schools not to include the results of students with special educational needs in the assessment data, because they would depress the school's scores. The inherent unfairness of such comparisons has meant that some schools have become losers in this new competitive environment. Research has emphasised the negative consequences of such high-stakes assessment (Firestone, Mayrowetz and Fairman, 1998), particularly when educators feel that the competition is not fair. More sophisticated 'value-added' systems of accountability based upon children's progress in learning would have provided a more meaningful measure of a school's academic effectiveness. However, these were distrusted by many politicians in the previous government, who argued that raw score league tables provide a mechanism for comparing schools that is easily understood by the public. The current Labour Government has recently decided to introduce an element of value-added into the league tables.

As a result of various implementation problems, together with a growing awareness that the curriculum was overloaded, the government set up a review of the National Curriculum and its assessment under the chairmanship of Sir Ron Dearing. The major outcomes of the Dearing Review (SCAA, 1994) were:

- a simplification of the National Curriculum;
- the reporting of teachers' assessment alongside test results and giving each equal status;
- the suspension of league tables of schools' performance at ages 7 and 14 (but retaining their use at ages 11 and 16).

Much of the vision of the TGAT Report was forgotten, though its principles remain valid (Lewis, 1996). Although there was rhetoric that formative assessment is important to the teaching and learning process, it is clear that the summative use of assessment in many schools prevails (Black, 1996; Lewis, 1996). This is due in part to the fact that much legislation on assessment has tended to emphasise its summative and evaluative functions, to the neglect of the formative uses of assessment (Harlen and James, 1996). More importantly, the prominence given to summative assessment has had a dominant influence on teachers' thinking and assessment practice. Gipps and Stobart (1993) remind us that, 'The aggregated summative information is there for accountability and political purposes, it is there to evaluate and monitor schools rather than to help directly in the education of individual children' (Ibid., p. 98). It could be argued that the skills that teachers have developed recently are for accountability purposes and hence they are summative in nature.

The extent to which a common set of assessment techniques can provide all the necessary data for both formative and summative purposes is debatable. There are those, including DES (1988), who claim that it is possible. Others disagree: Gipps (1990) maintains that, 'The received wisdom at the moment among most educationalists is that the two cannot co-exist' (Ibid., p. 98). Goldstein (1989) argues that the same assessment instruments and procedures cannot serve two different functions. Cline (1992) identified the use of one kind of assessment for different purposes as central to problems associated with national curriculum assessment in the United Kingdom. He states categorically that:

> All too often a variety of outcomes is anticipated from the same procedure that does not work. The assessment arrangements associated with the National Curriculum assessment in the UK offer a vivid example of the difficulties that can arise.
>
> (Ibid., p. 122)

Because the previous government saw the accountability purpose of assessment as the means by which they could raise standards in schools, it is not surprising that issues relating to students with special educational needs did not feature in the proposed national system of assessment. It is interesting to note, however, that within these reforms was the re-emphasis of the Warnock (DES, 1978) principle that educational aims are the same for all children. This idea was reiterated by the 1988 Education Reform Act, which stresses the entitlement of pupils to a broad, balanced and relevant curriculum (SCAA, 1994). The Act further challenged schools with the duty of providing all children with access to the curriculum. Much later, Dearing's final report on the revision of the National Curriculum was more explicit:

> what the National Curriculum should and must do is to allow teachers and schools to meet the particular needs of pupils with special educational needs in ways which they judge to be relevant.
>
> (SCAA, 1994: 6.2)

Students with special needs and national assessment

Dearing reiterated the view that the National Curriculum is an entitlement for all children and therefore implies that, to the maximum extent possible, children with special needs must participate in this national educational and assessment framework. Evidence suggests that few children have been taken out of the National Curriculum (Lewis and Halpin, 1994). Thus, teachers seem to have been using their professional judgements to make their teacher assessments and to adapt (the National) Curriculum to individual children's learning needs (Lewis, 1995).

In England and Wales modification of the standard assessment tests are possible for students with learning difficulties by using permitted special arrangements, but there is considerable uncertainty about the validity and reliability of these adapted tests. Unlike the United States which is considered below, there has been little or no systematic research into the effects of modification of National Curriculum assessment.

A problem arises from the way in which the National Curriculum is constructed as a series of eight progressive levels of achievement (level 1 to level 8) to cover the age range 5–16. Consequently the steps are too big for many children to demonstrate learning and the starting point is too high for many who have special educational needs. Thus there is the anomaly of having some pupils assessed at level 'W'; that is, working towards level 1 of the National Curriculum. In response to these difficulties, the National Foundation for Educational Research (NFER, 1995) produced a report on assessment and recording of small steps within the National Curriculum. More recently the Schools' Curriculum and Assessment Agency (SCAA, 1996) has issued guidance to help overcome such problems for children with profound and multiple learning difficulties.

Considerable professional effort has gone into making national assessment meaningful for children with special needs, and according to Lewis (1996), there is evidence of good practice emerging when teachers are clear in their understanding of the purpose and nature of the task. Others remain sceptical; Rouse and Agbenu (1998) reviewed the use of national assessment in a number of schools and reported that the standard assessment tasks present particular difficulties for pupils with special educational needs. The Schools Curriculum and Assessment Agency claim that national assessment should, 'provide a standard, summative assessment of attainment . . . which can properly be assessed under controlled conditions' (SCAA, 1994). However, in order for such pupils to have access to the tests, they have to be modified to such an extent that they no longer constitute a standard means of assessment. The modifications are often so substantial that the tests become a form of teacher assessment, but one that is separate from the ongoing process of teaching and learning. Furthermore, it is difficult for the tests to be carried out under controlled conditions. Attempts to provide controlled assessment conditions for the tests create circumstances which prevent an accurate reflection of children's level of attainment. Similar problems of involving students with special needs in national assessment are also being encountered in the United States. These difficulties are considered in more detail later in this chapter.

These and other problems mean that many teachers have conflicting views about national assessment. Recent work (e.g. Rouse and Agbenu, 1998), suggests that many of the problems result from confusion about the nature and purpose of assessment, the teachers' role in this process and the participation of students with learning difficulties in national systems of assessment. The notion that teachers are confused about the purpose of assessment in schools is in part due to the summative requirements of the National Curriculum assessments which are seen to oppose their need to use assessment to help them in teaching (Lewis, 1995). Furthermore, the narrow academic focus of summative assessment does not provide the necessary indicators for evaluating the outcomes of special education. Indeed, it could be argued that this emphasis on academic standards is a major impediment to many children's learning and the development of more inclusive practice.

Although there have been many problems with the introduction of national assessment in England, there is increasing evidence that teachers are becoming more skilled at carrying out teacher assessment. This is partly the result of the learning that has occurred during the group moderation process (Gipps, Clarke and McCallum, 1998).

Assessment and national standards in the United States

In the United States several federal laws are cited often in discussions of reform efforts and students with disabilities: Goals 2000: Educate America Act (Goals 2000), the Improving America's Schools Act (IASA), and the Individuals with Disabilities Education Act (IDEA). Each law includes requirements for the setting of standards and the use of assessment, and all have implications for how students with disabilities are to be viewed and valued by society.

The Individuals with Disabilities Education Act is, perhaps, the most prescriptive of the laws with respect to the role of the assessment as part of the education of students with disabilities. The law requires non-discriminatory multi-disciplinary assessment of educational needs in order to determine the eligibility of students with disabilities for special education. Section 614(d) of IDEA outlines several new requirements concerning the participation of these students in state or district-wide assessments. The committee report accompanying IDEA specifically cites a desire to reduce the unnecessary exclusion of students with disabilities from assessments because such exclusion may place severe limits on students' opportunities for post-secondary education and employment. Table 4.1 is a listing of the requirements for assessment found in IDEA.

Goals 2000 encompasses assessment issues primarily in relation to Goal 3, Competency in Challenging Subject Matter, and Goal 4, Mathematics and Science Achievement. State and local control for developing and adopting assessments related to the voluntary National Goals is stressed. Children with disabilities are to be participants in state assessments with 'adaptations and accommodations necessary to permit such participation' (Goals 2000, 1994, p. 20). The Improving America's Schools Act (IASA) requires that districts and schools receiving federal Title I funds implement a standards-based

Table 4.1 IDEA requirements for assessment – ss. 612(a)(17) and 614(e)(1)

Key points	Explanation
Participation	• Children with disabilities are to be included in general state and districtwide assessment programmes with appropriate accommodations where necessary
Guidelines	• SEA or LEA develops guidelines for participation of children with disabilities in alternate assessments for those unable to participate in regular assessments
Alternate assessments	• SEA or LEA must develop, and beginning not later than July 2000, conduct alternate assessments for children who do not participate in regular assessments
Reporting	• SEA will report to the public on performance of children on regular assessments by July 1998 and on alternate assessments by July 2000
Individualised Education Program	• IEP must list modifications needed to participate in state/district-wide assessments, reasons if not participating, and means of assessment

accountability system (see Chapter 5) that includes multiple sources of assessment data. All children, including students with disabilities, are to be included in assessments from which achievement results can be disaggregated for several groups including 'special education status' (US Department of Education, 1997, p. 2).

The important thing about these laws, and specifically the requirements of IDEA, is that they show a concerted effort by the federal government to align major legislative and regulatory requirements affecting states so that some degree of congruence is achieved. Rather than promoting the establishment of separate standards and assessment systems in all states, Goals 2000, IASA, and IDEA encourage the view that, to the maximum extent possible, those standards and assessments employed for these laws can and should be the same. Each law seeks to improve student achievement and attainment through challenging content standards and vigorous assessment of student performance.

Participation of students with disabilities in assessments

The inclusion of students with disabilities in state and national assessments has been the focus of ongoing research by the National Center on Educational Outcomes (NCEO) at the University of Minnesota. A major task of NCEO since 1991 has been to track participation of students with disabilities in state assessments. Over time, NCEO has documented an improving trend in the overall participation of students with disabilities in both state and national assessments (Shriner *et al.*, 1995). In the 1994/95 school year, forty-three states estimated participation rates – up from nineteen states in 1990/91. State estimates of participation have ranged from zero to 100 per cent of the special education population. In 1993, most state estimates were for less than 10 per cent participation; in 1994 most states said between 50 per cent and 75 per cent of their students with disabilities were participating in state assessments (Shriner, Spande and Thurlow, 1994, 1995). The rather dramatic one-year rise was most likely not a true increase across the board. Rather, it appeared states had been prompted by earlier NCEO surveys and were better prepared to answer. We do not know if participation had been better than earlier reported. Still, participation of students with disabilities was not a consistent and routine practice nation-wide.

Participation documentation challenges fall into four major categories. First, there is a great deal of variability in the states' rules about participation. While states should maintain their individuality in deciding exact procedures, without more consistent basic rules across states, meaningful national data are unlikely to result from the reports prepared in conjunction with IDEA requirements. Second, there is also significant variability in the degree to which the guidelines that are prepared by the states are implemented. Differential implementation of guidelines by Individualized Education Program teams (Thurlow and Ysseldyke, 1997) sometimes occurs when team members are concerned about the effect of participation on particular students with disabilities. In some cases students are excluded from testing because the IEP team does not wish to place the student in unduly stressful situations. While this is an altruistic motivation, it may be the case that when these students are excluded, a possible disservice to their long-term educational programme might be taking place, especially when higher stakes are attached to the performance on state and district-wide assessments (Roach, Dailey and Goertz, 1997).

A third reason why participation rates have languished in the past is the fact that these decisions rarely have been monitored by either districts or state agencies. It is sometimes the case that these decisions are made in error because not all members of the decision-making team have had adequate explanation and training, resulting in possible inconsistency and inappropriateness of participation decisions. With participation rates coming under increasing scrutiny, there is likely to be more follow-up and evaluation of decisions by both districts and states.

Finally, some research has examined the way in which students are counted and calculations for participation rates prepared. For example, Erickson, Thurlow, and Ysseldyke (1996) have found that states often have difficulty deciding just how many students with disabilities should be included as the basis for participation calculations. Some states do not know how many students with disabilities take part in their assessments. Other states, have issues in defining the eligible population for participation rate calculations.

Table 4.2 Possible scenarios for assessment under the Individuals with Disabilities Education Act (s. 612)

Curriculum goals addressed by student	Assessment scenario
1. General education goals	1. Participation in all parts of general education assessment with no accommodations
2. General education goals	2. Participation in all of general education assessment with accommodations for some parts
3. General education goals	3. Participation in all parts of general education assessment with accommodations for all parts
4. General education goals + student-specific goals	4. Participation in some parts of general education assessment without accommodations and alternate assessment for student-specific goals
5. General education goals + student-specific goals	5. Participation in some parts of general education assessment with accommodations and alternate assessment for student-specific goals
6. Student-specific goals	6. No participation in general education assessment with alternate assessment for student-specific goals

Because of these issues, participation rates, as currently reported, are very often misleading. Beginning with the newly reauthorised IDEA, states will no longer have the option of guessing about the rate of participation of students with disabilities. Rather, these data will be reported annually to the federal government. The newly passed reporting requirements suggest that a standardised counting and reporting mechanism should be given strong consideration. Whether or not national agreement about the reporting mechanism can be achieved remains uncertain at this time.

New participation patterns?

IDEA requires that states and districts prepare assessment participation rules that are based upon the degree to which a student's educational pro-gramme addresses the general curriculum. Table 4.2 is a listing of six possible assessment scenarios under IDEA. The IEP team must document which portions of the curriculum, and therefore which assessments, are relevant for each student in special education. It may be that all curriculum goals are pertinent regardless of where the student is instructed. Perhaps, the student may receive instruction in general curriculum goals in the special education setting. In this case, the student should participate in all parts of the state assessment, with or without testing accommodations for participation (see below). If the student is working on part of the general curriculum goals,

Table 4.3 Examples of accommodations for assessments

Flexible time	Flexible setting	Alternate presentation format	Alternate response format
• Extended time	• Test alone in test carrel or separate room	• Braille or large print edition	• Pointing to response
• Alternating lengths of test sections (e.g. shorter and longer)	• Test in small group setting	• Signing of directions	• Using template for responding
• More frequent breaks	• Test at home (with monitor)	• Interpretation of directions (paraphrasing)	• Giving response in sign language
• Extended testing sessions over several days (multiple sessions)	• Test in special education classroom	• Taped directions (audio/video)	• Using a computer
	• Test in room with special lighting	• Highlighted keywords	• Allow answers in test book

and has some goals specifically set for his or her unique needs, then the student should be afforded the opportunity for partial participation in the district assessment system. In this case the student should have a modified assessment plan as part of his or her IEP. Finally, if the student is working on goals and standards that are uniquely written for his or her curriculum needs, and no portion of the general curriculum is being addressed for that student, then the student should be assessed in an alternate assessment system (see below). Alternate assessments are designed to reflect the individual circumstances of the student and are prepared so that the state may collect outcomes data on students who are correctly excluded from the general assessment. A plan for how any student is assessed via alternate assessments must be included in that student's IEP.

Accommodations in assessment

Increased attention also has been focused on the issue of provision of accommodations to students with disabilities in national, state, and district-wide testing programmes. IDEA and its regulations make it very clear that the consideration of appropriate accommodations to improve the participation rate of students with disabilities is to be given priority in the future.

Four main categories of accommodation types are often discussed (see Table 4.3). These include changes in the setting of an assessment, the presentation of an assessment, the responses that a student makes, and in the timing or scheduling for the assessment (Thurlow, Scott and Ysseldyke, 1995; Thurlow, Ysseldyke and Silverstein, 1995). In 1996 thirty-nine states had written guidelines for use of accommodations (Erickson and Thurlow, 1997).

It is difficult to get a clear picture of accommodations in testing across the nation, because some of the same issues affect states' use of accommodation guidelines as were found for participation guidelines. The variability with which accommodation rules are applied is just as great as for participation decisions. Also, it has been shown that a particular accommodation may be permitted in one state's testing program, but be prohibited in another state's assessment (Thurlow, Scott and Ysseldyke, 1995). As the use of performance-based measures becomes more frequent, the numbers and types of accommodations that are offered to students also have changed in order to keep pace with the change in assessment practices (Braden, Elliott and Kratochwill, 1997).

The IDEA regulations will expedite the push for states to have comprehensive policies on accommodations. Several important factors must be considered in order to make defensible decisions about the use of accommodations in assessments. First, accommodations for testing should reflect those used during instruction. It does not make sense to use accommodations during assessment that have not previously been used with a student with disabilities during his or her instruction. Second, accommodations used for a particular student must be related to the student's particular educational need. Decisions for accommodations should be made on the student's level of functioning and learning characteristics, not on the type of disability for which they are receiving special education services. Third, consideration should be given to the possibility that a student might need accommodations for some portions of the general education assessment, but not need those same accommodations, or need different accommodations, for other portions.

More recently, the Americans with Disabilities Act (ADA) extended and reinforced the law, and reiterated that the focus should be on individual decision-making regarding the appropriateness of accommodations. Persons with disabilities are a heterogeneous group, and all legislation and litigation protecting their educational and civil rights emphasise the unique case-by-case factors that must be considered in making defensible accommodation decisions.

Phillips (1993a, 1993b) points out that common practice in the past was to grant accommodations in testing procedures to persons with physical or sensory disabilities. However, accommodations should not alter what is measured by the tests. Accommodations in testing are to be made in order to protect a person from being disqualified or penalised solely because of a disability.

Because accommodations are intended to level the playing field for persons with disabilities, valid accommodations should benefit them during assessments. A different accommodation should not benefit the same person if it is not needed. This differential functioning of accommodations is easiest to understand in the case of sensory and physical disabilities. Most people accept that a large-print version of a test would benefit a person with low vision, but not significantly help a person who is in a wheelchair, or a person without disabilities. In instances of cognitive disabilities (e.g. mental retardation learning disabilities) the same reasoning may or may not hold. Phillips (1993a, 1993b) presents the possibility that an accommodation may not always serve the levelling function; rather, accommodations for cognitive impairments may alter the skills being assessed. Added to this concern is the issue of 'content specific' accommodation effects (e.g. calculators or oral reading of directions for math examinations). Is it really the same to allow a calculator for a mathematics exam or a word processor for a writing test as it is to provide wheelchair access to test facilities or large-print versions of an assessment?

Research on accommodations

Research is beginning on the degree to which accommodations used in assessments affect the reliability and validity of the state and district-wide assessments. The main issue addressed by most research is the degree to which the provision of accommodations affects the technical adequacy of the assessments that are used. Many states have extensive lists of accommodations that are allowed by type of test, but we do not know the true extent to which these accommodations are being used and if these accommodations that are used are having significant effects on the results that are obtained. Early research studies suggest that the answers to accommodations research questions will be just as complex as the legal and philosophical surrounding these same issues. There are alternate views of accommodations' utility and effects being voiced at this time.

Koretz (1996), for example, has examined participation of students with disabilities and accommodations used in the Kentucky state assessment system. He found that many IEP teams were making accommodation decisions without regard to the reasons for which the student is receiving special education services and that the provision of accommodations was not always tied to specific criteria. For example, over half of the children with mental retardation or learning disabilities in the assessment were receiving questions in paraphrased form even though there was no logical reason for this accommodation. According to Koretz (1996) these kinds of accommodations result in scores that are implausibly high and the connection between a student's disability and the accommodations provided is rarely clear, especially in the case of cognitive impairments. Thus, accommodations are often overused, resulting in poor quality assessment data.

Tindal and his colleagues at the University of Oregon (e.g. Tindal *et al.*, 1997; Tindal *et al.*, 1998) have studied the effects of specific accommodation allowances on the validity of assessments by looking at student performance under standard and non-standard administration conditions. These efforts are attempts to find out the effects of accommodations by looking at their effect on targeted subgroups of students, for example, students who have difficulty with reading. Important findings from one study of this research that employed a nested design (n = 122 regular education; 42 special education), in which not all students received both accommodations, are worth noting. The opportunity to mark in the answer booklet (response accommodation) did not significantly affect the performance of either general education or special education students in the study. Scores for students with disabilities were not raised to levels that they could not have obtained without that accommodation. When looking at the provision of assistance for the reading of instructions and problems to students taking a math test (presentation accommodation), the authors found that the performance of students with disabilities was raised to a level that was significantly higher than in the condition in which the students had to read the examples, questions and problems on their own (no accommodation). As such, Tindal *et al.* have shown that for students in state-wide assessment, 'access skills like reading appear to prevent some students from performing well in math. Likewise, [response accommodations] that result in no differences in performance can be made without creating non-comparable outcomes' (1997, p. 10).

This work is a careful step toward more complex and robust accommodations research by showing the differential effects of accommodations that can eliminate the distortions of student performance that are caused by a student's disability while not changing the performance of students without disabilities for whom an accommodation is not necessary. Tindal *et al.*'s work emphasises the importance of *a priori* consideration of the effects of accommodations on obtained scores and their validity without imposing category-specific assumptions about students' possible performance.

Other researchers such as Braden, Elliott, and Kratochwill (1997) have looked at teachers' perceptions of accommodation use as a function of task type (performance assessment versus multiple choice) and degree of disability (mild versus severe). Braden *et al.* found that students with documented disabilities were receiving accommodations in state-wide and district-wide assessments because the teachers believed that the students need these accommodations in order to participate meaningfully in assessments. Accommodations were considered more important for performance assessments than for multiple choice tests, and more accommodations were used for students with severe disabilities than for students with mild disabilities.

Olson and Goldstein (1996) reported on investigations of participation and accommodation of students with limited English proficiency and students with disabilities in the National Assessment of Educational Progress (NAEP). They report on the changes in procedures for determining participation and accommodations, brought about because 'many students with disabilities . . . who had been excluded from NAEP were, in fact, capable of participating in the assessment (Ibid., p. 61). The 1995 NAEP involved new criteria for inclusion and allowed the use of various accommodations in mathematics (e.g. large print booklets and calculators; Braille versions of booklets and talking calculators; allowances for time, grouping arrangements, oral directions and oral responses). Inclusion rates for students with disabilities were improved by about 10 per cent across grades 3, 8, and 12 with the new criteria (from about 32 per cent of Individualized Educational Program students in 1992 to 42 per cent in 1994). The revised rules are worded in a more inclusive tone and support participation with accommodations.

Data on the validity effects of accommodations are described as preliminary, but suggest that the scores under non-standard administrations may not be comparable to the data for students who received no accommodations. Olson and Goldstein (1996) summarise early accommodations research in their report as follows:

> The findings . . . did not clearly indicate if the results for accommodated students will fit onto the NAEP scale. An answer to this question is important because of concerns that the assessments may not be measuring the same constructs for the students [with disabilities] assessed under standard conditions, which would mean that inferences made from the results may not be valid.
>
> (Ibid., p. 77)

Several major projects sponsored by the Office of Educational Research and Improvement and the Office of Special Education Programs are under way (see Table 4.4). At the time this chapter was prepared, data and results from these projects were just beginning to be published. As one can see, these projects tend to focus on issues of test accommodations and the efforts of non-standard administration performance and the technical characteristics of the assessments.

Some preliminary results are presented below:

- Students with disabilities routinely are offered test accommodations; students without disabilities also may receive accommodations.
- Participation of students with disabilities in norm-referenced tests does not necessarily affect aggregate scores for schools, districts or states.
- Effects of accommodations on test results are primarily opinion-based at this time; empirical research shows little conclusive evidence of differential effects for most accommodations.

Table 4.4 Summary of assessment project and related efforts

Project/sponsor	Focus	Important findings or understandings	Issues to address
Inclusive comprehensive assessment system Delaware (OERI)	Effects of accommodations for students with disabilities and students without identified disabilities. Accommodations: 1. Content 2. Administration 3. Response	Linguistic demand is greatest barrier to assessment of higher-order skills. Teachers suggestions: 1. Use simple language 2. Give extra time 3. Use visual aids	Validity of items with accommodations. Consistent use of accommodations. Effects of accommodations on student behaviour during testing.
The Maryland Assessment System Project Maryland (OERI)	Impacts on curriculum, instruction, and assessment. Comparison of state assessment to other measures of student achievement.	Importance of review and revision for each item. Simultaneous development of item and scoring tools. No significant discrepancy between items for cognitive ability and for applied skills.	
Minnesota Assessment Project Minnesota (OERI)	Participation, performance, accommodation, and modification for students with limited English proficiency and students with disabilities. Collaboration for testing policy and procedure. Collaboration for graduate standards training and resource.	Project activities are aligned with graduation standards and system accountability assessment. Influence of collaboration for graduation standards and performance assessments.	Misuse of accommodations and modifications. Rule language that is clear.

Table 4.4 cont'd

Project/sponsor	Focus	Important findings or understandings	Issues to address
Oregon Assessment Development and Evaluation Project Oregon (OERI)	Assessment development in science. Bilingual assessment. Accommodations and participation research.	Minor adjustments of rater scoring may significantly influence pass/fail status for borderline students. Scorers may be more biased in high stakes assessment. Lower scores for special education students than for other students.	Influence of reading skills on other content area test. Difficult decisions for accommodations eligibility. Accurate reporting for accommodated tests.
Examining alternatives for outcomes assessment for children with disabilities. Kentucky, Maryland, Minnesota (OSEP)	Characteristics of students with disabilities in various assessment systems. Performance of students with disabilities in the assessment system. Effects of including students with disabilities on overall score distribution. Relationship between instructional and assessment accommodations. Validity of alternative portfolio system for students with severe disabilities. Impact of assessment information on instructional practices.	Maryland and Kentucky are more similar than dissimilar in alternate assessment. Alternative assessments can be managed with advance plan. Students with disabilities can perform well with accommodation. Needs of study relationship between instruction and assessment modification.	Cost of providing accommodations in large-scale assessment. Continuum of assessment options to alternate assessment. Training and awareness: parents, teachers, administrators.

Table 4.4 cont'd

Project/sponsor	Focus	Important findings or understandings	Issues to address
Rand/CRESST studies of Assessment of Students with Disabilities Washington, DC	Assessment of students with disabilities in Kentucky assessment programmes. Designing experimental tests of alternative assessment approach for students with disabilities for large-scale assessment.	More frequent use of accommodations in elementary than secondary grades. Scores for disability and accommodated groups were inflated. Discriminated items.	Difficulty level of assessments linked to high standards for low achieving students. Design of accommodation guidelines to increase proper use.
Performance assessment and standardised testing for students with disabilities: psychometric issues, accommodation procedures, and outcomes analysis. Wisconsin (OSEP)	Students with or without disabilities functioning on three types (knowledge and concept test, performance tasks, teacher-constructed classroom performance tasks) of math and science assessments. Develop of assessment accommodation checklist and performance task construction guidebooks.	Performance-based assessments were difficult for both groups. Students without disabilities performed better than students with disabilities. 96% of students with disabilities received accommodations. Most common accommodation was increased time. All students preferred performance assessment task over multiple-choice. Performance-based items were equally reliable for both groups.	Time Funding

Table 4.4 cont'd

Project/sponsor	Focus	Important findings or understandings	Issues to address
National Assessment of Educational Progress (NAEP) Washington DC	Increase participation of students with disabilities and LEP. Effects of accommodations.	Accommodations allowed more students with disabilities and students with LEP to participate.	Ongoing monitoring of inclusion/ accommodation approaches.
Education Statistics Services Institute (ESSI) study of the inclusion of students with special needs in assessment. Washington DC	Monitor and summarise current activities, ongoing projects and other efforts toward the inclusion of students with disabilities and students with LEP.	More accommodations are being permitted and additional students are being included.	The needs of questions regarding the scalability and comparability of the data by item and test.

Types of assessment in the reform movement

Along with a push for higher standards, there has been a shift toward increased use of performance-based assessments in the United States. Performance assessments are any type of test that allows the student to demonstrate knowledge in a natural context. They generally require students to give a response that demonstrates understanding of a certain topic, skill, or concept (Office of Technology Assessment, 1992). Performance assessment encompasses a wide variety of responses options from the student. Some of these include: (a) short answers to open-ended questions, (b) extended open-ended responses, (c) an individual performance of a skill or task, (d) a group performance of a skill or task, (e) portfolio preparation, (f) projects, exhibitions, or extended demonstrations. Vocational education, special education, and the arts have relied on performance-based assessments for support in decision-making about teaching and learning for individual students. It is not unusual to assess students' skills in on-the-job settings, to require demonstrations of adaptive behaviours, or display the portfolio of a student's artwork. More recently, performance assessment has been used in state and other large-scale testing systems (Office of Technology Assessment, 1992). This shift has generated interest in some very important research issues, notably technical adequacy.

Technical adequacy and the race to reform

Reform policies and their underlying philosophies are changing practice ahead of the research base to support some of the activities that are now ongoing. This sequence of events is not altogether unreasonable, since it is difficult to validate an assessment process before it is used.

Research on the technical adequacy of performance-based assessment is mixed, especially when large-scale accountability issues are raised. Baker, O'Neil, and Linn (1993) reported on the scoring reliability of performance assessments in the area of written language. These authors found that reliable scoring of large-scale performance assessment is feasible, although it does take a large degree of training of the scorers. Braden *et al.* (1997) reported on the reliability of several mathematics and science performance tasks developed for use with students with and without disabilities. They found that inter-rater agreement coefficients ranged from .49 (4th grade science) to .82 (8th grade math). They concluded that it is possible to develop reliable performance-based assessments for students with and without disabilities. Reliabilities of tasks and instruments was approximately the same for both groups. They caution, however, that the psychometrics of their performance assessment tasks and instruments were too unpredictable for accountability decisions. Koretz *et al.* (1993) investigated relationships between measures of performance assessment in the state of Vermont. They found only moderate correlations between the writing portfolio scores and direct writing assessments, and suggest that stronger evidence of within-group performance comparability is needed before sound accountability decisions can be made.

There is little agreement about what evidence should be provided about the technical quality of performance-based assessments (Worthen, 1993), as traditional concepts of validity seem ill-suited to serve as psychometric standards. Messick (1989, 1994) makes a distinction between the evidential basis for validity in terms of its construct validity and the consequential basis for validity. He expresses concern that in the development of performance-based assessments, tasks are chosen without sufficient attention to the constructs that are to be measured. Worthen (1993) summed up the issue in this way:

> The crux of the matter is whether or not the [performance-based] assessment movement will be able to show that its assessments accurately reflect a student's true ability in significant areas of behaviour that are relevant . . . Whether called reliability, validity, or even 'isomorphism', . . . some evidence of that the technical quality of the assessment is good enough to yield a truthful picture of student abilities is essential. Otherwise, the promise it holds for improving teaching and learning will go unfulfilled.
>
> (Ibid., p. 448)

Linn (1992) has proposed several methods for linking performance on different types of assessments in order to establish the degree to which student performance over time is comparable. Linn's linking model includes anchoring, benchmarking, equating, projection, social moderation and prediction as options for describing the extent to which student performance from time to time or grade to grade is consistent and, therefore, will provide some evidence of reliable and valid improvement or lack of improvement on the part of the student. Cronbach *et al.* (1995) point out that the degree to which reliability coefficients may be used to describe the behaviour of performance assessments in high stakes decisions might need to be rethought. For these authors, when stakes are high it is appropriate to insist that the conclusion about student performance is nearly a 'sure thing' (Ibid., p. 8).

The impact of these concerns is amplified when performance-based assessment is intended to serve as the cornerstone of large-scale and, sometimes, high stakes assessment. The reality is that performance-based assessments will be researched as they are used, and answers to critical questions about technical adequacy are unknown at this time. The issues surrounding the degree to which the information gathered from performance assessment is in fact the information desired for broader purposes has yet to be resolved. It is likely that in the future some degree of work will be looking to see if there are more expedient ways to use performance assessments such as matrix sampling in order to cut down the cost and increase the technical adequacy of large-scale assessments.

Alternate assessment

The IDEA regulations make it clear that the vast majority of students with disabilities are expected to participate to some degree in the state's general education assessments. These assessments may be traditional tests, an alternative performance-based assessment, or a combination of both. For a very small percentage, however, the best way for the district or state to gauge students' progress in their unique curricula may be through participation of that student in an alternate assessment system. The term 'alternate assessment' has been defined by Ysseldyke, Olsen and Thurlow (1997) as 'any assessment that is a substitute way of gathering information on the performance and progress of students who do not participate in the typical state assessment used with the majority of students who attend schools' (Ibid., p. 2).

For some time, we have been able to point to the activities of two states, Kentucky and Maryland, as leading the way in the development and implementation of alternate assessment systems. Both of these states have used the idea of portfolio assessment as a means of gathering achievement information when students cannot participate in the general state assessments. Typically, these students should be only 'those with the most significant cognitive impairments who are working on educational goals more closely aligned with independent functioning' (Ibid., p. 4).

Kentucky has an alternate portfolio that addresses a subset of the state's defined learner expectations for students who are not working towards the regular diploma that is available in that state. These alternate portfolios contain a defined sample of prescribed items: (a) a table of contents, (b) a letter to the portfolio reviewer, (c) entries that show the students work in several life domains, (d) a schedule of the student's work and school activities, (e) a summary of job activities and experiences to date, and (f) examples of the students' communication activities in the student's preferred or primary mode of communication (Kentucky Department of Education, 1996). These entries change in context by age of the student. For example, in the area of job skills, an eighth-grader might have an employment entry showing job exploration skills, whereas a twelfth-grader might have a prepared résumé for a potential employer. Portfolios are scored on a scale of 1 (Novice) to 4 (Distinguished) along six dimensions: (a) student performance, (b) evidence of natural supports, (c) instruction in multiple dimensions, (d) extent of inter-actions with peers, (e) contexts of instruction, and (f) alignment with the state's learning expectations (Kleinert, Kearns and Kennedy 1997). Scores for student portfolios in the alternate assessment are included in the overall accountability system for the student's home school district.

Maryland is close to implementing an alternate assessment strategy, called the Independence Mastery Assessment Program (IMAP). The purpose of IMAP is to assess those students who have severe disabilities, who are working on a curriculum that has unique goals, and who are not at all participating in the general state assessment programme (Maryland State Department of Education, 1996). The individual assessment consists of four content domains: (a) personal management, (b) community functioning, (c) career vocational skills, and (d) leisure recreation skills. Examples of specific activities that the student engages in as part of his or her normal school day, are submitted as evidence of the learner domains of communication, decision-making strategies, and academic or behavioural skills within each of the content areas. IMAP also includes on-demand defined tasks for the domains; these are specific to the student's age group (e.g. 5, 8, 10, 13). Examples include: making lunch, using a pay telephone, preparing a work station, and listening to music. Performance on the tasks is evaluated as part of the overall portfolio. Tasks are videotaped and are scored by a panel of three to five teachers. Scores generated include: (a) holistic scoring of performance on the task, (b) a rating of the student's opportunity to learn the task and supports provided by the school, and (c) parents' perceptions of the tasks and student performance.

All states must make an expedited effort to address alternate assessment issues. By the year 2000 states and/or districts must have developed an alternate assessment for those students who cannot participate in the general state assessment because all students must be part of the overall system. Research by Erickson and Thurlow (1997) showed that only four states were in the process of developing an alternate assessment and another thirteen states were discussing plans to develop an alternate assessment. Thirty-six states reported during the 1996/97 academic year that they had no activities in the development or implementation of an alternate assessment. The purpose of alternate assessment is to measure progress toward high expectations that are established ahead of time. Clearly, the new federal requirements are causing a great flurry of activity among states, that for many should begin with an analysis of the standards that the state has for all its students.

Conclusion

With the current emphasis on higher standards, issues related to disabilities have been raised, discussed, and often acted upon in a hurried manner. For example, the transition to more performance-based assessments and the provision of accommodations to students with disabilities has occurred without a thorough understanding of the impact of either practice at the student or system level. As we stated earlier, there is a convergence of reform legislation. Recent and proposed laws in both countries make it clear that all students are part of the learning community and should be included in all aspects of education including assessment.

Setting higher national standards is not a simple remedy for under-achievement in the two countries. There are real problems with how to set appropriate standards. If all children are expected to achieve the same standards, then the standards are likely to be low. There is also the likelihood that the standards would only cover a narrow range of basic skills. Evidence suggests that minimal competency requirements drive down, rather than improve achievement. This is a real dilemma facing educators and policy-makers: if differential rather than common standards are acceptable, who decides who should achieve what?

In both countries, when the standard-based reforms were first introduced, there was no consideration of the impact of, or place within, the reforms for students with special educational needs. They were later included only as an afterthought. Although recent policy developments have been couched in more inclusive language, there is an intrinsic contradiction relating to the assessment of students with special needs. On one hand, certain forms of assessment are used to identify some students who are different so that they can receive something additional or special. Indeed, special education depends on such approaches to decide who is eligible for these additional services. On the other hand there is the drive to create universal high standards together with a common system of assessment that can recognise the learning of all students. If such systems are to be inclusive then they will need to be criterion-based. This is because there is an inherent problem for students with special educational needs with systems of assessment that are predicated on comparisons with others. Typically, norm-referenced tests compare the achievement of an individual with a standard sample of (similar) students. It is obvious that normal distributions of ability and attainment make it extremely difficult for some children to demonstrate progress because of the assumptions that underpin this psychometric view of the world. Indeed normative assumptions in education and assessment 'carry the power to determine selectively the way in which issues are discussed and solutions proposed' (Broadfoot, 1996). In other words, the influence of psychometric thinking leads to deterministic views of ability and achievement which not only limit what we expect from certain students, but it also restricts developments in education and assessment.

In both countries there is confusion in many sections of society, including within the education community, about the various purposes of assessment. This lack of clarity about purpose is partly the result of mixed messages from the media and from politicians, but also the lack of sufficient training for teachers to enable them to carry out the task. Furthermore, assessment techniques designed to produce data for one particular purpose are often used for other inappropriate reasons. Thus, there is sometimes a lack of 'fitness for purpose' in which inappropriate methods are used.

The introduction of a national system of assessment in England and Wales was part of the previous government's strategy to improve standards and the current government seems unlikely to change these arrangements. The extent to which this aim has been achieved is questionable. Undoubtedly, schools are more accountable than they ever were in the past. In many schools there is a real sense of urgency and a growing emphasis on learning, albeit within the core areas of the National Curriculum. The competitive ethos in which schools are operating has focused attention on assessment systems and there is little doubt that in some cases there have been improved outcomes for students. But, as in all competitions, there have been losers as well as winners. Some schools, particularly those that are not doing well in the league tables are not comfortable places in which to work or be educated. These schools are often situated in areas of high social need and are likely to contain a large proportion of poor, underprivileged children, many of whom will have special educational needs. In this particular competition, the cost of losing is high because unpopular schools find that their resources are cut as student numbers decline. Such high-stakes assessment systems have their casualties. It may be that it is the victims of 'educational Darwinism' who are being punished for their failure to adapt to the new environment.

The accountability functions of assessment are essential and it is important that assessment used to support this purpose should be technically adequate and have acceptable reliability. The public has a right to know what is happening in schools – after all, they pay for them through taxes of various kinds. One way of providing this information is through making the results of assessment available to those who need to know. However, this is a necessary, but not sufficient means of providing the required information. Schools are more than places where students learn to do better on tests. The other functions of schooling will never be perceived as important until accountability systems include some judgements about these vital aspects of the educational endeavour.

Many politicians and policy-makers have realised that control over the assessment process gives control of the curriculum. But there is also a need to redefine the relationship between assessment and curriculum. Perhaps this might best be done by ensuring clarity of purpose in the assessment task and ensuring fitness for purpose. This will require the continued development of a new form of educational assessment which place teachers at the heart of this process. There is evidence from England and Wales that, after considerable setbacks during the past decade, teachers are becoming increasingly involved in making the national system of assessment work for the benefit of their own professionalism and also for the benefit of children's learning.

In the United States, with its different traditions of assessment and its different approaches to individual rights, there has been progress with the development of systems that are enabling greater levels of participation in state-wide assessment systems. At both the national and state levels, public policy is outpacing research and practice by several years. Characteristic of the current reform, is the desire to make changes in policy that align special education with general education. This is a crucial time in educational history because persons with disabilities and special educational needs are increasingly being seen as an integral part of the new developments – a step toward meaningful inclusion not only into national systems of assessment but into society and its educational system.

References

Ainscow, M. (1988) 'Beyond the eyes of the monster: An analysis of recent trends in assessment and recording', *Support for Learning*, 3,3: 149–153.

Ainscow, M. and Tweddle, D.A. (1988) *Encouraging Classroom Success*, London: David Fulton.

Baker, E.L., O'Neil, H. and Linn, R.L. (1993) 'Policy and validity prospects for performance-based assessment', *American Psychologist*, 48, 1210–1218.

Berlak, H., Newmann, F., Adams, E., Archbald, D., Burgess, T., Raven, J. and Romberg, T. (1992) *Towards a New Science of Educational Testing and Assessment*, New York: State University of New York Press.

Black, P. (1996) 'Formative Assessment and the improvement of learning', *British Journal of Special Education*, 23,2: 51–55.

Braden, J.P., Elliott, S.N. and Kratochwill, T.R. (1997) *The Performance of Students With and Without Exceptional Educational Needs on Performance*, University of Wisconsin-Madison: Wisconsin Center for Education Research.

Broadfoot, P. (1996) *Education, Assessment and Society*, Buckingham: Open University Press.

Bryans, T. (1994) 'The 1981 Education Act: a critical review of assessment principles and practice' in Wolfendale, S. (ed.), *Assessing Special Educational Needs.* London: Cassell.

Cline, T. (1992) 'Assessment of special educational needs: meeting reasonable expectations?', *The Assessment of Special Educational Needs: International Perspectives*, London: Routledge.

Cronbach, L.J., Linn, R.L., Brennan, R.T. and Haertel, E. (1995, Summer) *Evaluation comment: Generalizability analysis for educational assessments*, Los Angeles, CA: University of California, Center for Research on Evaluation, Standards and Student Testing.

Cullingford, C. (ed.) (1997) *Assessment versus Evaluation*, London: Cassell.

Department for Education (DfE) (1994) *The Code of Practice on the Identification and Assessment of Special Educational Needs*, London: HMSO

Department for Education and Science (DES) (1978) *Special Educational Needs (Warnock Report)*, London: HMSO.

—— (1988) *National Curriculum: Task Group on Assessment and Testing. A Report*, London: HMSO.

Erickson, R. and Thurlow, M.L. (1997) *1997 State Special Education Outcomes.* Minneapolis, MN: University of Minnesota, National Center on Educational Outcomes.

Erickson, R., Thurlow, M.L. and Ysseldyke, J.E. (1996) *Neglected Numerators, Drifting Denominators, and Fractured Fractions: Determining Participation Rates for Students with Disabilities in State Assessment Programs* (Synthesis Report No. 23). Minneapolis, MN: University of Minnesota, National Center on Educational Outcomes.

Firestone, W. (1997) 'Standards reform run amok: What the British experience can teach us' *Education Week*, 8 October 1997: 30–32.

Firestone, W., and Winter, J. (1998) 'Different Policies, Common Practice: Mathematics Assessment and Teaching in the United States and England and Wales', paper presented at the annual meeting of the American Educational Research Association Conference, San Diego, CA. 16 April 1998.

Firestone, W., Mayrowetz, D. and Fairman, J. (1998), 'Performance-based assessment and instructional change: The effects of testing in Maine and Maryland', *Education Evaluation and Policy Analysis*, 20,2: 95–113.

Frostig, M., and Horne, D. (1964) *The Frostig Programme for the Development of Visual Perception*, Chicago, IL: Follett.

Gersch, I.S. (1992) 'Pupil involvement in assessment' in Cline, T. (ed.) *The Assessment of Special Educational Needs: International Perspectives*, London: Routledge.

Gipps, C. (1990) *Assessment: A Teachers' Guide to the Issues*, London: Hodder and Stoughton.

—— (1994) *Beyond Testing; Towards a Theory of Educational Assessment*, London: The Falmer Press.

Gipps, C., and Stobart, G. (1993) *Assessment: a Teacher's Guide to the Issues* (2nd edn), London: Hodder and Stoughton.

Gipps, C., Clarke, S. and McCallum, B. (1998) 'The Role of Teachers in National Assessment in England', paper presented at AERA Conference, San Diego, CA. April 1998.

Goals 2000: Educate America Act (1994) (P.L. 103–227). U.S. Congress, 2nd Session.

Goldstein, H. (1989) 'Psychometric test theory and educational assessment', in Simons, H., and Elliot, J. (eds) *Rethinking Appraisal and Assessment*, Milton Keynes: Open University Press.

Gould, S.J. (1997) (2nd edn) *The Mismeasure of Man*, London: Penguin.

Harlen, W. (1994) *Enhancing Quality in Assessment*, London: Paul Chapman Publishing.

Harlen, W. and James, M. (1996) 'Assessment and Learning: Differences and Relationships Between Formative and Summative Assessment', paper presented at the European Conference of Educational Research, Seville, Spain.

James, M. (1989) 'Negotiation and dialogue in student assessment and teacher appraisal', in Simons, H., and Elliot, J. (eds) *Rethinking Appraisal and Assessment*, Milton Keynes: Open University Press.

Kentucky Department of Education (1996) *KIRIS: Kentucky Alternate Portfolio Project Teachers' Guide*, Lexington, KY: Kentucky Systems Change Project for Students with Severe Disabilities.

Kirk, S.A., McCarthy, J.J. and Kirk, W.D. (1968) *Illinois Test of Psycholinguistic Abilities (ITPA)*, Urbana, IL: University of Illinois Press.

Kleinert, H.L., Kearns, J.F., and Kennedy, S. (1997) 'Accountability for all students: Kentucky's alternate portfolio assessment for students with moderate and severe cognitive disabilities', *The Journal of the Association for Persons with Severe Handicaps* (JASH) 22: 88–101.

Koretz, D. (1996) *The assessment of students with disabilities in Kentucky*, CSE Technical Report No. 431. Los Angeles, CA: CRESST/RAND Institute on Education and Training.

Koretz, D., Klein, S., McCaffrey, D. and Stecher, B. (1993) *The Reliability of Vermont Portfolio Scores in the 1992–93 School Year*, Santa Monica, CA: RAND Institute for Education and Training.

Lewis, A. (1995) *Primary Special Needs and the National Curriculum* (2nd edn), London: Routledge.

—— (1996) 'Summative National Curriculum assessments of primary aged children with Special Needs', *British Journal of Special Education*. 23,4: 9–14.

Lewis, A., and Halpin, D. (1994) 'The National Curriculum and Special Education: A report of the perceptions of twelve special school headteachers', paper presented at the annual conference of the British Educational Research Association, Oxford.

Linn, R.L. (1992, September) 'Linking results of distinct assessments', paper prepared for the Council of Chief State School Officers, Washington, DC.

Lloyd-Jones, R. (1986) 'An overview of assessment' in Lloyd-Jones, R., and Bray, E. (eds) *Assessment: From Principles to Action*, London: Macmillan.

Madaus, G. and Kellaghan, T. (1993) 'The British experience with authentic testing', *Phi Delta Kappan*, 74: 458–469.

Madaus, G., Clarke, M. and O'Leary, M. (1997) 'The Kaleidoscope of assessment: disciplinary angles', *Assessment in Education*, 4,3: 431–438.

Maryland State Department of Education (1996) *Independence mastery assessment program: IMAP PILOT*, Baltimore, MD: MSDE.

Messick, S. (1989) 'Validity'. in R.L. Linn (ed.) *Educational Measurement* (3rd edn), New York: Macmillan.

—— (1994) 'The interplay of evidence and consequences in the validation of performance assessments', *Educational Researcher*, 23, 13–2.

NFER (1995) *Small Steps of Progress in the National Curriculum*, Slough: NFER.

OECD (1992) *The OECD International Education Indicators, a Framework for Analysis*, Paris: OECD.

Office of Technology Assessment (1992) *Testing in America's Schools: Asking the Right Questions*, Washington, DC: OTA.

Olson, J.F. and Goldstein, A.A. (1996) 'Increasing the inclusion of students with disabilities and Limited English Proficiency students in NAEP' (NCES document 96–894) *Focus on NAEP*, 2,1: 1–5.

Pearson, L. (1994) 'From the Task Group on Assessment and Testing to Standard Tasks and Tests', in Wolfendale, S. (ed.) *Assessing Special Educational Needs*, London: Cassell.

Phillips, S.E. (1993a) 'Update on testing accommodations: Part 1', *National Council on Measurement in Education Newsletter*, 2,1: 2–6.

—— (1993b) 'Update on testing accommodations: Part 2', *National Council on Measurement in Education Newsletter*, 2,2: 2–3.

Rampaul, W.E. and Freeze, R.D. (1992) 'Enabling schools for all: Assessment in the service of systemic reform' in Cline, T. (ed.) *The Assessment of Special Educational Needs: International Perspectives*, London: Routledge.

Roach, V., Dailey, D. and Goertz, M. (1997) *Opening the Door to Educational Reform: Understanding Educational Assessment and Accountability*, Boston, MA: The Federation for Children with Special Needs.

Rouse, M. (1991) 'Assessment, the National Curriculum and special educational needs: confusion or consensus', in Ashdown, R. *et al.* (eds) *The Curriculum Challenge: Access to the National Curriculum for Pupils with Learning Difficulties*, London: Falmer Press.

Rouse, M. and Agbenu, R. (1998) 'Assessment and special educational needs: teachers' dilemmas', *British Journal of Special Education*, 25,2: 81–87.

SCAA. (1994) *The National Curriculum and Its Assessment (Final Report)*, London: HMSO.

—— (1996) *Planning the Curriculum for Pupils with Profound and Multiple Learning Difficulties*, London: SCAA.

Shriner, J.G., Spande, G. and Thurlow, M.L. (1994) *State Special Education Outcomes: 1993*, Minneapolis, MN: University of Minnesota, National Center on Educational Outcomes.

Shriner, J.G., Gilman, C.J., Thurlow, M.L. and Ysseldyke, J.E. (1995) 'Trends in state assessment of educational outcomes', *Diagnostique*, 20: 101–119.

Thurlow, M.L. and Ysseldyke, J.E. (1997) 'Large-scale assessment participation and reporting issues: Implications for local decisions', *Diagnostique*, 22, 225–236.

Thurlow, M.L., Scott, D. and Ysseldyke, J.E. (1995) *A Compilation of States' Guidelines for Accommodations in Assessment for Students with Disabilities* (Synthesis Report No. 18). Minneapolis, MN: University of Minnesota: National Center on Educational Outcomes.

Thurlow, M.L., and Ysseldyke, J.E. and Silverstein, B. (1995) 'Testing accommodations for students with disabilities', *Remedial and Special Education*, 16: 260–270.

Tindal, G., Hollenbeck, K., Helwig, B. and Heath, B. (1997) *Summaries of Research on Accommodations in Large-Scale Testing in Written Expression and Mathematics* (Technical Report to Oregon Department of Education), Eugene, OR: University of Oregon, Behavioral Research and Teaching.

Tindal, G., Heath, B., Hollenbeck, K., Almond, P. and Harniss, M. (1998) 'Accommodating students with disabilities in large-scale assessments: An empirical study', *Exceptional Children*, 64: 439–450.

US Department of Education (1997) *Guidance on Standards, Assessments, and Accountability*, Washington, DC: Office of Elementary and Secondary Education.

Weddell, K. (1988) 'The new act: a special need for vigilance', *British Journal of Special Education*, 15,3: 98–101.

Worthen, B.R. (1993) 'Critical issues that will determine the future of alternative assessment', *Phi Delta Kappan*, 74: 444–454.

Ysseldyke, J.E. and Christenson, S.L. (1987) 'Evaluating students' instructional environments', *Remedial and Special Education*, 8,3: 17–24.

Ysseldyke, J.E., Olsen, K. and Thurlow, M.L. (1997) *Issues and Considerations in Alternate Assessments* (Synthesis Report No. 27), Minneapolis, MN: University of Minnesota: National Center on Educational Outcomes.

Chapter 5

Educational accountability and students with disabilities in the United States and in England and Wales

Judy Sebba, Martha L. Thurlow and Margaret Goertz

Introduction

The demand for educational accountability reflects the belief that the public education system, like most other public systems, must be held accountable for what it does. Typically, education is viewed as a system (see Oakes, 1986; Shavelson, McDonnell and Oakes, 1989; Shavelson, McDonnell, Oakes and Carey, 1987) involving inputs (e.g. teachers, students) with certain characteristics (e.g. qualifications/certification, socio-economic status), and resources (e.g. funds) that flow into an educational process. The process of education can be characterised according to its quality and quantity. Altogether, these produce the outcomes of education, its results, which may include student performance, graduation rates, and a host of other direct and indirect results. Schools can be held accountable for any or all of these aspects of the education system.

In both the United States and in England and Wales, the increased emphasis on educational accountability is seen as one of the ways in which schools will be improved. Yet, the ways in which educational accountability plays out in the two countries are quite different. In this chapter we provide overviews of the educational accountability systems in the United States and England, then draw some general conclusions about their similarities and differences.

Overview of educational accountability in the United States

The concept of accountability goes hand-in-hand with most of the educational reforms in the United States within the past two decades. The desire for accountability has been a strong driving force since the mid-1980s, when the National Commission on Excellence in Education (1983) decried American education, warning that it was producing students who were ill-equipped for a competitive global economy. Following the Commission's report, US education has gone through several waves of reform, the latest of which reflects a redirection from an emphasis on accountability for the inputs and process of education to accountability for the results of education.

In the United States, responsibility for the content and quality of public elementary and secondary education rests within each of the fifty states. As a result, there are multiple goals for accountability (e.g. public information, improved student performance) and multiple approaches to ensuring accountability (e.g. graduation exams, cash rewards for exemplary schools). These must be taken into account as we attempt to determine the role that educational accountability is playing as a reform in the United States, and its relation to special education.

In this section we address the topic of accountability: who is held accountable, how accountability is implemented, and its consequences. Each of these topics reveals tensions between how accountability is defined by special education and general education in the United States. They also reveal a current dovetailing of approaches, reflecting a new hope for a unified system of education for students with and without disabilities. Much of this dovetailing of approaches is due to the 1997 amendments to the Individuals with Disabilities Education Act (IDEA), which pushes special education on to a pathway more aligned with that of general education.

Accountability in general education and special education

We use data from several sources to provide a picture of the current status of accountability within the United States. Among these sources are a national survey of state directors of special education (Erickson and Thurlow, 1997), analyses of state policies on graduation (Thurlow, Ysseldyke and Reid, 1997), and analyses of state accountability reports (Thurlow et al., 1997), all conducted by researchers at the National Center on Educational Outcomes (NCEO).[1] Other sources of information include intensive case studies of twelve states,[2] and a national survey conducted by the Council of Chief State School Officers (CCSSO) and the Center for Policy Research on the Impact of General and Special Education Reform (CCSSO, 1996a; Rhim and McLaughlin, 1997).

Accountability for what?

The design of a state's general education accountability system is driven by the goals of the system. For example, states concerned with ensuring student access to a basic education programme will hold school districts accountable for the level and quality of education inputs (e.g. minimum standards for the number, mix and qualifications of staff; content of curriculum and instruction; and the size and nature of facilities). As states have turned their attention to issues of productivity, school improvement and school autonomy, student outcomes have become a larger and more visible part of accountability systems. These outcomes include tested achievement (generally using

Table 5.1 Examples of targets of accountability systems in the United States

Who is held accountable?	Accountable for what?		
	Resources	Processes	Outcomes
Students		• High school course credits • Community service	• Tested achievement • Grade point average
Teachers		• Professional development • Teaching performance	• Student achievement
Schools and school districts	• Number and type of personnel • Credentials of personnel • Student/teacher ratios • Staff salaries • Operations expenditures • Per pupil expenditures • Quality, size of facilities	• Curriculum • Programmes for special needs students • Length of school day, year • School climate • Goals • Improvement planning • Fiscal procedures • Student access to special programmes	*Students* • Tested achievement • Grade point average • Attendance • Drop-out rates • Completion rates • Transition to work, post-secondary education *Staff* • Staff attendance • Staff absenteeism

a state assessment), student grades, student attendance, school retention and completion, and transition from school to work or post-secondary education. The increased emphasis on state assessments (Bond, Roeber and Braskamp, 1997) is, perhaps, one of the most obvious indicators of the shift toward outcomes as the focus of accountability.

States, however, did not eliminate their input and process regulations when they added accountability for outcomes. Rather, 'policies have been layered on top of one another, like geological strata' (Elmore and Fuhrman, 1995, p. 438). As a result, schools and school districts currently are judged against a multitude of standards (see Table 5.1). In 1997, the indicators most frequently used by states were: assessment scores (40 states), dropout rate (31 states), student attendance (28 states), expenditures and use of resources (25 states), graduation rates (17 states), student behaviour, discipline, truancy, expulsion and/or suspension (16 states), and transition to post-secondary education or employment after high school (16 states) (ECS, 1997b).

In special education, on the other hand, until very recently, there has been an almost total emphasis on the input and process of education as the focus of accountability (Danielson and Malouf, 1994; McLaughlin and

Hopfengardner Warren, 1992; Olsen, 1994). Furthermore, there is a strong federal precedence together with standards for accountability. To receive federal funds, states must provide to the federal agency annual state reports that give details about the number and types of children receiving services, and the personnel providing services. The Individualized Education Plan (IEP) that is required for each child receiving services must contain federally determined information (at a minimum) and be developed and updated on a specific time-defined basis.

The emphasis on the inputs, resources, and processes of special education reflects the concern about access to education that drove the creation of a special education system in the United States. Since the implementation of P.L. 94-142, states have been required, on an annual basis, to submit to the federal government data on the number of students receiving special education services, the nature of their placement, the number of personnel serving them, and the exit status of those leaving school. In 1989, the National Council on Disability (along with numerous other entities) suggested that it was time to shift the focus in special education from access to education to the quality of education and student outcomes. Several years later, a National Research Council study (McDonnell, McLaughlin and Morison, 1997) endorsed two principles when considering students with disabilities and standards-based reform:

- all students should have access to challenging standards;
- policy-makers and educators should be held publicly accountable for every student's performance.

The 1997 amendments to IDEA add the requirement that states report the number of students with disabilities participating in regular state-wide and district assessments. The amendments also require that states publicly report the performance of these students, in the same ways that they report the performance of other students. These requirements pose significant hurdles for educational systems, if past practice is any indicator of ability to meet these requirements. For example, in the spring of 1997, only about one-half of states were able to report the assessment participation numbers (Erickson and Thurlow, 1997). Further, a recent analysis of over a hundred accountability reports produced by states (Thurlow *et al.*, 1997) revealed that only twelve states actually report separate test-based outcome data for students with disabilities. In general, state reports are vague about whether students with disabilities are included in most of the data.

Who is accountable?

The major targets of all general education accountability systems are students, teachers, schools, and school districts. Roeber, Bond and Braskamp (1997) reported that thirty-six states have accountability systems for schools and/or their staff. The extent to which students with disabilities are included in these accountability systems has varied considerably. Most often, they have not been included in the student performance aspects of accountability (see Chapter 4). In 1996, the National Council on Disability recommended that local education agencies be held accountable for the outcomes of students with disabilities, as well as for process variables. Essentially, the National Council on Disability was requesting that students with disabilities be considered as part of the general student body, not to be treated differently within the accountability system.

The 1997 amendments to IDEA encompass some of these recommendations. For example, students are to be included in state assessments with accommodations as needed, and alternate assessments are to be provided to those students unable to participate in the state assessment. Performance results from these assessments (both the regular state assessments and the new alternate assessments) are to be reported in the same way and with the same frequency that performance results of other students are reported. It is also evident that there is a desire that high educational expectations be held for all students, including those with disabilities. This is expressed in the requirement that the state establish goals for the performance of students with disabilities that are consistent with other goals and standards established by the state. State improvement plans are to be developed and used as a basis for assessing progress toward achieving the goals.

How held accountable?

While states are the managers of accountability in the United States education system, determining how districts, schools, teachers, and students are held accountable, they sometimes delegate this responsibility to local districts. In contrast, there is no option for local control in special education accountability. The federal special education agency can sanction states, and states must cite districts when there is non-compliance with federal or state rules.

Accountability can be a public or a private activity. It also can be focused on aggregate or individualised student performance. Beyond whether there can be local control, these describe the major differences between accountability in general education and special education in the past. In general education, accountability is much more public than it has been in special education, probably because general education accountability data have been required by state legislatures. Aggregate student performance takes on a greater role in general education accountability systems than in special education systems. Furthermore, students, teachers, schools, and/or districts are the focus of these accountability systems.

Student accountability

When students are the focus of accountability, it is usually at the high school level and based on the courses that students take, rather than on their academic performance. All but six states prescribe the number of courses high school students must take, and in which academic areas. In 1996, the modal state required students to complete four years of English, three years of social studies, and two years each of mathematics and science to receive a high school diploma. States, however, generally do not specify exactly which courses (e.g. algebra, geometry, chemistry) students must take to meet their credit requirements (CCSSO, 1996a). Sixteen states award an advanced or honours diploma to students who complete additional or advanced courses in these core subjects.

Many states also assess what their students have learned by the time they reach the 11th or 12th grade. When CCSSO (1996a) conducted its national survey, only seventeen states required students to pass a proficiency test to receive a high school diploma. While several states have implemented challenging high school assessments, a large number of states have 'exit' tests that currently focus on minimal skills (AFT, 1997). However, many of these states are in the process of revising their high school assessments so they will measure more rigorous content, and additional states are developing new high school assessments. The arguments for the importance of increasing standards in this way are many (see, for example, ECS, 1997a).

Students receiving special education services may or may not be held to the same individual standards. Analyses by Rhim and McLaughlin (1997) and by Thurlow, Ysseldyke and Reid (1997) revealed that there are numerous inconsistencies in the course requirements and whether students are required to pass exams to earn the same diplomas as other students. In addition, some states have alternate completion documents such as certificates of completion, attendance certificates, and IEP diplomas; furthermore, these may mean different things in different states.

Use of the IEP as a measure for student accountability (through measurement of progress toward IEP goals and objectives) has been of limited value. Typically, there are no consequences for students attached to completion or non-completion of goals (Roach, Dailey and Goertz, 1997). Furthermore, the IEP typically has served as an indicator only of the special education process – what goals and objectives have been set and what types of services are to be provided to the student.

Teacher accountability

Teacher accountability is generally limited to ensuring that teachers participate in periodic professional development. Forty states require teachers to engage in continuing education or professional development as a condition of maintaining licensure or certification. Several of these states require six to eight semester credits of coursework every five years. Few states, however, specify the field or discipline for the courses or for other professional development activities (CCSSO, 1996a).

The concept of holding individual teachers directly responsible for student performance is extremely controversial in the United States. While most states require school districts to evaluate teachers on a regular basis, teacher compensation, tenure and licensure are not tied to student achievement or student progress. A few states (e.g. Texas) are taking steps to include student performance in the evaluation of teachers. Some states use school-based accountability as a way of rewarding (e.g. Kentucky) or punishing (e.g. Texas) teachers for their students' performance. Inclusion of students with disabilities in teacher accountability systems is complex, because they are so tied to the students' participation in the accountability components.

School and school district accountability

State accountability systems focus primarily on schools and school districts. Analysis of case study states conducted by the Consortium for Policy Research in Education (CPRE) and the Center for Policy Research on the Impact of General and Special Education Reform indicated that some states with strong traditions of local control have developed accountability systems that emphasise local standards and local reporting (e.g. Nebraska). Other local control states also allow districts to establish criteria for school performance, but use strategic plans or district and school improvement plans to hold districts accountable for student performance (e.g. Colorado, Pennsylvania). A third group of states holds schools and/or school districts accountable for both school improvement plans and attainment of state-established performance goals (e.g. Kentucky, Maryland, Texas). The consequences of not meeting state (and local) goals can range from direct state assistance or indirect assistance in schools, to a loss of state accreditation, to reconstitution, meaning removal of staff and direct state or local management of schools. The performance goals of these and other states vary along several dimensions, including the mix of outcomes in the performance measure, whether the goal is fixed or relative, and to which students (or group of students) the goal applies.

States also vary in how they monitor school and school district performance on input, process, and outcome standards. Some states rely primarily on district reports and state data bases to monitor general education. Other states continue to conduct on-site reviews of inputs, process and outcomes, but with reduced emphasis on inputs and process.

Within this context of varying policies, special education has relied on the IEP as a primary aspect of its system accountability mechanism. While the IEP itself can possibly serve as an indicator of the special education process, there are no consequences for the system based on students' completion of goals (Roach, Dailey and Goertz, 1997). Because so few students with disabilities have been included in the general education reporting of achievement scores (see Chapter 3) and aggregating across IEPs has precluded transforming the IEP into a basis for public accountability, special education has retained a private accountability system. State compliance monitoring, accompanied by federal oversight, is the primary mechanism for monitoring special education.

Compliance monitoring is accomplished primarily by state department personnel. Section 1412 of the original P.L. 94-142 (Education of the Handicapped Act) essentially gives the state educational agency primary responsibility for monitoring to assess compliance with the statutes and regulations for programmes and services for students with disabilities. The Office of Special Education Programs (OSEP) Division of Assistance to States (DAS), however, requires that 'States include in their monitoring system a procedure to determine compliance with *every* State and Federal requirement' (Ahearn, 1992, p. 2; emphasis in original).

In general, this means that compliance monitoring focuses on the seven content requirements of the IEP (present levels of performance, annual goals, services provided, objective criteria, evaluation procedures, evaluation schedule, and regular education participation). Monitors also evaluate compliance with procedural safeguards, both in terms of establishment of the safeguards (ways for families to challenge the school system practices, meaningful notice to parents of proposed actions, impartial due process hearing review system) and safeguards not included in notices to parents.

The manner in which states carry out the requirement to monitor compliance with the law varies tremendously (Ahearn, 1992; Regional Resource Center Program, 1992). For example, states use anywhere from a one-year to a seven-year cycle for conducting comprehensive monitoring site visits. Nearly all states (forty-eight of fifty) have an IEP review form. Many states (twenty) indicate that their compliance review goes beyond legal obligations, to include elements like classroom observations and comparisons to best practice. In 1992, thirty-four states and other entities receiving special education funding indicated that they were making or considering major changes to their monitoring systems (Regional Resource Center Program, 1992). Ahearn (1992) indicated that most state monitoring systems include a review of records (the nature of which can vary tremendously), an on-site verification of implementation of policies and/or procedures, and a process for correcting identified deficiencies.

The National Council on Disability (1993) analysed three years of state compliance and monitoring reports submitted to the United States Department of Education and found that 150 of the 165 local agencies visited were cited as being in non-compliance with federal and state IEP requirements. The Council also reported that nearly all of the agencies visited were in varying degrees of non-compliance with the procedural safeguards system of the Individuals with Disabilities Education Act.

How these procedures for holding states and districts accountable for special education will change with the reauthorised IDEA is still being determined. As noted previously, states are required to report on the number of students participating in state-wide and district assessments as of 1 July 1998, something that they seemed unable to do just one year prior to that (Erickson and Thurlow, 1997). In addition, they will be required to report actual scores of students with disabilities on state and district assessments, another thing that few states had been doing, even in 1997 (Thurlow *et al.*, 1998). Whether other state reports provided to the United States Department of Education will provide a basis for compliance monitoring is unclear at this point.

Consequences of accountability

States attach different consequences to their accountability systems. These consequences range from the public reporting of student, school and school district performance that is intended to generate parental and public pressure for reform ('low-stakes' accountability) to rewards or sanctions, such as state intervention in school and district governance ('high stakes' for school systems) and/or withholding high school diplomas ('high stakes' for students).

Nearly all states report annually on the condition of their schools; forty-three of them publish reports with district-level data and thirty-eight states include statistics at the school level (CCSSO, 1996b). Many states require low-performing schools to develop corrective action plans and provide technical assistance with this planning process. Schools and/or districts that still fail to improve student performance are subjected, in some states, to the additional sanctions of students being given the right to transfer to other schools, staff being reassigned or dismissed, schools being reconstituted, the state taking over the management of schools or school districts, loss of state accreditation, and/or the closure or merger of schools or districts.

Some states also reward students, teachers, and/or school systems for their performance. A few states (e.g. Florida, Georgia) provide college scholarships to high-performing students. Eight states provide regulatory waivers to schools or districts that show positive performance (Bond, Braskamp and van der Ploeg, 1996).

School accreditation is another consequence used in accountability systems. Accreditation typically involves state and regional reviews of school data. Rhim and McLaughlin's (1997) analysis revealed that thirty-two states indicated that programmes or services for students with disabilities were included in accreditation review processes. The nature of these components, however, often was unclear.

Consequences have been associated with the federal special education compliance monitoring system, namely withholding of federal funds. However, this has only been applied when the non-compliance involves over-counting the number of special education students (see National Council on Disability, 1993). If a state is found to be in non-compliance for any of a number of other reasons, such as not having IEPs on file, or not completing re-evaluations within the three-year time frame required by law, it is expected that corrective action will be taken within one year of issuing the final monitoring report.

With regard to state-level compliance monitoring, Ahearn (1992) concluded that the one aspect of compliance monitoring systems that is most consistent across states is that 'most SEAs rely on negotiation to achieve corrective actions and seldom apply fiscal sanctions as punishment except in instances of errors found in an LEA child count' (Ibid., p. v). Ahearn also noted that there is a lack of correlation between compliance monitoring and programme effectiveness because compliance monitoring focuses on whether required policies are being implemented, but programme effectiveness would need information on programme quality or student outcomes, both of which require professional judgement and are not included in statute or regulations.

Issues and challenges

As a major approach to educational reform, accountability in education has evolved over time toward a system that incorporates not just information on resources (e.g. school personnel with specific qualifications, low student–teacher ratios) and processes (e.g. positive school climate, appropriate programmes for gifted students), but also information on outcomes (high graduation rates, student performance levels that meet defined standards). Because of oversights, different requirements, or outright exclusions, special education accountability systems have developed separately, with different foci, targets, implementation, and consequences. As a result, policy-makers and educators face several challenges as they seek to align and merge general education and special education accountability.

Building on a weak foundation

Including students with disabilities in an accountability system increasingly focused on outcomes depends on having an adequate foundation of outcomes assessment. Following from the belief that most students with disabilities should be pursuing the same educational goals as students without disabilities, students with disabilities should be in the same assessment and accountability systems. Yet, there is considerable evidence to suggest that we have a long way to go to make this so.

Establishing a solid foundation will require at least two major changes in data collection programmes. First, the basic data elements that are collected will have to be adjusted to make sure that students with disabilities can be identified and their data aggregated and disaggregated. Many states currently are not able to do this (Almond, Tindal and Stieber, 1997; Erickson *et al.*, 1996). Further complicating this effort is that special education child count data in the United States are based on age, not grade. This makes comparisons of students with disabilities participating in assessments at particular grade levels difficult.

Second, states will have to ensure that all students are included in their assessment systems and that the systems are appropriate for students with disabilities. Making assessment systems appropriate involves significant technical and policy changes, such as making sure that assessments cover a range of difficulty levels, allowing the use of accommodations during assessments, and establishing accommodations policies.

Overcoming separatist attitudes

Over time, special education has evolved into a separate system. This separateness has had several consequences, one of which is the fostering of separatist attitudes among educators in their policies, programmes and reporting. Nowhere is the separation more evident than in accountability systems, particularly in how the general education and special education systems are overseen. Special education has developed a prescribed compliance and monitoring system, one that is overseen by the federal government. Advocates are invested in this system, and are not likely to relinquish precedence anytime soon. General education accountability, on the other hand, is primarily a state and district level effort without the invested interests that are evident in special education accountability.

To overcome the separate policies and attitudes, changes will have to occur in both quarters. For example, general educators will have to be willing to assume responsibility for the performance of students with disabilities as well as the performance of other students. This means that when schools receive rewards or sanctions based on the performance of students in the school building, assessment results for all students must be included. In some states, this policy is reinforced by requiring that student performance be assigned to the student's home school, regardless of where the student is educated. This helps to ensure that good placement decisions are made for each student, and to avoid moving students who are expected to perform poorly out of the school. On the other hand, special education will have to accept that its resources may need to be used for school-wide improvements. The 1997 amendments to IDEA support some movement in this direction by allowing for special educators to serve other students, not just those on special education rolls.

Integrating monitoring systems

At the present time, general education is relaxing some procedural requirements, such as school-based budgeting, to give schools and educators greater
flexibility to improve student performance. Special education will have to be
willing to give up some of the safeguards that it has held on to in the past,
such as its control over the use of resources (e.g. how special education
teachers are used and how services are delivered in a school).

Overview of educational accountability in England and Wales

One of the main mechanisms through which all schools in England and
Wales are accountable is the external inspection system introduced in 1993,
although inspection is only one of many reforms in England and Wales
that have had a major accountability component. Monitoring the performance of schools through inspections or reviews is common practice in
many countries. In France, Sharpe (1993) notes that inspections in primary
schools are of the teachers' performance rather than that of the school and
focus mainly on whether the prescribed curriculum is being delivered. He
describes the outcomes of primary inspections in France as influencing
teacher promotion but unlikely to lead to school improvement. In Australia
(Cuttance, 1995) and Scotland (McGlynn and Stalker, 1995), inspections
have a clear emphasis on quality assurance aimed at assisting the process
of school improvement.

   This section of the chapter describes the external inspection system in
England and Wales and draws out some of the issues relating specifically
to provision for pupils with disabilities that have arisen in studies of its implementation. There appears to be a paucity of literature describing studies in
the impact of inspection specifically for students with disabilities, although
anecdotal stories are rife. The contribution made by inspection to school
improvement is critically considered. More recent educational policy in
England (DfEE, 1997a) suggests a move towards school self-review within
which schools' own approaches to monitoring and evaluation will be critical. Some examples of monitoring and evaluation of provision for pupils
with disabilities are given as illustrations.

External inspection of schools in England and Wales

Until 1992 the task of monitoring schools was irregular and unsystematic.
Stillman (1989) noted that less than 1 per cent of schools were receiving
whole-school (as contrasted with partial or 'thematic' focusing on one aspect
of their curriculum) local authority inspections, although, about another 1 per
cent were inspected centrally by Her Majesty's Inspectorate (HMI). By 1992,

Wilcox, Gray and Tranmer (1993) noted that the number of local authority inspections had substantially increased, perhaps due to the need to monitor the implementation of the extensive reforms such as the National Curriculum and local management of schools. For reasons explained by Bolton (1994), the government decided to replace rather than extend the existing systems. LEA inspectors were seen as being insufficiently independent, while HMI provided a 'Rolls-Royce' service but would take a hundred years to inspect all schools in the country.

The 1992 Education Act introduced a new system of 'privatised' school inspection under the Office for Standards in Education (Ofsted), an independent office of government. Its task was to organise, plan and oversee the regular and frequent inspection of all schools for all students. The system was to be based on a common framework (Ofsted, 1995), centrally controlled, market-driven, independent of local government and occur on a four-yearly cycle. In 1997, the cycle was changed to six-yearly. The written reports arising from these inspections are presented to the school governors within thirty-five days and are public documents. A summary is sent to all parents. The governors have forty days within which to draw up an Action Plan based on the key issues identified in the report. Special school inspection under the 1992 Education Act began in September 1994, one year after mainstream primary and secondary schools.

Purposes of inspection

The stated purposes of the current inspection process (Ofsted, 1995) are:

- accountability for the expenditure of public money;
- providing national information about the performance of schools;
- providing information for parents to assist them to make informed choices of school; and
- to enhance school improvement.

The balance between these purposes is not explicit and varies according to which stakeholders' views are sought. Parents have limited choice of school in practice, once they have opted for a special school or if they live in a rural area. Schools may be most aware of the accountability aspects, teaching staff assuming the main task is over once the inspection is complete, while senior managers and governors are focusing on the improvement agenda ahead.

Who undertakes the inspection?

The inspections are undertaken by private teams trained, accredited and subsequently monitored by the Office for Standards in Education (Ofsted), to which HMI transferred. Team leaders known as Registered Inspectors tender for the contracts to inspect the schools. Each team includes at least one 'lay' inspector with no background in education. Fletcher-Campbell (1995) noted the high proportion of teams initially, who were local authority inspectors and some of the role conflict that may have arisen through their need to maintain independence from schools they had traditionally supported and advised.

The criteria used for inspection

The same criteria for judging quality, stated in the inspection 'framework' (Ofsted, 1995) are applied in all schools, mainstream and special. Many of these criteria matched those which can be derived from the literature on school effectiveness (e.g. Mortimore *et al.*, 1988) none of which specifically focused on special schools. An attempt made by one of the authors (Sebba, 1992) to speculate about the applicability of the school effectiveness findings to special schools suggested that while management, administration and leadership issues may be similar, some curricular aspects may differ. For example, the balance of time spent on 'academic' subjects, as compared to that allocated to personal and social development, has been a source of conflict for many special schools undergoing inspection. The criteria for inspection have been revised annually and additional guidance provided for inspectors on their interpretation through both revisions to the handbook and regular newsletters.

Inspection of provision for students with disabilities

Those leading special school inspections are expected to have a background in special education usually relating to the specific type of provision (e.g. hearing impairment) that they are intending to inspect. Teams inspecting mainstream provision are not required to include a specialist inspector of disability or learning difficulty. In the revised framework for inspection, special educational needs provision in mainstream schools is perceived as a whole school issue and is not inspected separately. Each area of the provision inspected (e.g. curriculum subjects, accommodation, management, etc.) should take into account quality in relation to the full range of pupils in the school and any implications of the Code of Practice, for example, checking that the curriculum meets the needs identified in individual educational plans.

Concerns have been expressed (Chorley and Davie, 1997) about whether this 'permeated' model for assessing 'special educational needs' provision enables the inspection report to focus sufficiently sharply on the school's use of support services, and implementation of policy and procedures relating to special educational needs. Furthermore, some of those responsible for special education provision have expressed concerns about quality of provision in special schools being judged on the same criteria as those used in mainstream schools. Conversely, others regard the use of the same criteria as having provided a common framework, language and targets for all schools, as did the National Curriculum when it was introduced in 1991.

Acceptability of the inspection process and outcomes seems to be an important prerequisite for a school's willingness to act upon the recommendations made (Brimblecombe, Ormston and Shaw, 1995). Hence, doubts about the applicability of the model to inclusive mainstream schools or special schools may be expected to inhibit subsequent school improvement in these settings. The next section considers the limited studies addressing these issues.

Research on the impact of inspection

Research on inspections in mainstream schools has proliferated over the last couple of years (e.g. Earley, Fidler and Ouston, 1996; Ouston, Earley and Fidler, 1996; Wilcox and Gray, 1996). With a few exceptions most of the research does not draw out issues relating to pupils with disabilities. Those that do so include Wilcox and Gray (1996), who report on case studies of a special school and special educational needs provision in mainstream, Chorley and Davie (1997), who analyse the coverage of special educational needs within mainstream inspection reports and our own work (Sebba, Clarke and Emery, 1996, 1997) on school improvement following inspection in special schools. Three major issues emerge from these studies. These relate to the quality and consistency of inspectors, the interpretation of the criteria in contexts in which there are significant proportions or all pupils with disabilities, and the lack of agreement about the priorities for education of these pupils. Each of these issues is discussed in more detail.

Quality and consistency of inspectors

The quality and consistency of judgements made by inspectors in all types of school emerged as a factor in the consultation process on the government's White Paper, *Excellence in Schools* (DfEE, 1997a). Parents, teachers, governors, unions, professional associations and local authority staff (some of whom are inspectors themselves) share unanimous concern about the consistency of inspections, suggesting that the monitoring of inspectors provided by Ofsted is insufficient (in quantity, quality or both). A few of the problems undoubtedly reflect the behaviour or personality of individual inspectors (Brimblecombe, Ormston and Shaw, 1995; Thomas, 1996) in a situation in which stress levels are so high that a single incident (of late arrival in class to observe a lesson, brusque questioning or lack of feedback) can have far-reaching consequences.

In schools providing for pupils with disabilities, these problems may be more common due to several factors. From the introduction of formal inspections there has been a relative shortage of inspectors for primary and special schools. This led to Ofsted introducing a scheme for recruiting additional inspectors on short-term contacts, drawing on current headteachers and deputy headteachers of schools. Some of these inspectors lacked experience beyond their own school and may have been more inclined to stick rigidly to the rules, perhaps inappropriately so. In mainstream inspection teams, the balance between ensuring that at least one team member has appropriate experience of disability and the need for all team members to inspect the special needs dimension, may be difficult to achieve. This is observed most clearly in the inspection of schools developing inclusion, whose reports provide evidence that inspectors are less than clear whether they should be inspecting 'special needs provision' or effective provision for all.

Interpretation of the criteria in inclusive or special contexts

There is some evidence to suggest that there are variations in the interpretation of the criteria given by inspectors in different settings. In most special school inspections, progress is assessed against the perceived capabilities and previous attainments of the pupils, not on national norms since these do not exist for special school populations. Judging capabilities is difficult in pupils whose communication difficulties or behaviour may be inhibiting their responses. Levels of acceptable behaviour, amount of time needed for counselling, physical positioning or feeding are all areas in which the context may alter the judgement.

In mainstream schools developing 'full' inclusion, pupils' individual priorities may be addressed within small group or whole class activities with support provided by the peer group. Judging quality on the amount of time spent on individual work would not be appropriate in this context, since it is applying traditional special education criteria to inclusive education settings. As yet, there are too few schools with the diversity of pupil population to have generated sufficient experience of making appropriate judgements in these schools.

The priorities for education of pupils with disabilities

The purpose of special school provision has lacked clarity in government policy in the past. Is specialist provision for pupils with emotional and behavioural difficulties serving the needs of mainstream schools who want to offload difficult pupils? These pupils are unlikely to contribute helpfully to the school's results in national assessment. Under the inspection criteria it is unclear whether a special school should aim to reintegrate their students back into mainstream or instead put their resources and energies into providing a broad curriculum and full range of opportunities within the segregated setting. There is also confusion about the extent to which vocational, functional and life skills should be a part of the curriculum in such schools. Little central or regional direction has been provided by policy-makers on these issues, yet when the inspectors arrive, the school is accountable, but accountable for what?

These tensions emerged from our own study of special school inspections (Sebba, Clarke and Emery, 1996, p. 87) in which, for example, a headteacher reported:

> In the inspection report the comments on quality of learning in the core subjects (English, maths, science) and personal and social education are very positive, but negative about the quality and range of the curriculum. If we shift the balance of our present curriculum to meet the statutory requirements, we inevitably give our children less of what is evidently proving very successful.

Furthermore, analysis of the published inspection reports demonstrates that the rate of schools classified as failing to meet appropriate standards (referred to as under 'special measures') is higher amongst special schools than mainstream, and is particularly high for schools for pupils with emotional and behavioural difficulties. It is in this latter category that the least clarity about purpose is to be found. In their attempts to achieve the combination of conflicting aims, these schools are more likely to fail to meet the standards required. Some, although by no means all, of this failure, may reflect confusion and difference of opinion about purpose of such schools on the part of inspectors and the subsequent difficulty of making judgements against the inspection criteria.

The role of inspection in school improvement

The previous points have been critical of the inspection process. However, for all the difficulties that have emerged in our study of post-inspection action planning and subsequent school improvement in just under 50 special schools (Sebba et al., 1997), there was evidence in all the schools of some improvements. These tended to be in terms of managerial, resource and administrative targets, rather than in those targets addressing improvement in teaching and learning. There are two major reasons for this.

The first noted in mainstream studies (e.g. Gray and Wilcox, 1995; Sebba and Loose, 1996) relates to the ways in which inspectors present the key issues for action in their reports. Action points such as 'developing the role of the curricular co-ordinator', 'producing a policy on health and safety' or 'improving the library accommodation', leave the school to make the connection between these managerial and administrative tasks and the pupil outcomes that they are supposed to bring about. We noted in our studies that the written action plans frequently confused targets and tasks, failed to define success criteria in terms of pupils' learning and lacked clear plans for evaluating the outcomes. More recently, inspectors have been instructed in the revised guidance to present key issues for action in terms of pupil outcomes rather than leaving the schools to make these connections.

The second reason why most schools could not demonstrate improvements in teaching and learning relates to the timescale of the research. We are repeatedly reminded in the literature (e.g. Fullan, 1993) of the time needed to achieve change, particularly at the classroom level. These schools were followed up one year after inspection when the writing of documents or redefining of roles may have been achievable, but staff acknowledged that implementing changes in teaching and learning take longer.

Recent government policy (DfEE, 1997a) indicates proposed changes to the inspection system. These include less advanced notice of inspection (two to three months, instead of up to a year), more focus on classroom practice, clearer reports, better availability of inspection evidence, extensive professional development for inspectors and the introduction of an appeals mechanism. With all these possibilities for improving the system, does this external inspection offer the most effective and efficient method of accountability and provision of an agenda for school improvement?

School self-evaluation: a way forward

Since the election of a new government in 1997, there has been an attempt to increase the emphasis placed on school self-improvement, one of the stated principles underlying government policy being that 'intervention will be in inverse proportion to success' (DfEE, 1997a). This principle is expanded upon by noting that the main responsibility for improving schools lies with the schools themselves. While there is little disagreement with the notion of schools taking principal responsibility for school improvement, there is evidence from our own and other work (e.g. Southworth, 1997) that good quality external support for schools is critical. Furthermore, the principle of inverse proportion as stated, fails to recognise that schools are not simply 'good' or 'bad', but have differential strengths and weaknesses. In addition, in order to continue to improve, so-called 'good' schools need to be further challenged. For these reasons external support and challenge will be needed by all schools to improve. If this involves a partnership between local advisory services and the schools evaluating progress, external inspection may become less disruptive as reviewing practice becomes the norm.

School self-evaluation involves a cycle of evaluating current practice, deciding what the school should be achieving, setting targets, taking action to implement the targets and reviewing progress. In England, all schools are required to set and publish targets annually. Since the government has set ambitious targets in literacy and numeracy for the year 2002, there need to be targets from every school which when aggregated will meet the national targets. In addition, local education authorities will be required to set and publish targets through their education development plans which reflect both the national targets and the aggregated targets for the schools in their area. Hence, some negotiation is likely to take place between local education authorities and their schools about the appropriate targets to set.

Simultaneously, the government's Green Paper *Excellence for all Children: Meeting Special Educational Needs* (DfEE, 1997b) promotes inclusion of pupils with identified special educational needs in mainstream schools. Concerns have been expressed that mainstream schools will not want to admit more pupils with disabilities because this will depress their targets. There is some evidence from the performance tables for 1997 that schools developing greater inclusion can simultaneously raise their examination results, supporting the thus-far speculative notion that developing inclusion challenges teachers to teach more effectively, benefiting a wider range of pupils than those with identified special educational needs (Sebba and Ainscow, 1996).

Defining the targets in special schools brings us back to the same problem of the need for clarity about the purpose of such schools. Should the targets include reintegration figures, life skills, or be restricted to National Curriculum attainment levels? Special schools cannot develop their targets on the basis of the national benchmarking data that inform mainstream schools of what other 'similar' schools are achieving. These data are not available for special schools and may become problematic for mainstream schools which are relatively inclusive, since there may be few 'similar' schools to which they can be compared. Further development will be needed to help these schools to define appropriate targets which genuinely reflect their priorities and set challenging expectations.

In the 1980s, a range of procedures were available to assist schools in self-evaluation. However, they tended to focus exclusively on process, with little or no attention to outcomes. The current standards agenda requires a combination of process and outcomes in self evaluation procedures. The Centre for Studies on Inclusive Education and University of Manchester Centre for Educational Needs (1997) have led the development of an index for inclusive schooling, informed by the work of Eichinger, Meyer and D'Aquanni (1996) on 'Program Quality Indicators'. The index is a form of self-review for schools to use to determine where they are in terms of inclusive education and exclusion in order to move thinking and practice forward (see Table 5.2). It is aimed at promoting both teacher and school development simultaneously, drawing on research evidence on processes that facilitate participation for students who might have been marginalised and on processes that enhance school improvement. It is based on the following assumptions:

- all pupils have a right to the same range of educational choices;
- schools should value all pupils equally and celebrate diversity;
- schools should be developed to facilitate the learning of all pupils;
- effective development requires the involvement of all members of the school community.

Table 5.2 Index for inclusive schooling: draft dimensions and indicators (CSIE/University of Manchester, 1997)

This draft index covers five dimensions; organisational arrangements, communication, classroom experiences, social climate and relationships. For each dimension there is a set of indicators. For example, the draft indicators for the dimension of classroom experiences are as follows:

3.1   Pupils are entitled to take part in all subjects and activities
3.2   Teaching and learning are planned with all pupils in mind
3.3   The curriculum develops understanding and respect for differences
3.4   During lessons all pupils participate
3.5   A variety of teaching styles and strategies are used
3.6   Pupils experience success in their learning
3.7   The curriculum seeks to develop understanding of the different cultures in society
3.8   Pupils take part in the assessment and accreditation systems
3.9   Difficulties in learning are seen as opportunities for the development of practice

The indicators for the five dimensions are presented through three rating scales and evidence is collected to determine where the school is at through observation, discussion and any other methods available. One of the rating scales is aimed at seeking staff views of the current practice in the school, a second one invites their views on what they believe the school should be like, and a third is for eliciting pupils' views. The responsibility for the review rests with the school. The cycle of activities designed to review, develop and evaluate practice includes negotiating with all interested parties such as parents, governors, staff and the pupils before starting. A co-ordinating group is identified to steer the use of the index. An initial audit is carried out by the school staff using the rating scales and other available evidence in order to identify a focus for development. The progress made during the development phase is evaluated.

During 1997/98, four primary schools and two secondary schools have piloted the draft index and the evaluation led to further development and modification of the materials. The development of this index drew on previous work in Australia and the United States on quality indicators for inclusive education. It represents an exciting new challenge in finding ways of encouraging, monitoring and evaluating developments in inclusive education at a time when school self-review is a priority.

Summary

This section of the chapter has reviewed briefly some of the issues relating to pupils with disabilities that emerge from the introduction of a formal external inspection system in England and Wales. The role of inspection in school improvement was critically considered and systems for self review presented. We are entering a new era of reform in England and Wales in which the balance between challenge and support for schools is being explored within a climate in which teacher morale must be boosted if we are to recruit sufficient numbers of good teachers necessary to improve our schools.

There is a strong commitment at all levels, nationally, locally and in the classroom, for provision for pupils with disabilities to be accountable within the same framework as all other provision. However, the tension remains between national reform aimed at preparation of a skilled workforce and competition with other countries and the equity goals that are needed to ensure high expectations for those students who may not make a major contribution economically or competitively. At the school level, this is reflected in the tension between the traditional focus of special educational needs provision on individual support for pupils with disabilities and the national standards agenda which focuses on group outcomes. The policy of developing inclusion may help by emphasising each pupil's progress in the context of the group and by acknowledging group collaborative achievements. Ultimately, the accountability for improvement in schools should be to the pupils and for the benefit of their learning. Approaches such as the inclusive schools index begin to address this. Some exciting challenges lie ahead if it is to be realised.

Conclusions: accountability in England and Wales and in the United States

School improvement is the rationale for educational accountability systems both in England and Wales and in the United States. Yet, the ways in which educational accountability plays out in the two countries are quite different. These differences permeate both the general education and special education systems. They are evident in the mechanisms of accountability, the ways in which results are reported and used, and the consequences attached to accountability information.

Accountability context

The content within which accountability systems are established defines those systems. For this reason, it is important to understand some of the basic differences in the educational contexts in England and Wales and in the United States. Both countries have well-defined systems of special education services for students with disabilities.

In England and Wales, significant educational reforms focus on the development and implementation of a national curriculum and local management of schools. Within this context of major reforms, there is a need to monitor and evaluate schools. Students with disabilities are viewed as part of the educational system and programmes for them require monitoring and evaluation.

In the United States, educational reforms reflect a mixture of federally driven and state and locally driven changes. Those reforms that are nationally driven, however, ultimately rely on states to implement them in the ways that meet their preferences and needs. Thus, a system of individual state or locally derived reforms form the foundations for accountability. It is not surprising, then, that the systems to monitor and evaluate schools are extremely varied across the fifty states, as well as across individual school districts and schools. Special education, however, almost always has been viewed as a separate programme, one that takes care of itself and has its own system of monitoring and evaluation. It also has a highly centralised monitoring process driven by federal requirements and demands. As a result, the United States federal special education law has supported its own compliance monitoring system, and has required states to feed information into this system.

Mechanisms of accountability

In England and Wales, inspections of schools by the Office of Standards in Education (Ofsted) are guided by an inspection 'framework' which is based to a large extent on school effectiveness literature. The criteria within the framework (e.g. leadership, management, administration, curriculum) are reviewed annually. Special education needs are viewed as a whole school issue within the framework and individual educational plans are monitored within the framework. The process is subjective, and relies predominately on qualitative information rather than quantitative indicators.

In the United States, there generally has been until recently a dual system of accountability, one for general education and one for special education. Within the general education accountability realm, there has been a wide range of practices, reflecting the state and locally defined nature of these accountability systems. Within the special education accountability realm, there has been a single monitoring system that has come from the federal agency, then been translated down to the states for implementation. Sometimes special education is included in the general accountability system; most often it is not.

The special education accountability system involves 'compliance monitoring' that historically has been focused on ensuring access to services. Thus, there has been a focus on inputs, such as counting children receiving services. Also, there has been a focus on ensuring that each eligible student has an IEP, a document developed for each child receiving special education services. Monitoring has focused on the extent to which required components are included on IEPs, on the timeliness of evaluations and re-evaluations, and on other 'process-focused' variables.

Accountability reporting

In England and Wales there is public reporting of the results of Ofsted inspections. The results are presented in a widely disseminated document. The general public in England and Wales is well aware of the inspections, and of the results for schools in which they have an interest. Each local education authority is now required to produce an education development plan in which annual targets are published, taking account of what has emerged from the inspection of schools in the area. The chief inspector publishes an annual report synthesising all school inspections from that year.

In contrast, accountability reporting in the United States is extremely varied across the fifty states. While nearly all states report the results of student assessments, large numbers also report on drop-out rates, student attendance, and expenditures. Yet, there are more than thirty other indicators that some states include in their reports, but most states do not. Individual states (and some local districts and schools also) produce their own reports on the status of education. Frequently, these reports have no information about students with disabilities. More often, it is impossible to tell whether data from students with disabilities are included in the reports.

The results of special education compliance monitoring in the United States generally are not reported publicly, although the reports are available to the public. When the federal education agency monitors a state, it presents its findings back to the state department verbally, and in a written report within sixty days. The report provides a Corrective Action Plan that identifies needed changes. The state can respond to the report prior to the publication of a final report. In general, these reports have not been disseminated widely, probably because they identify numerous problems in state compliance.

Changes are planned to occur in public reporting of the results of education for students with disabilities. With the enactment of the 1997 amendments to the Individuals with Disabilities Education Act, states now must report on the number of students with disabilities participating in state-wide and district assessments, as well as on the performance of these students. Furthermore, it is likely that State Improvement Plans, which now must include these data, will become a focus of monitoring efforts. In England, local education authorities are required to publish an education development plan that is based on local data and performs a similar function.

Use of accountability information

The use of accountability information can vary widely, from instructional improvement purposes to marketing purposes. The ways in which accountability information is used can, in turn, influence other aspects of the accountability system.

In England and Wales, schools use information derived from the Ofsted inspections to attract pupils, as well as for school improvement purposes.

Thus, data are used in a marketing approach to education, thereby becoming extremely important not only to schools but also to a number of individuals within the school community.

In the United States, state practices again vary tremendously. While nearly all states argue that accountability information is used for instructional and programme improvement, many also will suggest that accountability information is used in different ways. Some use assessments to determine whether students receive graduation diplomas. Others use accountability information to determine whether schools will receive cash rewards for good performance, or be sanctioned for low performance.

Special education data are almost never used for accountability purposes. As a result, they generally are not a key element in accountability reporting or use. Of course, there are some states that effectively use special education accountability information to influence those programmes.

Consequences attached to accountability results

The inspection system in England and Wales results in the allocation of extra resources for schools showing an extreme need for assistance, known as being 'in special measures'. Schools receive feedback that describes key issues for action, but these are sometimes viewed as confusing and unrelated to student outcomes, although they are improving.

In the United States, accountability data are used by some states and local districts to determine whether schools receive cash rewards or are sanctioned, and whether students receive diplomas or are promoted from one grade to the next. These approaches to accountability appear to be increasing in recent years. For the most part, however, data on students with disabilities have not been included within the data used to determine school-level consequences. Only recently has this changed in some locations. The special education compliance monitoring data rarely have had any significant consequences attached to them.

Summary

The pictures portrayed of England and Wales and the United States reveal quite different approaches to accountability overall, and specifically related to students with disabilities. These differences in many ways reflect the different educational contexts in the two countries. For example, the centralist nature of inspection in England and Wales most certainly would be viewed as too intrusive in the United States. Despite their differences, both countries continue to work on their systems, to strengthen them so that they might meet the needs of students with disabilities. This work may be pushed forward more rapidly by the movement toward more inclusive schools and the philosophy that all pupils are the focus of school improvement efforts.

Notes

1 Results from a 1997 survey of state directors of special education are included here. That survey was supported by a co-operative agreement (H159C50004) between the Office of Special Education Programmes (OSEP), US Department of Education, and the University of Minnesota.

2 These case studies were conducted by the Consortium for Policy Research in Education (CPRE) and the Center for Policy Research on the Impact of General and Special Education Reform (the Center) in 1996/97. Funding for this work was provided by the United States Department of Education's Office of Special Education Programmes (Grant #H023H40002) and National Institute on Educational Governance, Finance, Policymaking and Management (Grant OERI-R308A60003), the Annie E. Casey Foundation and the Pew Charitable Trusts.

References

AFT (1997) *Making Standards Matter*, Washington, DC: American Federation of Teachers.

Ahearn, E.M. (1992) *Analysis of State Compliance Monitoring Practices*, Alexandria, VA: National Association of State Directors of Special Education.

Almond, P., Tindal, G. and Stieber, S. (1997) *Linking Inclusion to Conclusions: An Empirical Study of Participation of Students with Disabilities in State-wide Testing Programs* (State Assessment Series, Oregon Report 1), Minneapolis, MN: National Center on Educational Outcomes.

Bolton, E. (1994) 'Alternative education policies: "School inspection",' in S. Tomlinson (ed.) *Educational Reform and Its Consequences*, London: IPPR/ Rivers Oram Press.

Bond, L., Braskamp, D. and van der Ploeg, A. (1996) *State Student Assessment Programs Database: School year 1994–95*, Washington, DC: Council of Chief State School Officers and North Central Regional Educational Laboratory.

Bond, L., Roeber, E. and Braskamp, D. (1997) *Trends in State Student Assessment Programs*, Washington, DC: Council of Chief State School Officers.

Brimblecombe, N., Ormston, M. and Shaw, M. (1995) 'Teachers' perceptions of school inspection: a stressful experience', *Cambridge Journal of Education* 25: 53–61.

Centre for Studies on Inclusive Education/University of Manchester (1997) *Index for Inclusive Schooling: Pilot version*, Bristol: CSIE.

Chorley, D. and Davie, R. (1997) OFSTED *Inspection Reports and Special Educational Needs*. Tamworth: NASEN.

Council of Chief State School Officers (CCSSO) (1996a) *Key State Education Policies on K-12 Education: Content Standards, Graduation, Teacher Licensure, Time and Attendance*, Washington, DC: CCSSO.

—— (1996b) *State Education Accountability Reports and Indicator Reports: Status of Reports across the States 1996*, Washington, DC: CCSSO.

Cuttance, P. (1995) 'An evaluation of quality management and quality assurance systems for schools', *Cambridge Journal of Education*, 25: 95–106.

Danielson, L.C. and Malouf, D.B. (1994) 'Federal policy and educational reform: Achieving better outcomes for students with disabilities', in J. Ysseldyke and

M. Thurlow (eds), *Educational Outcomes for Students with Disabilities*, Binghampton, NY: Haworth Press.

Department for Education and Employment (DfEE) (1997a) *Excellence in Schools*, London: HMSO

—— (1997b) *Excellence for All Children: Meeting Special Educational Needs*, London: HMSO

Education Commission of the States (ECS) (1997a) *A Policymaker's Guide to Incentives for Students, Teachers and Schools*, Denver, CO: ECS.

—— (1997b) *Education Accountability Systems in 50 States*, Denver, CO: ECS.

Earley, P., Fidler, B. and Ouston, J. (1996) *Improvement through Inspection*, London: Fulton.

Eichinger, J., Meyer, L.H. and D'Aquanni, M. (1996) 'Evolving best practices for learners with severe disabilities', *Special Education Leadership Review*, 1–13.

Elmore, R. and Fuhrman, S. (1995) 'Opportunity-to-learn standards and the state role in education', *Teachers College Record*, 96,3: 432–457.

Erickson, R. and Thurlow, M. (1997) *1997 State Special Education Outcomes*, Minneapolis, MN: University of Minnesota, National Center on Educational Outcomes.

Erickson, R., Thurlow, M., Thor, K. and Seyfarth, A. (1996) *1995 State Special Education Outcomes*, Minneapolis, MN: University of Minnesota, National Center on Educational Outcomes.

Fletcher-Campbell, F. (1995) 'Inspecting schools', in P. Potts, F. Armstrong and M. Masterton (eds) *Equality And Diversity In Education 1 – Learning, Teaching and Managing in Schools*, London: Routledge.

Fullan, M. (1993) *Change Forces*, London: Falmer.

Gray, J. and Wilcox, B. (1995) *Good School, Bad School: Evaluating Performance and Encouraging Improvement*, Milton Keynes: Open University Press.

McDonnell, L., McLaughlin, M. and Morrison, P. (1997) *Educating One and All: Students with Disabilities and Standards-based Reform*, Washington, DC: National Academy of Sciences.

McGlynn, A. and Stalker, H. (1995) 'Recent developments in the Scottish process of school inspection', *Cambridge Journal of Education*, 25: 11–19.

McLaughlin, M. and Hopfengardner Warren, S. (1992) 'Outcomes assessment for students with disabilities: Will it be accountability or continued failure?' *Preventing School Failure*, 36,4: 29–33.

Mortimore, P., Sammons, P., Stoll, L., Lewis, D. and Ecob, R. (1988) *School Matters*, Wells: Open Books.

National Commission on Excellence in Education (1983) *A Nation at Risk: The Imperative for Educational Reform*, Washington, DC: NCEE.

National Council on Disability (1989) *The Education of Students with Disabilities: Where do We Stand?*, Washington, DC: NCD.

—— (1993) *Serving the Nation's Students with Disabilities: Progress and Prospects*, Washington, DC: NCD.

—— (1996) *Achieving Independence: The Challenge for the 21st Century*, Washington, DC: NCD.

Oakes, J. (1986) *Educational Indicators: A Guide for Policymakers*, Santa Monica, CA: RAND, Center for Policy Research in Education.

Ofsted (1995) *The Handbook for the Inspection of Schools*, London: HMSO.

Olsen, K. (1994) 'Have we made progress in fifteen years of evaluating the effectiveness of special education programmes?' in J. Ysseldyke and M. Thurlow (eds), *Educational outcomes for students with disabilities*, Binghampton, NY: Haworth Press.

Ouston, J., Earley, P. and Fidler, B. (1996) *Ofsted Inspections: The Early Experience*, London: Fulton.

Regional Resource Center Programme (1992) *Profiles of State Monitoring Systems*, Lexington, KY: Mid-South Regional Resource Center.

Rhim, L.R. and McLaughlin, M.J. (1997) *State Level Policies and Practices: Where are Students with Disabilities?* College Park, MD: Institute for the Study of Exceptional Children and Youth, University of Maryland.

Roach, V., Dailey, D. and Goertz, M. (1997) *State Accountability Systems and Students with Disabilities*, Alexandria, VA: Center for Policy Research on the Impact of General and Special Education Reform.

Roeber, E., Bond, L. and Braskamp, D. (1997) *Annual Survey of State Student Assessment Programmes (Fall 1996)*, Washington, DC: Council of Chief State School Officers.

Sebba, J. (1992) 'Effective schooling for pupils with severe learning difficulties', in J. Bashi and Z. Sass (eds) *School Effectiveness And Improvement: Proceedings of the Third International Congress for Schools Effectiveness*, Jerusalem: Magnes Press.

Sebba, J. and Ainscow, M. (1996) 'International developments in inclusive schooling: mapping the issues', *Cambridge Journal of Education*, 26: 5–18.

Sebba, J. and Loose, T. (1996) 'Ofsted action plans: problems and possibilities for primary school improvement', paper presented at the BERA annual conference, England.

Sebba, J., Clarke, J. and Emery, B. (1996) 'How can the inspection process enhance improvement in special schools?' *European Journal of Special Needs Education*, 11, 82–94.

—— (1997) *Enhancing School Improvement through Inspection in Special Schools*, London: Ofsted.

Sharpe, K. (1993) An inspector calls: an analysis of inspection procedures in French primary education, *Compare*, 23: 263–275.

Shavelson, R., McDonnell, L., and Oakes, J. (1989) *Indicators for Monitoring Mathematics and Science Education*, Santa Monica, CA: RAND Corporation.

Shavelson, R., McDonnell, L., Oakes, J. and Carey, M. (1987) *Indicator Systems or Monitoring Mathematics and Science Education. Rand's Report to the National Science Foundation (NSF)*, Santa Monica, CA: RAND Corporation.

Southworth, G. (1997) 'Improving primary schools: shifting the emphasis and clarifying the focus', *School Organisation*, 16: 263–280.

Stillman, A. (1989) 'Institutional evaluation and LEA advisory services', *Research Papers in Education*, 4: 3–27.

Thomas, G. (1996) 'The new schools' inspection system: some problems and possible solutions', *Educational Management and Administration*, 24: 355–369.

Thurlow, M.L., Ysseldyke, J.E. and Reid, C.L. (1997) 'High school graduation requirements for students with disabilities', *Journal of Learning Disabilities*, 30,6: 608–616.

Thurlow, M.L., Langenfeld, K., Nelson, R., Shin, H. and Coleman, J. (1998) *State Accountability Reports: What Do They Say About Students with Disabilities?* (Technical Report 20), Minneapolis, MN: University of Minnesota, National Center on Educational Outcomes.

Wilcox, B. and Gray, J. (1996) *Inspecting Schools: Holding Schools to Account and Helping Schools to Improve*, Buckingham: Open University Press.

Wilcox, B., Gray, J. and Tranmer, M. (1993) 'LEA frameworks for the assessment of schools: an interrupted picture', *Educational Research*, 35: 211–221.

Chapter 6

Special educational needs policy and choice

Tensions between policy development in the US and UK contexts

Cheryl Lange and Sheila Riddell

Introduction

There are some broad similarities in the directions of educational policy in the United States and the United Kingdom over the past two decades in the areas of special education and parental choice of school, but also some key differences. Inspired by economists such as Milton Friedman, the Thatcher and Reagan administrations were both committed to the application of market disciplines and private sector management practices to the public sector. From this perspective:

> State intervention is admissible for two purposes: to police the boundaries of the market and to provide where necessary the essential minimum of resources that the market cannot for a variety of reasons secure for those in extreme poverty.
>
> (Deakin, 1994, p. 7)

In the sphere of education, the principle of parental choice was seen as crucial to the operation of the market. At the same time, legislation was being implemented which ensured certain rights to children with special educational needs and put in place a range of administrative and legal structures as guarantee. Kirp (1982) notes that in the United States, the approach to provide for children with special educational needs reflected an individual rights approach, whereas in Scotland the principle of professional discretion continued to be upheld. In this chapter, we explore subtle differences in the realisation of these two sets of policies before discussing the nature of the tensions between them.

The policy of parental choice in the United States and Scotland

The US context

Concern over educational standards appears to have happened almost simultaneously in the United States and the United Kingdom. A document published in 1983, *A Nation at Risk*, stated:

> We report to the American people that while we can take justifiable pride in what our schools and colleges have historically accomplished and contributed to the United States, and the well-being of its people, the educational foundations of our society are presently being eroded by a rising tide of mediocrity that threatens our very future as a nation and people.
>
> (NCEE, 1983, p. 5)

One of the proposed remedies for the alleged decline of the education system was the empowerment of parents as consumers through school choice. The national Governors Association under the direction of then Governor Bill Clinton of Arkansas highlighted this measure as a possible reform. In the document *Time for Results* (1986) the Governors noted:

> if we first implement choice, true choice among public schools, we unlock the values of competition in the marketplace. Schools that compete for students, teachers and dollars will, by virtue of the environment, make those changes that will allow them to succeed.
>
> (Governors Association, 1986, p. 84)

Given the information necessary to allow parents to make informed decisions, the policy of school choice became one of the reforms which, according to Chubb and Moe (1990) would 'demand' excellence in education. It joined other reform measures such as increased teacher standards, graduation standards, and school-wide accountability in the pursuit of excellence in education.

At the time of writing, over half of the states have passed or proposed some sort of school choice legislation (Bierlein, 1993; Cookson, 1994; Ysseldyke, Lange and Delaney, 1992; Bierlein, 1996). The types of school choice options available differ from state to state. However, the most popular options include open enrolment (interdistrict choice), intradistrict choice, second chance programmes for at-risk students, charter schools, post-secondary enrolment options and magnet schools.

Among academics, parents and the policy community in the United States, there has been strong support for the principle of parental choice because it appeals both to those who believe that it is likely to heighten motivation and commitment, and those who support the economic ideas that underpin it. In addition, it appears to widen opportunity of choice of school beyond those who have traditionally enjoyed it, that is people who have been able to pay for a private education or change their residence to a more desirable school attendance area. *Politics, Markets and America's Schools* (Chubb and Moe, 1990), provides an in-depth review of a governance orientation toward choice and makes the following claims about the efficacy of the policy:

> Without being too literal about it, we think reformers would do well to entertain the notion that choice is a panacea. This is our way of saying that choice is not like the other reforms and should not be combined with them as part of a reformist strategy for improving America's schools. Choice is a self-contained reform with its own rationale and justification. It has the capacity all by itself to bring about the transformation that, for years, reformers have been seeking to engineer in a myriad of other ways . . . The whole point of a thoroughgoing system of choice is to free the schools from these disabling constraints by sweeping away the old institutions and replacing them with new ones. Taken seriously, choice is not a system-preserving reform . . . It is a revolutionary reform that introduces a new system of public education.
>
> (Ibid., p. 217)

Not all commentators, however, reflected such a positive view of the transformative potential of school choice. In contrast to those who believe school choice will provide equal opportunity, opponents drew attention to issues of equity, quality, community and organization (Fowler-Finn, 1994; Hayes, 1992; Kozol, 1992; Marcoulides and Heck, 1990; McCollum and Walker, 1992; Molnar, 1992; Bastian, 1990). These writers pointed out that parents may move children from one school to another for a host of reasons that bear no relation to the quality of teaching. Such factors were likely to include the socio-economic make-up of a community, proximity to school, daycare arrangements and athletic opportunities (Sewall, 1991). They argued that if these are the reasons parents move their children, then increased accountability will not occur and districts will not be moved to change. They argue that as the policy of school choice is available, existing inequalities between schools will be exacerbated. The Carnegie Foundation for the Advancement of Teaching in its report *School Choice* (1992) reviewed the status of the policy in America and expressed the following concern:

> it was clear from our study [of inter-district choice plans] that few if any students transferred from a rich district to a poor one. If fair competition is to occur, all states with 'choice' programs must first resolve the financial disparities that exist from district to district.
>
> (Ibid., p. 60)

Others pointed to the danger that marketing might distort the free operation of choice, privileging those with access to the means of persuasion. Campbell (1993) posed the question:

> With the advent of school choice, will school districts change their programs or will they just become more proficient at marketing their schools? And what is the role marketing plays in the administration of an unfettered system?

Furthermore, the possibility that school choice was, in reality, a disguised method of operating a system of social selection was argued by some. Moore and Davenport (1990), for instance, reviewed intradistrict choice programs within three large cities and found that:

> school choice has, by and large, become a new improved method of student sorting, in which schools pick and choose among students. In this sorting process, black and Hispanic students, low-income students, students with low achievement, students with absence and behavior problems, handicapped students and limited-English proficiency students have very limited opportunities to participate in popular options high schools and programs.
>
> (Ibid., p. 188)

In the United States, then, among both the policy-making and academic communities, there were bodies of opinion both supporting and opposing school choice, with equity arguments being used by both sides. These arguments are set within a context where school choice laws and policies are set by the states and not the federal government. Though the federal government supports public school choice through grants and rhetoric, by and large, school choice laws are under the purview of state legislatures. This necessarily means that school choice laws vary by state in their breadth of choice and in their implementation. As a result, school choice laws in the United States sit on a continuum that includes those that remain highly tied to existing bureaucratic policies to those unfettered from bureaucratic intervention. The placement of a school choice law on the continuum impacts how it is implemented and perceived within the larger educational community (Lange, 1997).

The UK context

Anxiety about the quality of state education and its impact on economic performance appeared to take off in the United Kingdom at about the same time as in the United States. During the 1960s, a series of inquiries into the system was produced, starting with the Black papers in the late 1960s, continuing through the Plowden Inquiry into primary education and the Swan Report on ethnic minorities, and culminating in the 'great Debate' launched by James Callaghan in a speech at Ruskin College in 1976. The Parent's Charter in Scotland (Scottish Office, 1991) envisaged parental choice as a major engine for the delivery of more cost effective and efficient education. Parental choice provisions of the 1981 Education (Scotland) Act were considerably stronger than those in the 1980 Education Act, the equivalent legislation for England and Wales. Adler, Petch and Tweedie (1989) reviewed the impact of the legislation in Scotland and concluded that it had led to greater inefficiency in use of resources and, in the context of formula funding, an increased disparity between schools' financial circumstances. In Scottish cities, a two-tier system of education appeared to be emerging, although this differed somewhat from the junior and senior secondary school system in place prior to comprehensive reorganisation. Following the implementation of parental choice, schools in peripheral housing estates and disadvantaged inner city areas tended to experience falling rolls, loss of revenue and low morale among pupils and teachers. They also became increasingly non-cost effective because of the number of empty places within them. By contrast, the former senior secondaries, often in more socially advantaged neighborhoods, became overcrowded and their resources over-stretched. Adler (1997) describes this as a 'negative sum game' in which 'the gains achieved by some pupils and, by extension, some parents, were more than offset by the losses incurred by others and by the community as a whole'. The 'tyranny of small decisions' (Hirsch, 1977) had produced an outcome (rump schools and congested schools) which could only be described as irrational (Schelling, 1978) for the community as a whole.

Gewirtz, Ball and Bowe (1995), in a study of the effects of parental choice of school in England and Wales, similarly concluded that education had acquired the status of a positional good, and that families now undertook the task of class selection which had previously been undertaken by a process of academic selection. In addition, they noted that the process of pupil selection by schools had not ceased, but ran alongside and in opposition to the principle of parental choice, since schools with a religious foundation, grant-maintained schools and the vestigial grammar schools were still permitted to select their pupils. The previous 'interrupters' of class structuring through education had been removed or significantly weakened. A chapter on 'Choice and class: parents in the market place' concludes thus:

> The use of cultural capital in the decoding of schools and interpretation of information and in the 'matching' of the child to school is a crucial component of choosing and then getting a school place, although economic capital is also important, most obviously in relation to the independent sector.
>
> (Ibid., p. 56)

To summarise, parental choice in the United Kingdom was enthusiastically advocated by the previous Conservative government. The Labour government, elected to power in May 1997, has maintained its commitment to choice, although its greater emphasis on public provision is indicated by scrapping both the scheme for opting out of local authority control in Scotland and the assisted places scheme which operated throughout the United Kingdom and provided financial support for able state school children who fulfilled certain selection criteria to attend independent schools. The academic community has tended to be critical of parental choice policy on the basis that it widened social segregation and resource disparity between schools. A common feature of parental choice policy in the United States and the United Kingdom is that although it ostensibly concerns all children, it was nonetheless produced with mainstream children in mind and its implications for children with special educational needs were largely ignored. In the following section, we briefly describe special needs policy in the United States and the United Kingdom and its articulation with parental choice policies.

Special educational needs policy in the United States and Scotland

Special educational needs: the US context

There were considerable similarities between US and UK special education policies until the late 1960s, and some interesting disparities. Throughout the 1950s and 1960s, both systems educated what were then referred to as 'handicapped' children in separate schools or units. Children with the most severe impairments were deemed uneducable. A sociological awareness of special education developed in the late 1960s and early 1970s. According to Kirp (1982):

> Isolating the mildly retarded from normal school life and depriving the seriously handicapped of any schooling were both depicted as iniquitous and, like so many other iniquities, were brought to the courts.
>
> (Ibid., p. 166)

The outcome of campaigns for more equitable treatment of disabled children was the 1974 Educational for All Handicapped Children Act (P.L.94-142) which entitled disabled children to treatment as similar to that of all other children as possible. The Act requires an Individual Educational Plan to be drawn up for each disabled child, diagnosing the child's condition and specifying a prescriptive regime to be approved by the child's parents. States were not allowed to plead lack of money as a reason for failing to make educational provision for disabled children, thus establishing that appropriate education was a right rather than an act of largesse on the part of state or federal government. Kirp summarises the status of special education in the United States thus:

> Special education – 'appropriate' special education – has become a legally recognized right, not an artefact of governmental generosity or professional judgement. The due process hearing stands as a procedural safeguard for substantive claims to a suitable and individually determined education.
>
> (Ibid., p. 168)

This statement encapsulates the tensions between school choice policies, which encourage the release from bureaucratic constraints to allow individuals choice within and between the public educational systems. Special education policies, on the other hand, provide protection of the individual's rights through bureaucratic means. There are thus fundamental philosophical tensions between these two sets of policies.

Some school change advocates have suggested ways in which these tensions might be managed. Chubb and Moe (1990), for instance, suggested an incentive system to encourage schools to attract students with special educational needs as a way of overcoming possible discrimination. They suggest:

> Some students have very special educational needs – arising from economic deprivation, physical handicaps, language difficulties, emotional problems and other disadvantages – that can only be met effectively through specialized programs that are costly to provide. State and federal programs already appropriate public money to address these problems. Our suggestion is that these funds should take the form of add-ons to student scholarships. At-risk students would than be empowered with bigger scholarships than the others, making them more attractive clients to all schools (and stimulating the emergence of new specialty schools).
>
> (Ibid., p. 220)

However, they offered no suggestions as to how this would be implemented within the current context of federal laws, and did not explore the implications of the emergence of 'new specialty' schools for students with disabilities. Recent discussions of how charter schools, which are effectively independent schools funded by the state, should provide for students with special needs have indicated that financial and programmatic planning for students with special educational needs must form part of the overall package, rather than being considered as a later add-on. This is especially important in light of the variety of school choice issues that emanate from the decentralised education system versus a federally mandated choice system.

The tension between protecting individual rights to an education and the right to choose will need to be discussed and resolved.

Special educational needs: the Scottish context

We noted earlier the way in which special education policy in the United States and the United Kingdom ran along parallel lines until the 1970s. Whereas special needs policy in the United States embarked on an individual rights track following the 1974 Education for All Handicapped Children Act, UK special needs policy continued to be informed by a belief in the benevolent discretion of professionals (Tomlinson, 1982). The Warnock Report (DES, 1978) established the principle of partnership with parents and recommended the implementation of a system whereby children with significant and enduring special educational needs should be assessed by a multi-disciplinary team who should assess the support needed to enable them to progress in school. Warnock established a broad commitment to integration, but envisaged an ongoing role for special schools. The Education (Scotland) Act (as amended) embodied a number of Warnock's key recommendations, including the institution of recording procedures. However, it was far more restricted in the extent to which parents were granted legal rights to obtain the education they required for their child. Whereas the 1981 Education (Scotland) Act, which amended the 1980 legislation, gave parents of non-recorded children the right to choice of school, the education authority might refuse a placing request made by a parent of a child with special educational needs on the following grounds:

- if admitting your child would mean they would have to employ an additional teacher or spend a lot of money to adapt or otherwise extend the school;
- if your child's education would suffer from another change of school;
- if the kind of education provided in the school you want would not be suitable for the child;
- if your child's admission would affect the education of other children (because, say, he or she needs a very great deal of individual attention).

(Scottish Office, 1993)

These caveats meant in effect that although the Scottish Office and local authorities stated that a mainstream school would be the preferred placement for a child with special educational needs, in effect such a placement could be refused if professionals deemed it to be inappropriate. This contrasts markedly with the rights approach adopted in the United States, which reflected the view that neither financial grounds nor potential harm to the education of other pupils would be deemed acceptable reasons for refusing a child a place in a mainstream school. Parents' right to request a placement in mainstream school was also upheld, although the possibility that such choices might be manipulated by professionals with an interest in sustaining a separate special education sector was not addressed.

As we discussed above, in the United States during the late 1960s and early 1970s, civil rights activists struggled to establish the principle that a child with special educational needs should be regarded as having the same rights of access to education as other children. In the United Kingdom, this principle has never been fully established and groups of disabled people, such as the Integration Alliance in England and AccessAbility in Scotland, continue to campaign for equal rights rather than benign humanitarianism. Such campaigns sometimes highlight tensions within the disability movement itself, which appears willing to accept the demands of deaf people for separate schools but in general regards such preferences as either misguided or reflecting the inadequacies of provision in mainstream. The new Labour government in its Green Paper on special educational needs for England and Wales has restated its commitment to inclusive education:

> Where pupils do have special educational needs there are strong educational, social and moral grounds for their education in mainstream schools. Our policy for schools will be consistent with our commitment to rights for disabled people more generally. But we must always put the needs of the child first, and for some children specialist, and perhaps residential, provision will be required, at least for a time. That is compatible with the principle of inclusive education.
>
> (DfEE, 1997, p. 34)

The best way of ensuring that parents will choose a mainstream school for their child, it is suggested, is by improving the quality of special needs provision in integrated settings, rather than banning special schools. The transfer of resources from mainstream to special which the Green Paper proposes is likely to stimulate change in this direction.

In Scotland, as in the rest of the United Kingdom, a similar readjustment between market and social justice principles is evident. A Green Paper on special educational needs in Scotland, published in May 1998, outlined the future direction for special educational needs provision in Scotland. A commitment is given to the development of a policy framework which:

- places the child's educational needs at the centre of education policy and decision-making;
- ensures that special educational needs are routinely taken into account when framing and implementing education policies;

- develops the earliest practicable assessment of the educational needs of every child;
- promotes the earliest practicable intervention to tackle the needs identified;
- supports diversity of provision consistent with the diverse needs of the individual child;
- encourages and furthers the role of parents;
- places continuing and increasing priority on the development and training of staff working with children with special educational needs;
- ensures that every education authority prepares, publishes and makes readily available in consultation with relevant interests in this area a full policy on special educational needs.

(SOEID, 1998, p. 5)

Although there is a clear wish that special educational needs should move from the periphery to the centre of the policy arena, there continues to be an emphasis on the language of needs rather than rights. Needs are assumed to be identified by parents and professionals in partnership with each other, but a sense of the child as an individual with rights is largely absent. There is also a shrinking from a wholesale endorsement of the principle of education in mainstream classes, and considerable efforts are made to establish that education in segregated settings is consistent with ideas of social inclusivity:

In recent years, there has been much discussion about the development of integration and inclusion for pupils with special educational needs. However there is no single universal answer to how these are achieved. An inclusive society must ensure that the potential of each individual is fully developed through education and that their attainment and achievement are developed and respected. It is on the realisation of this potential that inclusiveness depends; an inclusive society and education system will therefore strive to ensure that it creates the range of approaches and opportunities to ensure that this is brought about.

(Ibid., p. 4)

A reading of recent Scottish and UK policy documents indicates that within official discourse, tensions between special educational needs policy and choice continue to cluster round the extent to which parents of children with special educational needs should have access to mainstream schools on the same terms as other parents and whether choices between special and mainstream should be construed as equally valid. A detailed discussion of wider school choice policies on the parents of children with special educational needs is absent from official policy discussion.

The implications of parental choice of schools for students with special educational needs: research evidence from the United States and Scotland

US research on school choice and special educational needs policy

The issues relating to school choice and students with disabilities have begun to bubble to the surface in the past few years. Charter schools and their place on the bureaucratic continuum appear to have led policy-makers and others to consider how the two policies work together. Here we briefly review some research findings before looking more closely at the experiences of Minnesota, the first state to pass comprehensive school choice legislation.

The Center for Policy Research examined special education and charter schools in Colorado (McLaughlin, Henderson and Ullah, 1996). After reviewing ten Colorado charter schools they concluded that 'two major issues impact charter schools' ability and desire to service students with disabilities: responsibility for service provision and learner characteristics of students enrolled in charter schools' (Ibid., p. 9). McLaughlin *et al.* note that in relation to the inclusion of students with disabilities in charter schools, there is concern with regard to student access, funding and familiarity with special education law and requirements within these schools. The Great Lakes Regional Resource Center (1995) also drew attention to the complexity of funding when charter schools, based on the principles of moving away from bureaucratic control, begin to implement mandated services:

> Funding special education students is a complex process. Often when a charter school is set up, the administrators are not familiar with the rules governing special education funds. They may have to hire someone to teach them the process. Also, many times they are not aware of the costs of testing and evaluating these students. The money may not be supplied by the resident district, depending on the law, but charter school administrators may not be aware of this until later.
>
> (Ibid., p. 2)

Lack of knowledge in charter schools of the Individuals with Disabilities Education Act, of mandatory evaluation and testing of disabled children and a shortage of special education professionals to serve in such schools were highlighted by Szabo and Gerber (1996). Buechler (1996) in his review of charter schools mentions the complexity of funding and the lack of planning involved when charter school laws are proposed and passed. He noted:

> There is generally no mechanism specified in the law for these schools to share costs or personnel with other district schools or to draw upon

the expertise of district staff members who specialize in special education assessments and funding.

(Ibid., p. 31)

The most comprehensive examination of the impact of school choice on
special education has been conducted by the University of Minnesota's
Enrolment Options Project for Students with Disabilities. Early in the
1990s researchers at the University of Minnesota recognised the importance
of examining school choice and its impact on students with disabilities. Issues
for students with disabilities and school districts implementing parental choice
strategies were defined in three areas: demographics/participation, implementation, and outcomes (Ysseldyke *et al.*, 1991). Using these three areas
as the framework for future research, several school choice options have been
examined in Minnesota, the first state to pass comprehensive school choice
legislation. Given that students with disabilities are accessing these options
in percentages that are equal to or greater than the proportion of special
education students in the state (10 per cent), Minnesota provided an excel-
lent laboratory for examining the issues.

The Minnesota experience

Fourteen studies examining four of the most popular school choice options
have been conducted over the past eight years. These studies examined the
participation, implementation, and outcomes for students with disabilities
and their programmes. Four of the most popular options are examined in
these studies. In Table 6.1 a description of each option is provided.

Demographics/participation

The question of whether students with disabilities would be denied access
has been central to those closely watching these two policies. The historic
exclusion of students with disabilities from educational settings and the lack
of discussion about how these two policies would interact led some to believe
that access would be a major issue for students with disabilities.

Most of Minnesota's school choice laws directly addressed access for
students with disabilities. However, there was still some ambiguity about
whether all schools, charter schools, or school choice programmes had to
take all students with disabilities, or whether the resident district bore the
educational responsibility. Research found there to be considerable participation by these students in the various Minnesota school choice options;
with the exception of post-secondary enrolment options, students with disabilities were represented in numbers higher than their state-wide proportion
(10 per cent). Participation varied by disability group, with a broader range
of disability groups participating in open enrolment and charter schools

Table 6.1 Minnesota enrolment options programmes

Post-secondary enrolment options programme	Provides 11th and 12th grade students, who qualify for the post-secondary institution of their choice, the opportunity to take college courses for high school credit. The programme gives the student choice of a wider variety or more advanced courses than may be available in their high school.
Open enrolment programme	Allows students from kindergarten to 12th grade the opportunity to apply to attend a school outside the district in which they live. Applications are due in the non-resident district before 15 January, except for those choosing to enter or leave districts with desegregation plans.
Second-chance Option (high school graduation incentives programme)	Designed for students who are not likely to graduate or who have dropped out of school before getting their diplomas. These learners may choose from a variety of education options including alternative schools or Area Learning Centers (12-month schools) to complete the requirements needed to graduate.
Charter schools	Educationally, financially and legally independent from a school district. They can be started by licensed teachers who get permission from the State Board of Education and their local school board. They are run by an independent elected board of directors.

Source: Minnesota Department of Education.

and more specific groups participating in second-chance option for at-risk students (students with learning disabilities or emotional behaviour disorders) and post-secondary options (students with mental retardation or learning disabilities). It should be noted that high participation in charter schools was explained, to some extent, by the fact that some of these schools were special schools, thus reintroducing segregation of special needs students, albeit based on the choice of parents rather than on the basis of professional judgement. There was some evidence that a number of districts were encouraging students with emotional behaviour disorders to move out of their area through open enrolment or second-chance options (Lange, Ysseldyke and Delaney, 1995). Findings also suggest, however, that parents and students are using these options to provide a fresh start for students with this label (Ysseldyke, Lange and Gorney, 1994).

Each of the options examined in the Minnesota studies can be placed somewhere on the school choice continuum. Established school choice options have more bureaucratic ties and less accountability requirements. Newer options, such as charter schools, are moving further and further away from bureaucratic rules and regulations and relying more and more on accountability, measured in terms of student performance. In relation to each type

Table 6.2 Selected school choice options and their place on the characteristics continuum (high, medium, or low factor)

	Bureaucracy	Competition	Accountability	Student/parent choice
Charter schools	Low	Medium	High	High
Inter-district Choice (i.e. Open Enrolment)	High	Medium	Low	High
Second-chance programmes for at-risk students	Medium	Low	Low	High
Post-secondary enrolment options	High	Medium	Low	High

of choice option, particular issues arise for student with disabilities. A summary of where the more popular options are placed on the continuum is presented in Table 6.2.

Parental choice

The ability to choose a school for a child with a disability is present in all the options studied, although particular issues arise for students with disabilities. For options that have set admissions or enrolment criteria, students with disabilities may be excluded from the opportunity for choice (e.g. post-secondary enrolment options). In other cases, school choice options may be used as a means to encourage choice (e.g. students with emotional behaviour disorders may be expected to choose schools specifically designed for this group of pupils).

Bureaucracy

Minnesota options vary in their level of bureaucracy. Charter schools have less bureaucratic ties to the larger system; however, post-secondary options entail considerable bureaucratic regulations. Without a communication channel or a decision-making process about rules and regulations surrounding special education, confusion will result. Since charter schools were established to liberate educational establishments from bureaucratic constraints, students with disabilities might well be unwelcome clients since they bring with them expectations of compliance with legally established procedures, which might be seen as at odds with providing an unfettered educational system.

Accountability

Though the raising of standards is a central factor in arguments for or against school choice, there was little data available in the state that could provide information about the success or failure of these options for students with disabilities. This illustrates that improving educational outcomes may be a key factor in legislating choice options, but not one that has been closely monitored. Monitoring the inclusion of students with disabilities in the accountability process will be important, since charter schools have much at stake when implementing an accountability system. The rhetoric from politicians and advocates suggests charter schools will provide the impetus to improve student achievement, and in many states, charter schools must demonstrate improved student outcomes in order to continue operating. When such high stakes are involved in the school choice option and its future, who is tested and how they are tested is a critical issue.

Accountability will also be an issue for those charter schools or school choice options that only serve students with special needs. In Minnesota, the second-chance programme serves only those who are at risk of school failure. Teachers and administrators of these programmes are struggling with the difficult task of how to measure success with at-risk students. Will these programmes or options be penalised if the rate of success is different than other schools? Should they be penalised if students are not achieving at the rate expected by the general public? These are issues that arise when the stakes are high and results will determine whether a school or school choice option is continued.

Competition

Each of the Minnesota options is designed to promote competition to varying degrees and in different ways. The post-secondary enrolment option is intended to provide enhanced curricula at the secondary level, and charter schools and open enrolment are intended to foster competition between and among charter schools and school districts. How participation of students with disabilities in these options affects the ability of institutions to compete with each other raises some interesting questions. Will charter schools tailor their programmes to encourage students with disabilities or special needs to attend, or will they take the position that special needs students may damage their competitive advantage? Will more schools be designed to meet the exclusive needs of students with disabilities, thus impacting other school district programmes and services? In short, what role will competition play for students with disabilities who desire choice or who are encouraged to seek an educational alternative?

Scottish research on choice and special educational needs policy

Scottish research on the impact of choice on special needs policy is very different in its concerns from the US research described above. Unlike recent US studies, which have explored the impact of the marketisation of education on students with disabilities, Scottish research has tended to restrict its analysis to the nature of parental choice between mainstream and special schools. Research commissioned by the Scottish Office to investigate the impact of the 1980 Education (Scotland) Act (as amended) (Riddell, Dyer and Thomson, 1990), suggested that professionals continued to control the decisions made by parents and manipulated statutory procedures to ensure that parents chose the school they felt was most appropriate. A subsequent study of policy and practice in relation to parents of children with specific learning difficulties indicated that this group of parents, who were predominantly middle class, were much more likely to challenge professional judgement than other parents of disabled children, but even so felt short-changed by the system. They disagreed with educational psychologists who saw specific learning difficulties as lying along a continuum of special educational needs and maintained that the condition could not readily be distinguished from other types of learning disability. Parents, on the other hand, maintained that dyslexia was a specific impairment, physiological in origin, which required specialist forms of assessment methods to diagnose, and particular methods of reading instruction which were different from those provided by the learning support teacher in the mainstream class. Parents and professionals disagreed about the extent to which parents' wishes were acted upon with regard to their children's education. According to professionals, this group of parents exerted a powerful, many maintained unhealthy, grip on the system, extracting an unfairly large amount of financial support for their particular children to the disadvantage of other groups lacking powerful advocates. Parents, on the other hand, felt that they were prisoners within an unwieldy bureaucratic system which went to great lengths to ignore their requests.

A further piece of research, exploring the effectiveness of mainstream and special schools for children with special educational needs (Riddell, forthcoming) showed that despite the cautious endorsement of mainstreaming since the 1980 Education (Scotland) Act (as amended), the proportion of children in special schools had remained remarkably constant at 1.8 per cent, although there was a national move away from special schools and towards special units attached to mainstream (between 1983 and 1993, the number of special schools decreased from 213 to 159 and the number of special units increased from 108 to 168). There was some inflation in terms of the number of pupils with Records of Needs (an increase of 3 per cent from 1995 to 1996). A major change, however, occurred in relation to the proportion of pupils with Records of Needs who were in mainstream schools, which increased from 6 per cent in 1983 to 42 per cent in 1993. Interviews with parents about their experience of choice of schools suggested that this was seen in terms of opting for the local mainstream school or a special school, rather than exploring a number of mainstream options. Significant factors influencing the choice included geographical location (few special schools in rural areas), social class (middle-class parents were much more likely to succeed in obtaining their choice of school, whether mainstream or special, because of their familiarity with professional discourse) and the nature of a child's impairment (those with profound or multiple learning difficulties were usually placed in special schools). The researchers encountered parents from socially disadvantaged backgrounds who were clearly unhappy with their child's placement in special schools, but who had lacked the assertiveness to insist on their preferred option. Professionals manipulated parents' awareness of available options by, for example, arranging visits to a number of special schools but to only one mainstream school.

Very little research in the wider UK context or in Scotland has explored the impact of choice policy and its effects for children with special educational needs, and this is probably indicative of the fact that these mainstream and special school sectors continue to be viewed separately. A study of classroom experiences of lower-achieving pupils in secondary schools of varying levels of effectiveness and socio-economic status (Riddell, Brown and Duffield, 1998) indicated the salience of the latter variable. The teaching methods used in socially disadvantaged schools were designed to control rather than encourage individual pupil attainment. Thus long reading or writing tasks were set, rather than ones involving group discussion and interaction. Ironically, although the proportion of pupils with learning difficulties in the most socially advantaged school was lower than in the disadvantaged schools, it had acquired an additional learning support teacher because of the number of dyslexic pupils identified. Because of their disproportionately high number in socially disadvantaged neighbourhoods, it is likely that pupils with Records of Needs and learning difficulties receive less learning support than similar pupils in socially advantaged schools. For example, 57 per cent of pupils with Records of Needs in Glasgow City attend schools within priority partnership areas. More empirical research is required to understand the home/school experiences of pupils with special educational needs in advantaged and in disadvantaged localities.

Conclusion

This chapter has provided an account of the development of school choice and special educational needs policy in the United States and Scotland, and reveals fascinating divergence from the situation in the late 1960s and early 1970s, where 'normal' pupils attended their local school apart from those who were educated privately and disabled students, who were sent to special schools. From the mid-1970s, there was divergence in special educational needs policies in the United States and Scotland, the former developing an individual rights approach and the latter continuing to give precedence to professional judgement. Parental choice policy, introduced earlier in Scotland, also took different forms. Although parents increasingly took up the option of 'shopping around' for an appropriate school, draining pupils and resources from those in the poorest areas, nonetheless the types of choice available remained limited even compared with the rest of the United Kingdom. Very few schools opted out of local authority control and the Scottish equivalent of city technology colleges were never established. The assisted places scheme was abolished by the incoming Labour government, and education action zones, freeing schools from a range of bureaucratic controls to enable them to raise standards, have not yet been introduced north of the Border. Recent research suggests that choice for parents of children with special educational needs is still seen in terms of opting between special and mainstream placements. In the sphere of special educational needs, which has always preferred the language of needs rather than rights, professionals still exert great powers in mediating school choice, and parents, often struggling with multiple disadvantages, find it difficult to challenge this control. Although the area remains largely unexplored, it would appear that children with special educational needs are very likely to find themselves in rump schools with falling roles and resources.

In the United States, although introduced slightly later than in Scotland, parental choice of school has been adopted enthusiastically, with considerable diversity emerging within the system. The tension between the federal laws that ensure a 'free and appropriate education' to children with disabilities and the state school choice laws that seek to dismantle bureaucratic policies puts students with disabilities in the middle of a policy debate that must be resolved for the best implementation of school choice.

In order to retain the gains made in the 1970s and 1980s, when special needs emerged from its previous backwater, it will be important to ensure that the inclusion of such students is a preliminary consideration in the establishment of future choice options. At the same time, it may be necessary to question the wholesale embracing of choice as the overriding principle in education. Although many policy-makers in both the United Kingdom and the United States maintain that the market should be the ultimate arbiter of educational provision, there are manifest dangers if the legislative protection of the 1970s for students with disabilities is dismissed as no more than a cumbersome piece of bureaucracy. Much research on parental choice has demonstrated the ways in which such choices are socially structured and that the incremental effects of individual choices may have negative effects for minority groups and for the social whole. Such insights need to be applied to further research on the interaction of special educational needs and choice policies. Comparative work, such as we have undertaken in this chapter, may be helpful in highlighting the commonalities and differences within national systems. However parental choice is interpreted, expanded or curtailed, it seems evident that it will remain a potent ingredient of education systems in western industrialised countries, and therefore it is important to engage with it to ensure that it does not work to the detriment of those children with special educational needs.

References

Adler, M. (1997) 'Looking backwards to the future: parental choice and educational policy', *British Educational Research Journal Special Issue, Reflexive Accounts of Educational Reform*, 23,3: 297–315.

Adler, M., Petch, A. and Tweedie, J. (1989) *Parental Choice and Educational Policy*, Edinburgh: Edinburgh University Press.

Allan, J., Brown, S. and Riddell, S. (1995) *Special Educational Needs Provision in Mainstream and Special Schools in Scotland. Final Report to the Scottish Office*, Stirling: University of Stirling.

Bastiam, A. (1990) 'Unwrapping the package', in W.L. Boyd and H.J. Walberg (eds), *Choice in Education: Potential and Problems* (pp. 177–186), Berkley, CA: McCutchan.

Bierlein, L.A. (1993) *A National Review of Open Enrolment/Choice: Debates and Descriptions*, Morrison Institute for Public Policy: Arizona State University.

—— (1996) *Charter Schools: Initial Findings*, Denver, CO: Education Commission of the States.

Buechler, M. (1996) *Charter Schools: Legislation and Results after Four Years* (Policy Report PR-B13). Bloomington, IN: Indiana Policy Center.

Campbell, M.A. (1993, July 8) 'In era of choice, public schools must develop marketing plans', *Education Week*, 3–4.

Carnegie Foundation for the Advancement of Teaching (1992) *School Choice*, Princeton NJ: Author.

Chubb, J.E. and Moe, T.M. (1990) *Politics, Markets and America's Schools*, Washington, DC: Brookings Institution.

Cookson, P.W., Jr (1994) *School Choice: The Struggle for the Soul of American Education*, New Haven: Yale University Press.

Department for Education and Employment (1997) *Excellence for All Children: Meeting Special Educational Needs*, London: HMSO.

Department of Education and Science (DES) (1978) *Special Educational Needs* (The Warnock Report), London: HMSO.

Deakin, N. (1994) *The Politics of Welfare: Continuities and Change*, London: Harvester Wheatsheaf.

Fowler-Finn, T. (1994) 'Why have they chosen another school system?', *Education Leadership*, 51,4: 60–62.

Gewirtz, S., Ball, S.J. and Bowe, R. (1995) *Markets, Choice and Equity in Education*, Buckingham: Open University Press.

Governors Association (1986) *Time for Results: The Governor's 1991 Report on Education*, Washington, DC: National Governors Association Center for Policy Research and Analysis.

Great Lakes Regional Resource Center (1995, October) *Information on Charter Schools*, Coloumbus OH: GLRRC.

Hayes, L. (1992) 'An interview with Jonathan Kozol: A simple matter of humanity', *Phi Delta Kappan*, December: 334–337.

Hirsch, F. (1977) *Social Limits to Growth*, London: Routledge and Kegan Paul.

Kirp, D. (1982) 'Professionalisation as policy choice: British special education in comparative perspective', *World Politics* XXXIV, 2: 137–174.

Kozol, J. (1992) 'I dislike the idea of choice, and I want to tell you why . . .', *Education Leadership*, 50,3: 90–91.

Lange, C.M. (1997 March) 'School choice, charter schools, and students with dis-abilities', paper presented at the meeting of the American Educational Research Association, Chicago, IL.

Lange, C.M., Ysseldyke, J.E. and Delaney, T.J. (1995) Open Enrollment's Impact on School Districts When Students With Disabilities Transfer Schools (Research Report 14), Minneapolis, MN: University of Minnesota Enrollment Options Project.

McCollum, P. and Walker, C. (1992) 'Minorities in America 2000', Education and Urban Society, 24,2: 178–195.

McLaughlin, M.J., Henderson, K. and Ullah, H. (1996 April) 'Charter schools: a hopeful response to the education of students with disabilities in colorado, paper presented at the meeting of the American Education Research Association, New York, NY.

Marcoulides, G. and Heck, R. (1990) 'Educational policy issues for the 1990's – Balancing equity and excellence in implementing the reform agenda', Urban Education, 25,3: 304–316.

Molnar, A. (1992) 'Choice, orientation, discussions, and prospects', Education Policy, 6,2: 105–122.

Moore, D.R. and Davenport, S. (1990) 'School Choice: The new improved sorting machine', in W.L. Boyd and H.J. Walberg (eds), Choice in Education: Potential and Problems (pp. 187–224), Berkley, CA: McCutchan.

National Commission on Excellence in Education (NCEE) (1983) A Nation at Risk: The Imperative for Education Reform, Washington DC: NCEE.

Riddell, S., Brown, S. and Duffield, J. (1994) 'Parental power and special educa-tional needs: the case of specific learning difficulties', British Educational Research Journal, 20,3: 327–344.

—— (1998) 'The utility of qualitative research for influencing policy and practice on school effectiveness' in R. Slee, G. Weiner, with S. Tomlinson (eds) School Effectiveness for Whom? Challenges to the School Effectiveness and School Improvement Movements, London: Falmer.

Riddell, S., Dyer, S. and Thomson, G.O.B. (1990) 'Parents, professionals and social welfare models: The implementation of the Education (Scotland) Act 1981', European Journal of Special Needs Education, 5,2: 96–110.

Schelling, T.C. (1978) Micromotives and Macrobehaviour, New York: Norton.

Scottish Office (1991) The Parents' Charter in Scotland, Edinburgh: The Scottish Office.

—— (1993) A Parents' Guide to Special Educational Needs, Edinburgh: The Scottish Office.

Sewall, G.T. (1991) 'America 2000, an appraisal', Phi Delta Kappan, 73: 204–209.

SOEID (1998) Achievement for All, Edinburgh: SOEID.

Szabo, J.M. and Gerber, M.M. (1996) 'Special education and the charter school movement', Special Education Leadership Review, 135–148.

Tomlinson, S. (1982) A Sociology of Special Education, London: Routledge.

Ysseldyke, J.E., Lange, C.M. and Delaney, T.J. (1992) School Choice Programs in the Fifty States (Res. Rep. No. 7), Minneapolis MN: University of Minnesota, Enrollment Options for Students with Disabilities Project.

Ysseldyke, J.E., Lange, C.M. and Gorney, D. (1994) 'Parents of students with dis-abilities and open enrollment: Characteristics and reasons for transfer', Excep-tional Children, 60,4: 359–372.

Ysseldyke, J.E., Algozzine, B., Thurlow, M.L., and Nathan, J. (1991) *Open Enrollment and Students with Disabilities: Issues, Concerns, Fears, and Anticipated Benefits* (Monograph No. 91-001), Minneapolis, MN: University of Minnesota, Enrollment Options for Students with Disabilities Project.

Chapter 7

The changing governance of education and its comparative impact on special education in the United Kingdom and the United States

Jennifer Evans and Michael M. Gerber

Introduction

This chapter begins with an analysis of the effects on the organisation of special education, as a school-based enterprise, of recent and current changes in school-based governance and management in both countries. To illustrate and evaluate this discussion, the chapter will then present descriptions of particular governance reforms in those parts of the United Kingdom (England and Wales) and the United States that focus on local management of schools. Specifically, we discuss the impact of local management of schools and grant maintained policies in the United Kingdom and the movement to establish site-based managed and governed and charter schools in over twenty-five states in the United States. The chapter then presents a comparative discussion and analysis of key similarities and differences observed in the UK and US reforms. We conclude with arguments for keeping special education goals in view as both countries continue to experiment with reforms in school site-based governance and management.

Governing and managing schools

The major reforms in the United Kingdom and the United States that are of interest in this chapter are those that have shifted authority away from more centralised governance of schools, investing schools themselves with varying degrees of autonomy to pursue educational goals. We use the term 'school-site governance and management' to serve as a broad categorical umbrella covering a host of different labels used to connote recent changes in the way individual schools are governed and managed. These include: local management of schools; local management of special schools; administrative decentralisation; building-based management; decentralised management; responsible autonomy; the autonomous school concept; shared governance; school-based management; school-based budgeting; school-site management; school-centred management; school-site autonomy; and school-based curriculum development. The concepts underlying these terms are not precisely the same, of course, but they all have as their primary intention a portrayal of some vision of radically increased organisational autonomy for schools and empowerment of the communities they most directly serve.

Impact of governance on education for students with disabilities

The empirical literature reporting effects on provision for students with disabilities or special educational needs (SEN) of reforms in school-site governance and management is surprisingly thin, given the attention these ideas have received over the past decade. This is an unfortunate state of affairs because, without empirical evidence, it varies from difficult to impossible to project why and how changes in school-site governance and management might impact the welfare of students with disabilities, or which changes might enhance the capacity of schools to provide substantive educational opportunity for these students.

The dearth of literature on school-site governance and management and special education may be explained by several factors. First, the administration of special education provision historically has tended to come from central administration to personnel offering special programmes in mainstream schools, or to special schools, in lines of authority and responsibility that are different and separate from administration of the general educational programme. In general, those responsible for day-to-day administration of schools have had only ambiguous and limited administrative involvement with special education provision, even when such provision is based at mainstream school sites. With some variations, special education administrators at some level beyond the school traditionally have managed special budgets, promulgated and implemented policies, hired and disciplined personnel, conducted in-service needs assessments and training, and established curricular requirements.

Second, although great attention has been given to the implementation of special education policies in both the United Kingdom and the United States, mostly this has been directed towards study of how national policy is or is not implemented nationally. Occasionally, implementation variations between local education authorities (LEAs) are noted for analysis. Variations at the school level are often ignored. Indeed, little special education research exists in which 'school', rather than student or teacher or parent, is the unit of analysis.

Third, the field of special education tends to mistake the study of children with disabilities for the study of special education. Although they are clearly related, one does not simply reduce to the other. The study of special education, we would argue, is not child study, nor is it the study of what unique or specific instructional methods or tactics might be employed most successfully with regard to any specific class of child differences. Rather, special education is something that schools do in their capacity as education organisations. Special education involves explicit resource arrangements and an organisation of activity designed to implement stated or unstated policies and plans for an entire school. It seeks to meet the joint needs of all students, teachers, staff, parents, and community members, not just the needs of any particular student with disabilities. Variations in school organisation are active forces that shape how individual differences in children are perceived, how and if these differences are recognised as disabilities at all, how effectively instructional efforts are organised and provided.

Normally, variations in school governance cannot be induced experimentally. However, some school reform efforts produce something very much like an experimental manipulation by urging or prescribing highly specific changes in school governance and management. The reform proposals we address in this chapter have brought about significant relocation of authority to the school site and away from centralised authorities, thereby bringing classroom activities, school building management functions, and the exercise of authority into greater proximity. The differential impact of these changes in the United Kingdom and the United States provides the opportunity to focus on the construction of special education at the school, rather than the national or LEA levels.

School governance reforms in the United Kingdom and the United States

Recent changes in the United Kingdom

In this section, we explore the nature of changes in governance and their impact on special education in the United Kingdom (or more precisely in England and Wales, since Scotland and Northern Ireland have different governance structures in place). The argument will draw on data collected as part of an ESRC-funded research project[1] which studied the impact of local management of schools (LMS) on special education, as well as published findings from other research in the field.

Over the last two decades, LMS and local management of special schools (LMSS) are among a number of school reforms that have altered the relationship between LEAs and schools in fundamental ways that have had a direct impact on special education, whether offered in segregated or integrated settings. At the same time, the creation of grant-maintained (GM) schools and a national Funding Agency for Schools (FAS) has diminished the power of LEAs in planning and funding schools in their local areas and has centralised decision-making at the national level. Thus, there has been a two-way squeeze on local authorities – many of their powers and responsibilities have been delegated to schools and school governing bodies, while other aspects of their work have been taken over by civil servants at the

Department for Education and Employment, or by non-elected bodies whose officials are appointed by the government. One significant organisation which has been set up to make decisions about funding special educational provision for individual children is the Special Educational Needs Tribunal, a quasi-judicial body which hears appeals by parents about LEA decisions on funding or placement of individual children.

There has been new legislation (School Standards and Framework Act 1998) which will create three new types of publicly funded schools – 'community', 'voluntary' and 'foundation' schools – to replace the current system of locally managed and grant-maintained schools. Community schools will have the same governance structures as the former LEA schools under LMS, but with more parent governors.[2] That is, they will have control of their budgets, but still have close links with the LEA, especially for the provision of services, such as support and advice for children with SEN. The LEA will own the land and buildings of these schools, and, although staff are appointed by the schools, the LEA will be the employer.

Both voluntary (usually church) schools and foundation schools will be similar in governance to the former GM schools. They will own their premises and be the direct employers of their staff. They are similar, in these respects, to charter schools in the United States. Foundation schools (unlike the GM schools which they are replacing) will have a small representation of governors appointed by the LEA. All schools will be able to choose which status they wish to adopt, but the assumption is that most schools will choose that which is closest to their present status (i.e. LEA schools will become community, voluntary aided church schools will become voluntary, and GM schools will become foundation schools). GM special schools (of which there are very few) must become community schools, thus reinforcing the rather ambivalent attitude of government policy-makers towards special education, which is nominally a partnership between parents and professionals, but, in reality is heavily dominated by professional concerns (Kirp, 1982; Fulcher, 1989).

Some commentators have argued that these changes are merely cosmetic, and the existing differentials of prestige between GM and LEA schools will be perpetuated by the new system. Currently, GM schools have tended to cater for middle-class children, and have been allowed to select a proportion of their pupils on the basis of ability. Many fully selective (grammar) schools currently have GM status. Thus, pupils with special educational needs have effectively been denied access to these schools, which have operated overt or covert selection processes to screen out pupils who may be problematic (Evans and Lunt, 1994; Gewirtz, Ball and Bowe, 1995).

The role of the LEAs

The 1998 Act promotes a new role for LEAs, compared with the minimalist approach of the previous government. In essence, the LEA has been co-opted as an arm of the surveillance regime put in place by the creation of an inspectorate – the Office for Standards in Education (Ofsted), whose focus is on promoting higher standards in schools through regular inspections of individual schools and the publication of inspection reports. The duties of LEAs, under the new legislation, include the preparation of Education Development Plans, which will involve providing information for schools and governors to help in setting targets for school improvement. A code of practice in LEA/school relations is to be issued, to give guidance about the respective roles of LEAs and schools.

The government is also planning to increase financial delegation to schools. Currently, a proportion of the education budget can be retained by the LEA to fund administrative and other services. This is now to be strictly limited and the LEAs will only be able to retain funding for certain clearly defined purposes (which include some support services for students with special educational needs (such as the educational psychology services). It is not yet clear what differences these changes will make in the relative autonomy of schools to manage their own affairs, but it seems clear that site-based school governance and management will continue to be the key organising principle for the delivery of education in schools in the United Kingdom.

What is local management of schools?

In common with many other western industrialised nations, the United Kingdom has moved from a hierarchical, bureaucratic system of school administration by officials employed at the level of the local authority to one where schools and their governing bodies have the major role in decision-making about how schools are run (Whitty, Power and Halpin, 1997; Lawton, 1992). Schools have their budgets delegated to them, and decisions about how to use their funding and other resources, such as staff and premises, are up to them. The official power within this system lies with the governing body, although, unofficially, the headteacher (school principal) is the key decision-maker. This system applies to special and mainstream schools.

This change in power structures has had a significant impact on relations between LEAs and schools *vis-à-vis* the education of children with special educational needs. LEAs still have a responsibility to fund special educational provision for those children who have a Statement of their special educational needs. This is a contract between the LEA and the child which is issued after a formal multi-professional assessment and which details the child's special educational needs and the provision that must be made for those needs. Around 3 per cent of the total school population has such a Statement, and the proportion is increasing. However, another 18 per cent (at least) of children in schools are presumed to have special educational needs, and these needs should be met by the school out of its delegated budget. Each LEA (apart from those funded through the FAS) allocates money to its schools on the basis of a formula, most of which is based on 'pupil-related factors' (i.e. the age of the pupils and some weighting for SEN). The rest of the formula consists of additional weightings for a variety of other factors, including social deprivation indices and special educational needs. For some schools, these additional factors make up a large part of their budget. Once the money is delegated to schools, it can be spent according to the priorities of the head and the governors, so money intended for special educational needs (for example) need not necessarily be spent on pupils with SEN. LEAs currently have to delegate 85 per cent of their potential schools budget to the schools, leaving only 15 per cent of the budget available for centrally provided services, such as specialist teachers, educational psychologists and funding for Statements of special educational needs. The proportion delegated is likely to increase under the new proposals, described above, which are currently out for consultation. This would leave less money for the maintenance of the central support role of the LEA.

Effects on special education

This division of responsibilities between LEAs and schools has several important consequences for the development of policy and practice. First, schools are increasingly seeing obtaining a Statement for a child as a way of acquiring guaranteed extra funding. Although funding for Statements is legally retained by the LEA, many LEAs are now adopting a policy of devolving the funding of Statement provision to schools and expecting schools to use those funds to find the appropriate support for the child. Thus, the rate of issuing Statements is rising each year, and LEAs are finding it very difficult to stem this tide. The result of this is that LEAs are finding that more and more of their education budget is tied up in funding support for individual children, leaving fewer resources available for the general support of schools through advice and in-service training for teachers. Since schools are becoming increasingly unwilling to support special educational needs from their own delegated budgets, a culture is growing up in which children with SEN are seen as 'someone else's problem', and schools will not take responsibility for meeting the needs themselves.

The original concept of a Statement was that it would apply to around 2 per cent of the pupil population (those with severe and long-term special educational needs) (Warnock, 1992). The extension of the provision of Statements to a much wider population with problems of literacy, behaviour or general under-achievement has meant that LEAs are constrained in their policy-making about funding priorities and are finding it difficult to implement policies for inclusive education, since schools are unwilling to accept pupils without extra funding to support them. In some cases, schools are excluding pupils with a variety of learning and behaviour difficulties, leaving LEAs to deal with the consequences of this.

Case examples

One recent high-profile case involved a school where the headteacher had excluded a pupil and the governors had ordered the school to take the pupil back. Other parents had protested and withdrawn their children from the school. The parents of the excluded pupil had refused a place at a special school for children with behaviour problems and insisted on their child's right to remain in the school. The LEA maintained that it was powerless to intervene in the dispute, which was eventually resolved when the parents of the child withdrew him from the school and sent him to another primary school in the area.

This incident illustrates a key aspect of LMS, that is, the funding of schools on a 'per capita' basis, which means that schools are keen to attract pupils who will enhance the school's reputation and raise its status in the local area. School governors, who have a statutory responsibility to ensure that, if a child in their school has special educational needs, those needs are being met, find themselves torn between their duty to individual children with SEN and their responsibility to keep their school viable by attracting pupils. Governors are responsible for schools' admission policies, and, as mentioned above, many governing bodies have taken the opportunity to introduce selection by ability (although this is now to be outlawed).

Head teachers are also, obviously, aware of the need to attract 'desirable' pupils. One example from our research illustrates this. The school in question was an LM comprehensive school which had experienced a drop in numbers since open enrolment (parental choice) had been in force. It was, as one teacher described it, the 'poor relation' among the schools in the area. Its published results were way below those of neighbouring schools. The school had a reputation of being 'good at' catering for special needs, but this had its down side, in that, according to the headteacher and chair of governors, this discouraged parents of more able children from sending them to the school.

In order to attract a broader range of ability social class into the school, the governors had decided to dilute its commitment to an inclusive education policy, where children with special needs were integrated into all classes and there was mixed ability teaching (rather than grouping by ability). The school changed its name, in order to dissociate itself from the area of public housing in which it was located. It abandoned mixed ability teaching and introduced setting (tracking). Thus, special needs policy was being driven by the headteacher and governors whose interests reside in the future viability of their own school, and who do not take responsibility for the education of children in the local community as a whole.

Code of Practice and the SEN Tribunal

Two ways in which the United Kingdom government has attempted to standardise good practice in schools have been through the publication of a Code of Practice for the Identification and Assessment of Special Educational Needs (DfE, 1994) and by the establishment of a Special Education Needs (SEN) Tribunal in 1993 to mediate disputes concerning the statutory assessment procedures. Schools are expected to 'have regard to the Code' and its five-stage assessment process when exercising their duties towards children with SEN. The Tribunal's decisions are binding on LEAs and it exercises its functions independently of central and local government. Some LEAs are concerned that the decisions of the Tribunal have restricted their ability to meet the needs of all children with special educational needs equitably, because they have been forced to fund expensive provision for a few high-profile cases, where parents have appealed to Tribunals (Evans, 1998). It is no coincidence that the implementation of the Code of Practice and the SEN Tribunal has coincided with a huge rise in the number of Statements issued by some LEAs (Garner, 1995).

A number of reports have suggested the need for a complete review of the system of allocating resources through statements. A House of Commons Select Committee issued a report on this in 1993 (House of Commons, 1993), during the course of which they took evidence from LEAs, voluntary organisations and schools. A common theme was the reduction in the power of LEAs to influence what was happening in schools, and, in a later inquiry, the Committee heard evidence that the opportunity parents had to take their case to an independent tribunal was distorting policy-making and provision in LEAs across the country (House of Commons, 1995).

Some commentators (e.g. Fish and Evans, 1995; Bibby and Lunt, 1996) have suggested that articulate parents would dominate the use of the Tribunal, and that has appeared to be the case. An analysis of the appeals made in the first year of the Tribunal showed that the majority of appeals were for children with specific learning difficulties (dyslexia), and that LEAs were being obliged to pay for expensive provision for a number of children with this type of problem, thus distorting their spending on other areas of SEN provision (House of Commons, 1995).

Recent changes in the United States

Major changes in special education national policy in the United States have occurred against a backdrop of two decades of general school reform efforts as well as a shift in power in the national government. Changes in special education national policy may be better understood in the context of strong movements to dismantle the federal role in a broad array of social welfare programmes.

Most states have resisted persistent conservative pressure to make public schools subject to some sort of market discipline including, for example, so-called voucher schools (e.g. see Chubb and Moe, 1990). In 1991, Minnesota introduced an alternative school reform strategy, based on the idea of a 'charter' school. It proved an irresistible compromise concept for both the moderate left and right. At little or no additional cost, charter schools would be autonomous individual schools that, in return for a planned commitment to educational improvements, would be completely self-governing and released from most government requirements. In this section, we report some of the initial evaluative reports on charter schools and special education, including preliminary studies conducted by the California Charter School Research Project (CCSRP) at the University of California, Santa Barbara.

In 1997 the United States Congress reauthorised the Individuals with Disabilities Education Act (IDEA) (originally the Education of the Handicapped Act of 1975). It contains the most extensive revisions and was the most politically contested reauthorisation in the twenty-three years of this federal mandate. The overall impetus for change in the IDEA can be described by two overarching themes. The first is a concern for increasing efforts to integrate students with disabilities into the same physical settings, social experiences, general curriculum and system of accountable academic standards as their non-disabled peers. The second expresses the desire for local administrators to have greater discretion in how special education – its funding, its procedures, and its students – is managed at the level of local agency and school building.

The two themes are somewhat contradictory. For example, the new IDEA suggests schools make stronger efforts to integrate students with disabilities while, on the other hand, permitting increased authority for suspension of students thought to be dangerous. The federal contribution to implementing IDEA is still so small that states and local educational agencies must carry well over 90 per cent of the real costs that special education incurs. However, in the name of greater integration, the reauthorised IDEA is much more liberal than previous versions in allowing LEAs to use special education money for general education expenses when such expenditures will also benefit students with disabilities. Likewise, in an attempt to remove a possible incentive towards over-identification, IDEA now will fund special education at one rate times a fixed proportion of resident population. Although it is unclear that federal funding ever acted as an incentive to maximise revenue, it is quite clear that the new approach to funding might encourage schools to minimum expenditures on identifications and individualised education plans (IEPs) in order to hold direct programme costs as low as possible. (See Chapter 8 for more detail of current funding policy changes.)

During these years of debate over revision of federal special education policy, the charter school movement has grown swiftly with much federal encouragement, from about forty schools in two states in 1993 to nearly 700 schools in twenty-five states by 1997. California, accounting for 125 schools, removed its legislated cap in 1998 and further rapid expansion is anticipated.

Creation of charter schools

Charter schools generally emerge from a process of conversion or creation. In conversion, existing public schools request a charter from the local school district or a specially empowered state body. Some states also permit public and/or private individuals to create new charter schools as well. Newly created schools tend to have smaller enrolments than converted schools.

The first national study of charter schools (RPP International, 1997) estimated that only about 32 per cent of charter schools were converted from pre-existing public schools while over 56 per cent of charter schools were newly created. The terms within specific enabling legislation in each state, however, constrain how schools become charter schools. Some states allow only conversions. Some states allow conversion of private schools; others do not. California, the state serving as our case study, had approximately half converted and half newly created.

Moreover, some states allow the state to sponsor charter schools while other states require that local education agencies approve charter school status. However they came into being, most charter schools reported that they faced significant financial barriers and maintained fiscal relationships with sponsors. Most converted schools, especially, had no experience and no expertise for completely managing their own fiscal or personnel affairs. Although most charter legislation permits the possibility of total autonomy, few charter schools, at least in the first years of this 'experiment', actually attempted to achieve complete autonomy, although over 50 per cent of converted schools reported 'autonomy' as the most important reason for seeking charter status (RPP International, 1997).

Charter schools and special education

Charter schools represent a unique class of reform proposals that pivot on the prediction that increasing school site autonomy will improve desirable educational outcomes (e.g. achievement). In addition to some degree of governance autonomy, charter schools are usually released from obligation to comply with most rules and regulations imposed by outside governing bodies except, notably, for laws regarding health, safety, and civil rights. The latter laws include federal and state mandates for special education. However, both national (RPP International, 1997) and state (Powell et al., 1997) surveys show that charter schools often were unaware of the obligation to serve disabled students. When cognisant of such responsibilities, many charter schools relied upon sponsoring LEAs to provide special education services. On the other hand, there are a few charter schools that have identified special education as central to their charter and actually serve proportionately more students with disabilities than average for other schools in their respective states. In rhetoric, at least, the improvement predicted for charter schools will include students who currently perform poorly on measures of desirable outcomes. Generally speaking, the legislation that enables charter schools in each state does not overtly consider issues of special education (RPP International, 1997; Szabo and Gerber, 1996). However, just as it is reasonable to ask if claims to 'effectiveness' by school officials include evidence of 'effectiveness' with students who are disabled, so it is reasonable to inquire whether charter schools established on the claim that they will improve 'effectiveness', also can demonstrate that they improve outcomes for students with disabilities as well.

Of the three major categories of decision-making autonomy thought to be reliably descriptive of charter schools – budget, personnel, curriculum – either by design or structural complexity, budgetary autonomy has proved thus far to be most variable. School finance in the United States is complex, with multiple streams of revenue and a host of matching regulations and practices regarding expenditures. Some of the budgeting for school districts is only distally related to instructional operations at the classroom or school building level. Generally, tax revenues are distributed to schools in proportion to their enrolments.

Therefore, loss of students to a new charter school represents a loss of revenue for the parent district. The charter school, on the other hand, stands to lose costly services that are prohibitively expensive without the economies of scale enjoyed by multi-school agencies, including some costs associated with special education (e.g. low incidence programmes, transportation, related services). Moreover, although granted relative autonomy, most charter schools are still considered public schools and are, therefore, restricted in their ability to raise revenue independently, especially by charging any kind of fee-for-service. For these and a variety of other reasons, either charter schools or parent districts, or both, have shown reluctance to suddenly or absolutely sever all financial ties.

Attitudes and organisation for special education

Some data are now emerging about how charter schools establish and manage special education. As stated above, researchers found in their first year of national study of charter schools that these schools were unclear about their responsibilities to students with disabilities. Were they to seek to enrol a proportion equal to that enrolled in the parent school district? Were they to search aggressively among their enrolment for students with disabilities? Over a third of nationally surveyed schools reported that inability to serve some disabled students might have created a barrier to their admission (RPP International, 1997). In both state (cf. Powell et al., 1997) and national surveys, charter school respondents admit confusion over if and how they are to provide for students with disabilities. Although they have been reported to serve equivalent percentages of their enrolment as disabled compared to local or state averages, our analysis by category of disability reveals potentially significant differences. For example, compared to the state, California's charter schools identify approximately the same percentages of disabled students they serve as having speech and language impairments (i.e., about 25 per cent) and specific learning disabilities (i.e., between 55 per cent and 60 per cent). These so-called 'mild' and high incidence disabilities are also associated with lower instructional costs per pupil. However, charter school rates of identification are consistently lower than California schools in general for very low incidence disabilities for which regionalised services are usually available (e.g. visual impairment, 0.5 per cent vs. 0.8 per cent; deafness, 0.1 per cent vs. 0.8 per cent; autism, 0.3 per cent vs. 1 per cent; and other health impairments, 1.8 per cent vs. 2.5 per cent). This pattern is not found, however, for multiple handicaps, and traumatic brain injury (i.e., 1.3 per cent vs. 1 per cent and 0.3 per cent vs. 0.1 per cent, respectively). It is highly likely that students identified with these disabilities received services elsewhere before schools had charter status and continued, by arrangement with sponsoring LEAs, to receive services elsewhere after charter status was conferred. However, schools in general in California identified almost 6 per cent of all disabled students as mentally retarded, but charter schools only identified 3 per cent. Similarly, California schools in general identified 3.2 per cent of their disabled students as severely emotionally disturbed, while charter schools identified only 1.1 per cent. Compare these large differences with comparative rates for identifying students with orthopaedic impairments. Charter schools' identification rates were twice as great (i.e., 5.2 per cent vs. 2.4 per cent).

These patterns suggest that, where charter schools vary in rates of identification by category, they favour disabilities that, although low in incidence and perhaps somewhat higher in cost, involve mostly physical accommodations (i.e., orthopaedic and multiple handicapping disabilities). Students with disabilities associated with high management costs – e.g. emotional disturbance and mental retardation – are identified at far lower rates; similarly for very low incidence disabilities involving sensory impairments.

Charter schools in California – some examples from research

Our research has focused on how California's charter schools organise instruction and other supports to accommodate individual differences and disabilities. This line of research examines educational arrangements, specifically special education, at the level of school and investigates how reform and restructuring of governance and management creates or diminishes substantive learning opportunities for students with a variety of learning difficulties.

Charter arrangements in California have to be negotiated with local school authorities not with an independent state agency. California's legislature left intact – at least in the short term – the existing arrangement whereby state education funds (including both basic and categorical programmes, such as special education) go only to the parent districts rather than directly to the charter schools. The practical effect of this system is that every charter school has generally needed to negotiate its own revenue and spending arrangements with its parent district. Some schools – but by no means all – make maximum use of their new flexibility to promote fund raising and elaborate 'development programmes', although all charter schools are prohibited from charging tuition. While the enabling legislation gave maximum flexibility to the participants, the resulting variations in charter school finances have given rise to concerns about equity and efficiency.

Analysis of charter proposals

As most charter schools began their third or fourth year of their initial five-year charter, we conducted a text analysis of California's first charter school proposals followed by interviews with principals to examine the 'mid-charter' progress of these schools. The documentary review found very few proposals that seemed fully realised and the result of a long, systematic process of community building or deliberation with stake-holders other than teachers.

Findings from the follow-up interviews were consistent with what we inferred from the documentary review and with findings from the first year national survey of charter schools. They were very variable in their vision, organisation, demographics, and motivations for becoming charter schools. Most reported that they were involved in school-wide restructuring efforts, innovations, and experiments, with significant parent participation, before the charter legislation passed. One principal confided that, in fact, his school was doing nothing as a charter school that they had not done or could not have done previously. In general, charter status seemed a logical next step for schools and seemed to promise the autonomy they perceived they needed to protect themselves from any unforeseen policy shifts at the local or state level. Very few schools reported that they pursued charter status because it was perceived as holding more opportunities than they already enjoyed under existing laws and funding mechanisms. However, many also admitted that they were only now, after several years, coming to grips with what autonomy really meant, its risks as well as its opportunities.

Our research on proposals also investigated school-site governance and management variations among a sample of California charter schools, focusing generally on how management of budget, personnel, and curriculum might impact the capacity of these schools to improve educational outcomes for students who are very difficult to teach. Specifically, we examined variations in number of members on governance councils, what constituencies are represented, how representatives are selected, their length of service, with whom ultimate decision-making power resides, and how strong or weak is the role of the person holding day-to-day administrative responsibility. From interviews with the principals of the charter schools, we attempted to further clarify and delineate the degree of autonomy maintained over budget, personnel, and curriculum issues.

Most (about 70 per cent) of California's charter schools did not specify in their proposals the number of people that would serve on their governance councils. For those that provided explicit numbers, membership ranged from three to thirteen members. About 42 per cent of charter schools explicitly planned to elect their council members, or use a combination of election and appointment. Only about 20 per cent specified the length of service for council members. When stated, length of service ranged from one to four years. Parents were listed as participants in over 75 per cent of charter school proposals, with slightly fewer explicitly listing teachers as participants. Others included in school governance were community members, representatives from teachers' professional associations, representatives of local school districts, public agencies, and the business community, as well as students. Of the remaining five that provided information, parents and teachers were found to fill the greatest number of positions. Information regarding the voting rights of participants was not provided or was not clear in most cases.

Few proposals specified voting privileges (21 per cent) for all participants (sometimes explicitly excluding students). Significant variation was found also in the assignment of ultimate decision-making power. In about half of the schools, ultimate decision-making power was vested in a school governance committee, council or advisory board. Most of these schools (about 25 per cent of the total) did not place the responsibility for day-to-day operation of the school on one person. It appears that school governance is constituted from a much wider community pool than would exist in traditional schools. The lack of explicit planning information in proposals we reviewed may indicate uncertainty on the part of new charter schools regarding how they planned to carry out their new governance structure. Many might wish to develop positions on these issues over time as the charter school gains experience and determines its needs. However, the majority of schools had determined whom they wished to participate in the governance of the school and who was representative of the general community. This may indicate a desire to expand empowerment to stakeholders who in the past have not held such roles.

The future of charters and the IDEA

To characterise differences between charter and same-district, non-charter schools in both governance and predisposition towards students with disabilities, Szabo and Gerber (1996) conducted a mailed survey of both teachers and principals in California's charter schools. Matching non-charter schools were selected from the same district for a subset of surveyed charter schools. Schools were the units of analysis, with teachers' and principal's surveys within schools as data sources.

Comparison of charter with nearby, non-charter schools revealed strong confirmation of greater school site governance and management although, overall, charter schools only showed a moderate level of involvement in activities associated with autonomy of governance and management. Analysis also showed that charter school principals perceive somewhat greater attention to and change for accommodating students with special needs in their schools compared with their colleagues in comparison schools, but, in absolute terms, it was clear that special education was a low priority for charter as well as non-charter school principals.

Similarly, when we surveyed teachers in charter and comparison non-charter schools, we found that similar percentages of teachers in both charter and comparison non-charter schools had positive attitudes toward sharing responsibility with special education teachers, the adequacy of their instructional and collaborative skills, and the likely success of collaborative teaching. The percentage of teachers responding positively to these items tended to be over 70 per cent in both kinds of schools. But, even though more teachers in charter schools held positive expectations for success of disabled students who were integrated for instruction (52 per cent vs. 40 per cent), it is worth noting that, in either type of school, these figures reveal a startlingly low overall confidence in teachers' perception of the likely success of integration. These findings are slightly improved, but basically confirm the relative pessimism about inclusion expressed by a sample of teachers surveyed some years ago before reauthorisation of IDEA and before the charter school movement began (see Semmel *et al.*, 1991). What makes these findings so striking is that charter school teachers choose to work in their schools as a sign of their commitment to a change process aimed at improving outcomes for all students in their school. They enjoy greater power and more autonomy than fellow teachers in non-charter schools. And yet, despite their high degree of motivation and increased ability to influence resource allocations to support the work they do, the fact that only half of them view the likelihood of success for fully integrated instruction in their schools is sobering. It seems clear that they make a clear-eyed assessment of what resources would be necessary for success and do not see those resources forthcoming on the basis of organisational change and greater autonomy of governance and management alone.

Comparative analysis and conclusions

National special education policy in the United States is mandated by federal legislation that, in part, draws on constitutionally protected rights in its formulation. Federal law in the United States, under IDEA combined with several related items of legislation (e.g. Section 504 of the Vocational Rehabilitation Act, and the Americans with Disabilities Act), means parents may pursue a legal redress of grievances with local school authorities across the entire range of special education provisions. Such legal and constitutional foundation for special education is without precedent anywhere else in the world. In contrast with parents of special education students in the United Kingdom, this has meant that parents in the United States have enjoyed a relative advantage in pressing schools to meet the educational needs of their children with disabilities. They have substantial legal standing in disagreements with LEAs, a standing which historically they have frequently and vigorously exercised in the federal judicial system. At least one of the lines of attack on the IDEA during the reauthorisation process sought to limit this substantial empowerment of disabled students and their parents. The new SEN Tribunal system in the United Kingdom is as close an approximation of the rights granted disabled children and their families in the United States as might be expected under the United Kingdom's different constitutional system. It is profoundly significant in that it establishes a binding authority external to the local schools, albeit authority limited to disputes regarding assessment and eligibility for statement processes. Florian and Pullin (in Chapter 2) discuss this in detail.

Nevertheless, this striking change has both an up side and a down side to it. On the positive side, governance of schools must accommodate the power that both countries have now invested in parents as educational clients of schools. However, both countries have established a strong means for parents to press for resources in a policy environment that has absolutely reduced the revenue-raising and resource allocation abilities of LEAs. Consequently, the United Kingdom now has experienced what has been seen in the United States for some time – a dramatic rise in formal disputes, with scarce resources drawn away to matters other than instructional accommodation as one unintended result.

The White Paper *Excellence in Schools* (DfEE, 1997) makes mention of this problem with respect to the United Kingdom:

> Within the substantial resources devoted to SEN, there is still too much emphasis on the processes leading to a 'statement' of SEN, rather than on preventative and remedial action. Statements will continue to have an important role, but they should not be the driving force in provision for SEN. We want to ensure that, over time, we put resources into direct support for children, rather than bureaucratic procedures. In particular, we want to look urgently at the scope for improved mediation, to reduce the need for disputes to get as far as the SEN Tribunal.
>
> (Ibid., para. 45)

As a further result of recent changes, then, the United Kingdom may have created a system in which identification of disabled students may create a general economic incentive for local schools to identify children with SEN, since differential support goes to schools with identified students. In the United

States, on the other hand, reauthorisation of the IDEA included new provisions meant to eliminate any incentive for schools to over-identify students as disabled.

More central to the theme of this chapter, both countries now also have measures to permit increased local autonomy in governance and management. This policy is pervasive in the United Kingdom but only undergoing relatively cautious, experimental expansion in the United States. In the United Kingdom thus far, local fiscal autonomy works together with funding mechanisms to encourage identification of students as disabled as a strategy for enhancing revenues. One can envision any number of policy initiatives that will soon develop to control this process.

On the other hand, only about half of the states in the United States currently have legislation permitting charter schools, and in the overwhelming majority of cases, complete fiscal autonomy, even if pursued by reluctant, ill-prepared school staff, is unlikely to make paying the real costs of special education any easier. The granting of autonomy without new revenue-raising mechanisms and without the economies of scale supporting special education for some high-cost disabilities will ultimately frustrate the intent of the innovation. Or, schools may simply discover some extra-legal method for excluding higher cost disabled students as an economic necessity.

Under these conditions, charter schools as a group already appear to enrol somewhat fewer students with disabilities than surrounding public schools enrol. However, the data are not clear. There are great variations from state to state and school to school, depending on whether schools are newly created or converted from existing public schools. It is clear, though, that teachers in these schools, despite significant empowerment to influence governance and management, are not sanguine about the chances of supporting disabled students in regular instructional settings in the absence of additional, appropriate, supportive resources.

Concluding thoughts

In the United States and the United Kingdom, site-based school governance and management has altered the relationships between LEAs, schools and communities. New funding arrangements and managerial autonomy have located decisions about the allocation of resources to students, including those with special educational needs, at the school level. The outcomes, in terms of the willingness of schools to accept and make provision for such students, has been variable, but, in general, it appears that there is an increasing tendency for schools to view such students as a drain on their resources and a threat to their status in the community.

In the United States and the United Kingdom, special education policy is in open contradiction to many general education reforms. Whereas special education policy calls for increasing integration of students with disabilities in curriculum exposure and high-stakes testing programmes, general school reform is pressing schools for high academic standards and accountability. Schools are caught in the squeeze between these potentially conflicting goals.

Another sort of squeeze is being experienced by schools in the United Kingdom. There, the current system appears to be as chaotic, fragmented and inequitable as the one which it replaced. The division of duties and responsibilities between LEAs, schools and central government continues to be highly contentious and unclear. The setting up of the Tribunal has shifted the onus of decision-making about individual cases away from central and local government. The pressure to integrate more students with special educational needs into regular classrooms has been signalled in a recently published Green Paper (DfEE, 1997b).

In both countries, there are short-term advantages for central government because these reforms shift accountability along with autonomy to local schools and appear to absolve it of blame for the decisions made. However, in the long-term, this abrogation of responsibility will have serious consequences as the unfair and arbitrary nature of decisions made on a case-by-case basis becomes more apparent.

The nature of LMS in the United Kingdom and school-site governance and management schemes, like charter schools, in the United States, along with increased emphasis on parental choice and legal standing, mean that schools, left to act autonomously, will develop individual policies about children with special needs depending on what moral and economic weight is given locally to the problem of educating students with disabilities. Growing inequities, created by a system of relatively autonomous schools abandoned to market forces without a reliable means for securing the additional resources needed to meet the exceptional needs of students with disabilities, will mean increasing litigation and political intrusions to redress grievances of all concerned.

The current governance arrangements in education in both countries, with their emphasis on local school autonomy, consumer choice and parental power combined with centralised direction through imposition of standards (e.g. the Code of Practice) and accountability (e.g. high-stakes testing programmes in the United States and Ofsted inspections in the United Kingdom), makes the respective systems increasingly unwieldy and unstable with regard to special education. In some cases, reforms result in wide variations in need based on differing instructional characteristics of actual student populations being funded at the same levels and, conversely, similar needs being funded at widely differing levels, depending on local circumstances, legislation, and the social class mix of the school (Gross, 1996). Merely moving allocation decision-making authority closer to the classroom does not appear to be sufficient for securing effective, quality, or even appropriate special education in autonomous or even semi-autonomous schools.

Notes

1 The project was funded by the Economic and Social Research Council, award number ROOO 23 3586.
2 Currently, the governing bodies of schools are related to their size and comprise LEA and local council nominees, parents, teachers (including the headteacher), church nominees (in the case of church-aided or controlled schools) and, for GM schools, foundation governors. Governing bodies are also able to co-opt members and usually try to have some members of the local business community as co-optees. A typical governing body would have between twelve and fifteen members.

References

Bibby, P. and Lunt, I. (1996) *Working for Children: Securing Provision for Children with Special Educational Needs*, London: David Fulton.

Chubb, J.E. and Moe, T.M. (1990) *Politics, Markets, and America's Schools*, Washington, DC: The Brookings Institution.

Department for Education (DfE) (1994) *Code of Practice on the Identification and Assessment of Special Educational Needs*, London: HMSO.

Department for Education and Employment (DfEE) (1997a) *Excellence in Schools*, Cm 3681, London: The Stationery Office.

—— (1997b) *Excellence for All Children*, London: The Stationery Office.

Evans, J. (1998) *Getting it Right: LEAs and the Special Educational Needs Tribunal*, Slough: National Foundation for Educational Research.

Evans, J. and Lunt, I. (1994) *Markets, Competition and Vulnerability: Some Effects of Recent Legislation on Children with Special Educational Needs*, London: Tufnell Press.

Fish, J. and Evans, J. (1995) *Managing Special Education: Codes, Charters and Competition*, Buckingham: Open University Press.

Fulcher, G. (1989) *Disabling Policies? A Comparative Approach to Education Policy and Disability*, London: Falmer Press.

Garner, P. (1995) 'Sense or nonsense? Dilemmas in the SEN Code of Practice', *Support for Learning*, 10,1: 3–7.

Gewirtz, S., Ball, S. and Bowe, R. (1995) *Markets, Choice and Equity in Education*, Buckingham: Open University Press.

Gross, J. (1996) 'The weight of parental evidence: Parental advocacy and resource allocation to children with statements of special educational needs', *Support for Learning*, 11,1: 3–8.

House of Commons (1993) *Meeting Special Educational Needs: Statements of Needs and Provision*, London: HMSO.

—— (1995) *Special Educational Needs: The Working of the Code of Practice and the Tribunal*, London: HMSO.

Kirp, D. (1982) 'Professionalisation as policy choice: British special education in comparative perspective', *World Politics*, 34,2: 137–174.

Lawton, S. (1992) 'Why restructure? An international survey of the roots of reform', *Journal of Education Policy*, 7,2: 139–154.

Powell, J., Blackorby, J., Marsh, J., Finnegan, K., and Anderson, L. (1997) *Evaluation of Charter School Effectiveness*, Palo Alto, CA: SRI International.

RPP International (May 1997) *The National Study of Charter*, in partnership with the University of Minnesota's Center for Applied Research and Educational Improvement (CAREI), Minneapolis, and the Institute for Responsive Education (IRE), Boston. Washington, DC: USDOE/OERI and the National Institute on Student Achievement, Curriculum, and Assessment.

Semmel, M.I., Abernathy, T.V., Butera, G., and Lesar, S. (1991) 'Teacher perceptions of the regular education initiative', *Exceptional Children*, 58,1: 9–24.

Szabo, J.M., and Gerber, M.M. (1996) Special education and the charter school movement. *Special Education Leadership Review*, 3,1: 135–148.

Warnock, M. (1992) 'Special case in need of reform', *Observer*, October 3.

Whitty, G., Power, S. and Halpin, D. (1997) *Devolution and Choice in Education: The School, the State and the Market*, Buckingham: Open University Press.

Chapter 8

Funding of special education in the United States and England and Wales

Tony Bowers and Tom Parrish

Introduction

Some thirty years ago, Hardin (1968) analysed an ancient parable, 'the Tragedy of the Commons'. In this a number of herdsmen (in those days, only men had herds) graze their cattle on a commonly shared pasturage. Since no one owns the pasture, it is clearly in each herdsman's interest to increase the size of the herd that he grazes there because each of his animals represents a potential profit to him. There is a cost attached to grazing the animal, of course, and this can be measured by the damage done to the common pasturage. The cost, though, is a shared one; unlike the profit, which goes directly to the individual, the losses are evenly distributed among all those who graze their herd on the common land.

Responding to this logical incentive to maximise what can be got out of the pasturage, each herdsman decides to increase the size of his herd. This decision is made all the more easy by seeing others doing so, or just suspecting that they may be doing it. The result is predictable and inevitable. As the carrying capacity of the commons is exceeded, the quality of grazing diminishes. Despite this, no individual herdsman find it advantageous to reduce the size of his herd unilaterally. Things go from bad to worse until, like all tragedies, it approaches its final conclusion. The pasturage can no longer sustain the expectation placed upon it and the animals begin to starve. Finally, the common land is destroyed and so, of course, are the herds that grazed upon it.

Hardin was addressing the problem of population growth. He concluded that only by taking drastic steps to control population size can we avoid the destruction of the 'commons' that are important for maintaining both the quality of our lives and our lives themselves. But a good parable has generalisable qualities. It is easy, for example, to see this one applying today to the utilisation of fossil fuels and global warming. It also doesn't need a great leap of the imagination to connect the tale to the perceptions of those concerned with financial provision for children and young people with special education needs. In the United States, for example, Hartman's

(1992) observation that special educational funding cannot be isolated from other equally deserving programmes in education or from other areas of public service such as health or welfare, suggests the capacity for infinite expansion. Parrish (1997) has drawn attention to a widely held suspicion that the cost of special education is rising too rapidly and so encroaching upon the common pool of resources available for public sector education.

This encroachment is paralleled by issues in the United Kingdom. Following a review of special education services in part of London, Bowers (1996) pointed to the increasing costs of providing special education having to be met by either a transfer of funds from regular education or from other services offered by the UK regional resourcing body, the local authority. Local education authorities (LEAs) are a sub-element of each local authority. Fletcher-Campbell (1996) referred to 'escalating special education budgets', linking these directly to overall education overspends in some local authorities. 'Controlling the special education budget', she observed, 'has become a critical management issue in a political-economic context of concern over public expenditure' (Ibid., p. 6).

On both sides of the Atlantic, the 'commons' of education spending are seen as being in danger of overgrazing by those claiming, for one reason or another, the right to additional resources for particular children or groups of children. In case the use of the story of the herdsmen and their grazing sounds a little too far from the mark, we will later justify its use by looking at some evidence from experiments on the psychology of economics and linking these with developments in policy and practice.

Accountancy and dilemmas

There was a stark reminder of the parable in the introduction of this chapter when we read a report commissioned by consortium of local education authorities, financed by the British government. Research for the report was undertaken by a large firm of accountants, Coopers and Lybrand (1996). As part of the report, they posited a situation confronting a local education authority where the budget available for schools is capped by government and an overspend has to be contained. Only one of two practices, they suggested, can result from such a situation. First, the 'unit value' of the 'non-SEN unit' can be reduced. In plain language, schools get less money per head for each pupil who isn't allocated additional resources for identified special educational needs. Alternatively, the unit value of the 'SEN unit' can be reduced. In other words, as the overall number of pupils identified as requiring additional resources because of their special needs increases, the average amount allocated to each one would decrease, thus keeping expenditure constant. The report goes on to suggest that such a situation creates a 'Prisoner's Dilemma'. In this dilemma, it is in the interest of all schools as a community not to bid for too many Statements (with a Statement, of which we shall say more later, usually comes additional money from the LEA), since more Statements do not bring more money into the system, yet it is in each individual school's interest to secure Statements, since these increase that school's share of funding.

Hardin's (1968) parable of the commons provides a classic example of a social dilemma, of which the 'Prisoner's Dilemma' is one. Such dilemmas typically involve two participants who must decide separately whether to co-operate or to seek to take advantage of the other. The former course leads to a 'win-win' solution, the latter always results in one loser and frequently leads to both parties suffering losses. In real life, of course, most dilemmas involve more than two participants, and the Coopers and Lybrand story provides an example of the N-person prisoner's dilemma (Bixentine *et al.*, 1966; Messick and Brewer, 1983). However, when we look at Coopers and Lybrand's two scenarios for a cash-limited schools budget, we can see that the elegant underpinnings of such a social dilemma have already been removed. Effectively, the commons (i.e. the budget for all schools) has a fenced-off area or corral within it, to which only certain members of the herd can gain access. Moreover, while the individual herdsmen (in our analogy, the school) may nominate particular herd members for that access, an intervening party (the LEA) actually decides who passes into the corral. A regulator has been introduced to the dilemma. Coopers and Lybrand's (1996) analogy becomes further suspect when we consider that in a typical N-person prisoner's dilemma, each participant has a shared interest in the same satisfactory outcome. This might be true if the players in the special education dilemma were confined to education authorities and schools. But they are not. They include parents, disability-focused groups, and charities, with multi-layered involvement in advocacy, service provision and schooling. All of these are becoming increasingly adept at exerting legal and political pressure upon the system, and some of them may have little or no interest in the long-term husbandry of a common resource.

Even if their model falls short of the requirements of a social dilemma, Coopers and Lybrand have attempted to reframe the situation as they see it in a way which other commentators on funding special education provision in the United Kingdom have largely ignored. If we are to step beyond the mere mechanics of funding, then we must seek to understand the processes which any funding mechanism supports or underpins. We shall borrow from the psychology of economics to look further at the social dilemmas and social traps which lie within our current initiatives for reform. We shall also look at the motivating forces which may assist or inhibit current initiatives for reform. First, however, we will endeavour to summarise the current funding position for special educational needs in England and Wales. Scotland is excluded from this discussion since it has a differently structured education system, although there are strong parallels in its provision for children with special educational needs.

England and Wales: a changing system

In 1998 there were 172 LEAs in England and Wales. Overall, around 5 per cent of all publicly funded schools were 'grant-maintained', or entirely independent of the LEA in which they were set. The picture is far from even, however. In some LEA areas, no schools opted out of LEA control, while in others the majority of secondary (11 years and older) schools chose to do so. Grant-maintained schools were much favoured by the previous Conservative administration, but recent legislation has changed the status and the terminology relating to them, making them 'foundation' schools. It appears that all schools will shortly gain full financial autonomy. The LEA's ability to influence what goes on will probably wane further.

From the perspective of special educational needs funding, the differences between types of publicly maintained schools are not that great. This is because the LEA retains responsibility both for identifying the special needs of their pupils if they require a Statement of SEN and for providing the additional resources required to meet what it specifies.

The significance of the statement

Statements have been defined elsewhere in this book. However, we will explain their significance for funding in England and Wales. Statements of special educational needs have been with us since 1982; their introduction therefore lagged behind the inception of the IEP in the United States. A recent government document (DfEE, 1997) observed that 'the statement has often come to be seen as central to SEN provision' (Ibid., p. 35) – hardly a radical insight, given that practically all the critical SEN judgments in our highest courts over the past ten years or so have revolved around the Statement and the obligations which accompany it.

Essentially, a child with a Statement has a legal entitlement to receive the provision specified in the Statement. The legal responsibility for ensuring that provision is made falls squarely on the LEA. Even when funds are delegated to a school for that purpose, the LEA retains the legal accountability for ensuring that the extra help, specialist teaching, additional equipment, etc. written into the Statement are provided. Recent judgments have confirmed that this accountability extends to the provision of speech therapy and other therapies, even though the relevant therapists may be employed by health organisations and not by the LEA.

While there are quite wide variations among LEAs in England in the proportion of their school populations with Statements, the overall figure is well below the number who might be expected to have IEPs in the United States. The UK government (DfEE, 1997) gives the overall figures for Statements at just under 3 per cent of the school population. It is perhaps more revealing to look at the raw data (available for England alone) for 1997, which show there are 234,900 pupils with Statements in all schools, with 134,500 of these attending publicly maintained mainstream schools. This last figure is substantially higher than it was just four years earlier, which in 1993 was just 84,894. The potential cost to the LEAs of this rise of nearly 60 per cent does not of course relate simply to extra staffing or money for the schools in order to meet the requirements of the Statement. The cost of assessing each child and preparing the Statement must be borne by LEAs, as must the cost of reviewing each Statement every year.

Getting a Statement, getting the funds

If an LEA decides resolutely to limit the number of Statements which it issues, or to restrict the type of provision to minimise expenditure (for example, specifying attendance at one of its own day schools or units, rather than at a specialist boarding school in another area), it faces another potential cost. A parent whose child is offered a Statement where the provision or school placement, or both, are not what the parent wants, can appeal to a specialist court: the SEN Tribunal. Unless parents hire a lawyer, the appeal costs them nothing. However, the cost to the LEA is potentially considerable. It has to administer its own case presentation and typically to send at least two members of its staff to what is usually, with travelling time, at least a day's hearing. The Tribunal's decision is legally binding of the LEA. If it rules in favour of the parent, the LEA must bear the cost of making the required provision. Because of Tribunal rulings, some LEAs are now obliged to fund boarding places for children at schools overseas. For example, one school in the United States, the Higashi School in Boston, which specialises in educating autistic children, now has a significant English contingent.

What forms the guidance as to who should have a Statement, and what yardsticks does the Tribunal use? The Audit Commission (1992), another accountancy-based organisation, suggested that there might be nationally laid-down criteria for which children should have a Statement. Underpinning that assumption, of course, was a view of special educational needs which saw deficits, whether cognitive, emotional, sensory or physical, residing squarely within the child. It ignored the essential interaction of the child with his or her school environment and overlooked the fact that some 'needs', manifested by low attainments and/or inappropriate behaviours, may owe much to an unproductive learning environment. So far, no definitive criteria have been proposed, and it is perhaps significant that the Coopers and Lybrand (1996) report has acknowledged that local circumstances may make national criteria for Statements undesirable. However, this medical view remains firmly with us. Indeed, it was enshrined in law when in the Court of Appeal in London in 1987 (cf. Bowers, 1991), Lord Justice Woolf likened key elements of the Statement to a medical diagnosis and prescription. When the author

(Bowers) represents parents in dispute with their LEA, he is often struck by the almost magical qualities with which the notion of a Statement can become imbued. Understandably, if not always justifiably, a link seemed to be drawn between a properly framed Statement and a 'cure'.

There are essentially two ways in which a Statement can be acquired. The school can ask the LEA to assess a child with a view to issuing a Statement or the child's parent can ask the LEA directly. LEAs tend to prefer the former route, since a school cannot appeal to the SEN Tribunal; only a parent can. Perhaps unsurprisingly, as Lunt and Evans (1994) have pointed out, schools vary considerably in the number of pupils they see a need to 'refer out' to the LEA. A Statement will guarantee extra money for the school to make specified provision, or it will carry with it the right to the time of specialists such as teachers of the deaf or speech and language therapists. However, most LEAs have formulae which offer schools extra funds for children without Statements but who have been assessed as requiring additional attention because of some identified area of need. Such children will be at one of the 'school-based' stages of the Code of Practice (DfE, 1994) which is intended to provide guidance on identifying and assessing special educational needs. Stage 3, seen as the stage before assessment for a Statement, will typically embrace students on IEPs in the United States. Some of those on Stage 2 of the Code might warrant an IEP also. The term 'IEP' is also used in the Code to describe a plan of action for a child at Stages 2 and 3, but this does not typically have the complexity of an IEP in the States and, unlike such an IEP, it currently has no legal force.

Funding 'additional' educational needs

A Statement carries legal accountability for the LEA. Without a Statement, even when a child may have special educational needs which have been identified according to the principles of the Code of Practice, all of his or her educational provision remains the responsibility of the school. The Code recommends that 'an appropriate specialist from a support service' (2:104) should be involved at Stage 3. Where this is an educational psychologist, there will usually be no cost to the school. Under the principles governing 'delegation' of funds from the LEAs to schools, the funds for psychology services cannot be passed on to schools. For specialist teachers, the picture varies widely from LEA to LEA, and from specialism to specialism. Some LEAs keep control of the money for services within the limits set by central government, while others pass on the funds and then charge back for specialist involvement with a child without a Statement (e.g. teachers of children with specific learning difficulties; teachers of children with communication difficulties). As an example, Table 8.1 shows the proportion of money that one London LEA retained for its special needs support services for one year. That amount will not be typical of all LEAs. Policy

Table 8.1 Special educational needs expenditure in one London Borough

Percentage of budget not delegated to mainstream schools' own budgets		£
1. Students with SEN and attending schools outside the LEA (mainly special schools)	3.33%	4,512,150
2. Students attending LEA's own special schools	2.00%	2,710,000
3. Support for students with statements in mainstream schools	2.78%	3,766,900
4. Specialist units in mainstream schools (e.g. hearing impairment, dyslexia)	0.18%	243,900
5. Educational psychologists	0.54%	731,700
6. Specialist support services working with non-statemented (Stage 3) students	1.51%	2,046,050
7. Education welfare service	0.22%	298,100
8. Units and services for students excluded from schools	0.53%	718,150
9. Transport for SEN students	1.65%	2,235,750
10. Administration	0.16%	216,800
TOTAL	12.90%	17,479,500
Percentage delegated to schools		
11. 'Transparently' through SEN audit	1.87%	2,533,850
12. 'Objectively' through free school meals uptake	1.8%	2,439,000
SEN CUMULATIVE TOTAL	16.57%	22,452,350
13. To this can be added a 'notional' or 'opaque' SEN sum included in the unit sum given for every child. If we assume this to be just 5.3% (see Coopers and Lybrand, 1996) then it will constitute 2.62% of the education budget, giving a final total of 19.19% in this LEA's education budget devoted to SEN.		
Total education budget:		£135,500,000
Total SEN budget (not allowing for amount in no.13 above):		£22,452,350
Total SEN budget (including 'notional' sum for SEN):		£26,002,450

and geography, together with the vagaries of accounting procedures, can produce very different pictures.

The funding of 'non-Statemented' special educational needs has the potential to be a major area of tension between schools and their maintaining LEA. Each LEA, within the formula which it uses to fund its schools, employs one or more yardsticks which are applied to fund these 'additional' educational needs. The point of tension can be found particularly at Stage 3. Schools get extra money and are expected to provide smaller groups or extra help when a child is placed at this stage. Yet the LEA has no power to see that

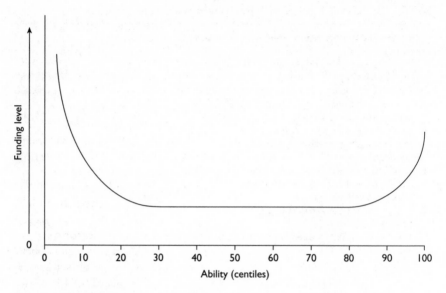

Figure 8.1 The 'ability/resource' relationship

the help is provided. Bowers (1997) has observed a continuing upward pressure towards assessment (Stage 4) and a Statement (Stage 5). These last two stages commit the LEA to substantial costs in implementing the process of assessment and statementing. It is therefore not surprising that LEAs attempt to apply stringent criteria, usually linked to pupil attainments and IEP-related evidence of school endeavours to the passage beyond Stage 3. If we apply Hardin's (1968) parable to the situation, this is the point where an attempt is made to limit the 'overgrazing' that the LEA knows will occur unless it is careful about who it lets through the gate.

In theory, increasing the funding which applies prior to statementing should reduce the demand to pass through that gate. Two factors stand in the way of that theory becoming reality, however. The first is a legal one. The Statement 'ring fences' funds, or guarantees resources being directed towards an individual child. Under the current UK system of financial delegation, funding for non-statemented SEN can easily be cut by the LEA, never reaching the school. If it does get there, the school's management can choose to use it for other purposes. The other is one of tradition. In our culture we tend to accept that increased resources should be devoted to those whose educational 'ability', however we define it, is significantly lower than that of the majority. Coopers and Lybrand (1996) remind us of this, suggesting that a 'U' curve, skewed in the way shown in Figure 8.1, underpins current conceptions of educational funding in the United Kingdom. Stage 5 (a Statement) indicates the greatest levels of deservingness, if we apply this thinking it must also carry the highest element of funding.

Funding mechanisms

A recent survey of eighty-five LEAs (Marsh, 1997) revealed at least nine different elements being used to make budgetary allocations to schools for students with SEN but without Statements. The most frequently cited indicator (92 per cent) relates to free school meals, although even this 'hard' indicator is not as reliable as it might be. The right to receive free school meals is not necessarily synonymous with the decision to eat them. Yet, the latter is what schools know about. The term 'entitlement' is cited frequently by Marsh (1997) in his report of LEA responses. Our own experience suggests that schools, whose returns would be used to determine this, are unable accurately to assess actual entitlement to this welfare benefit and are better placed to report on *uptake* of free school meals. It is not uncommon for families to choose to conceal their circumstances from a school by failing to claim all their entitlements.

In some LEAs, free school meals are seen simply as an indicator of social disadvantage, as they are in the United States, rather than of special educational needs. Marsh (1995), looking at 101 secondary or high schools in the United Kingdom, found correlations of between 0.71 and 0.84 between uptake of free school meals and scores below the twentieth percentile on a test of cognitive ability. Results from such tests, as well as from those relating specifically to literacy and numeracy, are also used, though less frequently, as a base for funding non-statemented SEN via school budgets (Marsh, 1997). Now, though, we are seeing increasing reliance placed on audits of special educational needs, conducted in every school in an LEA. Ostensibly their purpose is to establish the actual incidence and nature of special educational need rather than rely on counting student characteristics which may only be correlated with SEN. Such audits vary widely in structure and application, but a general feature is their attempt to establish criteria which can be uniformly applied. In addition, they usually involve LEA and school staff in collaborative activity in moderating allocation according to these criteria. Fletcher-Campbell (1996) devotes an entire chapter to audits and lists benefits they bring. However, in practice an audit can use a lot of personal and professional time. It can also provide incentives for schools to attempt to 'bid up' the incidence of need in order to increase budget share. Since a school's numbers on the Code of Practice's stages are often used to provide differential funding (Marsh, 1997), progressing a child towards a Statement can form a major part of the school's special needs co-ordinator's role (Bowers, 1997). This is tacitly acknowledged in a recent UK government document (DfEE, 1997), which recommends that when LEAs base funding on repeated incidence of SEN, 'they need to ensure that it does not influence assessment of children's needs' (Ibid., p. 92).

There is a final contentious funding element for special educational needs in every mainstream school's annual budget. This is the notional amount which many LEAs consider is built into the 'per pupil' allocation of money given to each school for overall funding of their educational offerings. Yet, because it is not spelled out in their budgets, many schools prefer not to acknowledge its existence. This is foggy territory indeed. Fletcher-Campbell (1996) suggests that government guidelines limit this element to 5 per cent, but this is probably a misreading of the current situation. The accountants Coopers and Lybrand (1996) offer several models, in one of which the 'non-specific' special needs element of the 'per pupil' funding is as much as one sixth of the overall unit of funding. In their lowest it is 5.3 per cent. The amounts in Table 8.1 do not allow for this element. Were it put in, even using the lower figure, it would amount to an additional £5 million-plus figure for SEN.

Controlling the budget

Coopers and Lybrand (1996) estimate that around 16 per cent of an LEA's total education budget goes on supporting special educational needs. Sixteen per cent or even 20 per cent does not seem an unreasonable figure, given that most of the discourse on special educational needs in the United Kingdom in the last twenty years has focused on a notional 20 per cent of the school population. What concerns many LEAs is their lack of control over the percentage share, and this is often linked to the unpredictability of Tribunal decisions. When just one judgment in favour of one parent wanting specialist outside education can easily cost over £60,000 annually, it is difficult to predict expenditure with any accuracy. As one administrator recently put it: 'You can *manage* a special education budget but *controlling* it is another thing' (Bowers, 1996).

In looking at Table 8.1, we should not ignore the cost of segregated special schooling and its impact on what can be spent to support inclusive education. Despite many recent calls to redirect money from special schools, LEAs are limited by several factors. The first is the unwillingness of many mainstream schools to accept or to retain students whose special needs render them challenging, unhelpful to their examination league table position, or both. Special schooling can provide the easiest option for the LEA. Since it retains the obligation to provide suitable education for a child with a Statement, and since it probably already has its own special schools which cost no more to run full than they do with empty places, it is not hard for an LEA to see special schools as a more efficient option than supported places in a mainstream school. Secondly, parents have the right under current law to express a preference for a special school and to have that preference respected unless more compelling reasons militate against it. Thirdly, and perhaps most importantly, administrators in LEAs are answerable to local politicians. Any reduction of resources for special schools is fraught with political uncertainties. Few politicians want to find the local media accusing them of seeking to disadvantage children with disabilities. Thus special schools remain and in many cases grow, to the detriment of inclusive education.

Motivating forces

As noted earlier, the accountants Coopers and Lybrand were key architects of the current system of funding schools according to the number of pupils they can attract. In this system, the allocation of school places according to place of residence plays only a minor role. A school must be attractive to parents and such attraction is linked closely to its compulsorily published position in a league table of examination results. There is therefore a certain irony in Coopers and Lybrand (1996) attaching much of the blame for the upward pressure on SEN spending to 'competition and suspicion between schools and LEAs' (Ibid., para. 582).

Underpinning the educational reforms of the past ten years in the United Kingdom has been the assumption that the forces of the market-place will drive schools to offer the kind of education that their 'customers' most want. By allowing schools to take as many students as they are prepared to and by permitting parents (in theory at least) a free choice of schools, the most popular schools should thrive. If the least popular are to survive, then they must change. This economic principle of Adam Smith (1776, 1976) has been imposed on local education authorities and schools through a variety of mechanisms. Central among these have been those which devolve decision-making to schools, so reducing the power of LEAs, and which redefine success in terms of academic attainments. If we believe in the power of market forces, then competition and the pursuit of self-interest should improve the lot of everybody.

Within such a framework the increasing demand for that share of education funds devoted to special education is entirely predictable. It may even be laudable. It is in each school's and every parent's interest to get as much as possible for themselves or their children, and self-interest is the engine of market economics. However, we have only to reconsider Hardin's tragedy of the commons to see the dilemma which presents itself when those resources are finite. If everybody seeks to get as much as they can from a system, then everybody will lose.

Two typical responses to this dilemma are to be found in the recent UK government (DfEE, 1997) consultative paper on SEN. The first is the call for LEAs to eliminate features in their funding procedures which provide 'purely financial incentives' (Ibid., p. 92) for identifying children as having special educational needs. The second is the call for greater co-operation or collaboration between the various parties involved. Both seem reasonable. Yet both proposals sit uneasily within an education system which is structured around competition and financial reward.

Possible solutions

What other arrangements could be made? If we look to the United States for ideas, we can find them. Dempsey and Fuchs (1993), for example, have demonstrated that the use of 'flat' formulae for SEN, which take little account of the types or severity of need, lead to less restrictive placements than 'weighted' formulae which take account of such factors. In the United States, of course, decision-making tends to be devolved to district special education directors rather than to school principals, but setting this distinction aside it would seem sensible for LEAs to avoid the financial incentives of weighting. Audits and differential funding may actually inhibit inclusive education. However, as was mentioned earlier, UK special education legislation as it is currently framed rests heavily on the rights of a child with a Statement of SEN to have his or her needs met on an individual basis. Without a legislative shift from the notion of difficulties residing within a given child, it is difficult to see any flattening of funding differentials going unchallenged.

Calls for collaboration and co-operation between what or whom are presumably based on an assumption of trust between parties. Unfortunately, a look at research into social dilemmas indicates that when uncooperative behaviour occurs it is frequently prefaced by greed (Poppe and Utens, 1986) or by the fear that somebody else is getting more than their fair share of resources (Rapoport and Eshed-Levy, 1989). However undesirable we may think these two emotions are, it must be remembered that they are central components of a competitive, market-driven system. Trust is harder to generate. Lopes (1994) supports the notion that increasing opportunities for communication between parties enhances co-operation. However, group identification and in-group bias in prisoner's dilemma situations can work against it.

Work with parents' groups and special education administrators (Bowers, 1995) suggests that both of these can be found in special education. The need to beat the other party appears at times to operate as dominantly as the need to maximise outcomes. It is not difficult to connect the apparent militancy of some disability-focused groups with this tendency, nor the spirited responses of some LEA administrators. Recent exchanges (Wright, 1997; McDonnell, 1997) lend support to this conflictual view. Trust comes with time. A look at Brann and Foddy (1987) suggests that people are more likely to respond to trust than they are to initiate it. Defensive behaviour accompanies low trust. It is probably reasonable to assume that the increasing litigiousness (SEN Tribunal, 1997, 1998) surrounding special needs education in England is a function of that defensiveness.

Cost and effectiveness

The provision of any public good tends to be suboptimal. What is offered falls below the actual level of demand and so, unlike Hardin's commons, which had free access, measures must be taken to restrict the uptake of resources. Restricting, controlling or rationalising funding constitute the measures we have grown used to. However, two central issues involve identifying the actual population of individuals seen as being in need of additional resources, and determining the type of resource (specialist placement, targeted assistance in mainstream) which should be allocated. The former is made easier if we conceptualise need as residing as a 'condition' or 'disability' within the child. But that doesn't always fit into reality. Our working models of special educational needs embrace low attainments and challenging behaviours and those are not easy to separate from what goes on in the school. They also encompass disabilities (dyslexia, dyspraxia, ADHD) which are subject to varying definitions and whose common nomenclature may disguise quite disparate aetiologies. While we use such thinking and such terminology, there will always be dispute about who is allowed onto the best grazing.

Coopers and Lybrand's (1996) survey was stimulated primarily by a perceived need to control costs. Attempts at control tend to be accompanied by the rhetoric of 'effective' and 'efficient' use of funds, just as they do in the United States (e.g. Hartman, 1992). It tends to be easier to define effectiveness and efficiency in terms of appropriately targeted and equitable resource allocation than it is to relate them to tangible outcomes for students. This has certainly been true in the United Kingdom, where relating effectiveness to value for money, quality of provision or outcome has seldom been attempted (Lunt and Evans, 1994). Matters are changing, and attempts at assessing the 'value added' components of interventions, however crude they may currently be, are to be welcomed as a major shift in thinking.

A good example of the tendency until now to fund without evaluating the effectiveness of outcomes can be found in the DfEE (1997) statistic that the full-time equivalent of 24,000 unqualified assistants are currently used to support SEN in mainstream school. A conservative estimate of the cost of their direct employment gives us the entire education budgets of more than two London LEAs or, put another way, enough to fund more than five hundred primary (elementary) schools. Yet so far little has been done to determine how effective this resource – the one most commonly funded through Statements for mainstream children – is in achieving educational goals.

How special education is funded in the United States

In the United States, a varied and diverse mix of programmes and services was transformed into a national system of special education when the United States Congress passed the Education for All Handicapped Children Act (P.L. 94-142) in 1975. Ever since, the federal government has continued to provide important leadership in the formulation of special education policy. However, in terms of financial support it remains a junior partner to state and local levels of government. Special education in the United States is funded through a complex set of arrangements between the local, state, and federal levels of government, with the federal government providing about 8 per cent of total support and the residual being about equally funded by school districts and the states.

The special education count for the 1995/96 school year exceeded 5.6 million children of ages 3 to 21, with an additional 178,000 receiving services in ages birth to 2. The percentage of students receiving special education services has grown every year since the passage of the federal special education law in 1975 (Parrish *et al.*, 1997). On a state-by-state basis, however, this percentage varies considerably across the nation, with 10.7 per cent being identified in Massachusetts as compared to 5 per cent in Hawaii (US Department of Education, 1997a). These substantial differences across the states may be less indicative of variation in the incidence of children with disabilities across the states than of varying rules, regulations, and practices.

While expenditures for special education services in the United States are estimated to be about $32 billion, exact current expenditures are unknown (Parrish *et al.*, 1997). This is because the states were last required to report these amounts for the 1987/88 school year and because the last independent national special education cost study was based on data from the 1985/86 school year. This study showed that, on average, expenditures for students receiving special education services were 2.3 times greater than general education students (Moore *et al.*, 1988).

Federal funding

Federal funding is based on each state's count of children with disabilities who are receiving special education services. No distinction is made for variations in the types of disabilities or patterns of placement of special education children across the states. The number of school-age children who may be counted for federal funding purposes is limited to 12 per cent of the general school-age population. However, states and local school districts must provide special education programmes and services to all eligible children with disabilities.

State funding

The major responsibility for education in the United States rests with the states and localities, with all states having special provisions in their funding formulae that acknowledge the excess costs of special education. State special education funding formulae vary from reimbursing a fixed percentage of actual special education expenditures (eleven states), to pupil 'weighting' systems (nineteen states) in which special education students generate a fixed multiple of the general education pupil allocation (e.g. twice as much as is allocated to a general education students), to systems that directly fund special education teachers (ten states), to fixed dollar grants per student (ten states).

The relative state versus local shares of funding vary considerably across the states, with a number of states unable to identify the amount of local funds going to special education. However, the best estimates available suggest that the local share has been steadily growing over the past decade and that nationally the states and local shares of special education funding are about equal (Parrish *et al.*, 1997).

Reform issues at the federal level and across the states

A recently published overview of special education finance reform reports very high levels of reform activity with sixteen states having implemented some form of special education finance reform in the past five years and twenty-eight others considering major changes in their special education funding policies (Parrish *et al.*, 1997). In addition, the 1997 Amendments to the federal special education law (IDEA) included significant changes to its funding provisions. The following are some of the major issues driving these reforms.

Flexibility in placement and use

An important provision relating to flexibility in the use of state special education funds is whether these funds must be spent only on special education students. Such policies provide more fiscal accountability, but they also reduce local control. Currently, twenty-seven states report that their policies do not require that all special education funds be spent exclusively on special education students.

Rising special education costs and enrolments

Policy-makers in a number of states are expressing concern about rising special education costs and enrolments. In Pennsylvania, for example, the primary objectives of reform were stabilising special education costs and enrolment and the promotion of 'best practice'. Previously, Pennsylvania was the only state that provided 100 per cent of the 'excess cost' of educating children with disabilities.

Encroachment

Concerns about continuing growth in special education enrolments have led to increased concerns about whether special education 'encroaches' on regular education expenditures, and if so, to what extent. Several studies (e.g. Lankford and Wyckoff, 1995; Rothstein and Miles, 1995), have produced data that suggest that substantial encroachment is occurring.

A closer examination of potential encroachment, however, does not allow such a clear conclusion. For example, what is 'regular' as opposed to 'special' education? Rather than discrete activities, these are complementary programmes designed to provide education to America's schoolchildren. Prior to the passage of the federal IDEA law, students now being served in special education were often receiving comparable services as a part of their general education. Thus, the question of encroachment is more complex than it seems at first. It requires a comparison of the cost of the additional services school systems provide in relation to the additional revenues raised for these purposes. More research is needed to better understand the extent of special education encroachment.

Concerns over the efficiency of special education services

Studies have shown that only about 62 per cent of the special education dollar is being used to provide instructional programmes to students (Moore *et al.*, 1988, p. 69). As a result, questions are raised about whether too much is being spent on such support activities as student assessment and programme administration. For example, the average special education assessment is estimated to cost $1,700 in current dollars (Moore *et al.*, 1988 as reported in Parrish, *et al.*, 1997, p. 49). These assessments are primarily used to determine whether a student does or does not qualify for special education services. After a student is placed in special education, teachers often report that their first activity is to reassess the student to determine their instructional needs because eligibility assessments are not useful for this purpose (Shields *et al.*, 1989). This raises questions about the usefulness of such assessments for students who are determined to be ineligible for special education services, as well as for many students who are deemed eligible.

Strict categorical nature of special education services

Categorical funding refers to dollars allocated for a specific purpose which generally have strict limitations on use. An important issue in special education finance is how strict these controls should remain. For example, as noted by a former Director of Special Education in Florida, 'When over one-half of our students qualify for at least one type of special, categorical program, it is no longer clear that it makes sense to refer to them as special.'[1]

Fiscal policies that work at cross purposes with special education inclusion policies

Questions are increasingly being raised about the relationship between segregated placement patterns and special education funding policies. An extreme example, recently reported for New York State, was based on a

12-year-old student with disabilities, who at the beginning of each week travelled for over an hour to get to the local airport to be flown to a special residential placement located at the opposite side of the state. At the end of the week, he again travelled this route, at a cost to the state in excess of $100,000 per year. This continued despite the obvious difficulties for the child and arguments presented by the child's district of residence that they could provide appropriate services at much less cost.

'Adequacy' determination for all children

In addition to questions of encroachment, a related question is whether too much is being spent on special education overall in relation to what general education students receive. While clearly a subjective question to which no clear answer can be provided, conflict may be inherent in the fact that an entitlement to an appropriate education is uniquely granted to special educa-tion children. While the United States courts have not ruled on this question directly, they have been approaching it indirectly over the past ten to twenty years. While early school finance litigation in the United States focused primarily on equity issues, the relative adequacy of the services being pro-vided has always been a complementary theme and as of late has become more predominant (Verstegen, 1998).

Federal and state fiscal reform initiatives

Federal reform

Important changes related to funding were made to the Individuals with Disabilities Education Act (IDEA) when it was reauthorised in 1997. When federal appropriations exceed the 'trigger' amount of $4.9 plus billion (expected to occur sometime after 1999), a new federal allocation formula will take effect. States will continue to receive a base amount of funding equal to their award in the year prior to this 'trigger' appropriation being reached. Beyond this base year amount, 85 per cent of funds will be dis-tributed based on states' relative share of the entire school-aged population and 15 per cent of the funds based on states' relative share of school-aged children living in poverty. This movement away from funding based solely on the number of students identified as requiring special education, toward criteria which are beyond district control (i.e. the total population of students and the percentages in poverty) represents an important new direction in special education funding policy across the states.

A second important provision of the reauthorisation pertains to a concept known as 'placement neutrality'. This requires states with funding formulas distributing assistance to LEAs based on the type of setting in which a child is served to have policies and procedures for assuring that their funding provisions do not result in an undue number of restrictive placements for students. Fiscal incentives promoting restrictive (i.e. more isolated) placements violate the least restrictive environment (LRE) requirement of the IDEA. This new requirement could affect about one-quarter of the states, whose special education funding systems are based primarily on placement, or with subsidiary provisions based on placement, such as additional funding for students served in separate schools or institutions.

Another federal change allows non-disabled students to benefit from special education services being provided for children with disabilities. Prior to this change, federally funded special education teachers could not easily serve children with disabilities in groups that included non-disabled students. Under new provisions, this type of 'incidental benefit' to non-disabled students is allowed.

State reform

Over the past decade, several of the nation's largest states have adopted census-based special education funding (i.e., formulae based on total district enrolment rather than counts of special education students) similar to that recently adopted for federal special education funding, as described above. These include California, Massachusetts and Pennsylvania. Other states that have adopted census-based special education funding models include Montana, North Dakota, Alabama, and Vermont.

However, this reform has not been embraced by all of the states considering it. After lengthy deliberations, Illinois decided against such a system. New York also completed the design for such a system several years ago, but so far has failed to adopt it.

In Alabama, the State Supreme Court found that their state's census-based formula violated the equal protection clause of the state constitution because under such a system, districts with higher percentages of special education students received lower levels of special education funding per child. However, the Alabama court also refused to endorse the major finance alternatives to a census-based system, expressing concerns that they may produce incentives to over identify special education children or to place them in more restrictive settings.

As a state that adopted a census-based funding approach in 1997, and addressed the issue of differing incidence rates of 'severe and/or high cost' students across districts in 1998, California provides an interesting case study for other states to consider. With the passing of the Poochigian and Davis Special Education Reform Act of 1997, California special education funding changed from a resource-based model to a census-based model.[2] Under the old approach, funding was linked directly to 'units' of special education services received and programmes provided at the special education local plan area (SELPA) level. Much criticism had been levied toward the old funding model on the grounds that it was inequitable, created incentives to place students in special education programmes, was complex, and inflexible regarding where children could be served.

According to the new law, the reform was enacted for five principal reasons: (1) to ensure greater equity in funding among SELPAs; (2) to eliminate financial incentives to inappropriately place pupils in special education programmes; (3) to enhance funding flexibility at the SELPA level; (4) to require fiscal and programme accountability; and (5) to create a funding formula that is understandable and avoids unnecessary complexity. This landmark legislation was approved with the recognition that questions relating to varying incidence rates of 'severe and/or high cost' students still needed to be addressed. In response, a study was commissioned to determine if these incidence levels are unevenly distributed across the state, and if so to recommend methods to adjust the census-based funding formula to allow for these variations (Parrish *et al.*, 1998).

Despite the considerable difficulties noted by the study team, they were able to derive several working definitions of 'severe and/or high cost' students. Based on these definitions, and using data from the state's student-level file, they were able to show with a high degree of statistical confidence that 'severe and/or high cost' students are not randomly distributed throughout the state, and therefore that some form of severity adjustment to the state's overall census-based formula was justified. Based on prior patterns of service, a 'severity service' funding factor was developed which provides supplemental funding to districts that have historically served larger proportions of 'severe and/or high cost' students. Importantly, these adjustments were based on prior district practices and will not be updated for at least five years with the intent of removing fiscal incentives to identify higher percentages of 'severe and/or high cost' students or to over provide extensive services.

While it will not be easy to replicate, the general direction of this approach may point the way for other states attempting to resolve the dilemma facing other states wishing to adopt census-based funding approaches. Census-based systems have considerable appeal because they provide local flexibility without creating local incentives for increased identification and escalating service provision. On the other hand, they can only be considered equitable if it is believed that the incidence of students with disabilities are fairly evenly distributed across school districts. The California severity adjustment provides one approach to having both a census base and adjustments for districts that are quite different from the norm in terms of the numbers of 'severe and/or high cost' students.

The final details of these new funding provisions are not yet finalised. Will they be well accepted after implementation? Will they result in unintended deleterious consequences? Can they be replicated in other states or jurisdictions without the types of detailed student-level information available at the state level in California? Despite these questions and limitations, however, a new approach to modifying census-based systems has been introduced that may have the potential to address some of the concerns commonly associated with census-based funding as well as the types of constitutional issues raised by the Alabama Supreme Court.

A look to the future

The birth to 21 special education population has consistently grown at a faster rate than the overall resident population for this age group. For example, during a ten-year span starting with the 1985/86 school year, the resident population grew by 4.3 per cent in the birth to 21 age group, while the number of special education children increased by 28.7 per cent (Parrish et al., 1997). Add to this the projection that total school enrolments will grow by approximately 2 per cent over the next ten years (US Department of Education, 1997b) and the estimate that special education expenditures per student have been growing at a faster rate than general education expenditures (Parrish et al., 1997), and it is not hard to imagine continuing strains on special education budgets over the next decade.

Current interest in special education finance reform is likely to continue and focus on efforts to increase the effectiveness of, as well as to contain expenditures on, programmes for children with disabilities. As states continue to control state-level expenditures on special education, but fail to develop service standards or other forms of limits useful to local districts in attempting to control their costs, pressures on local districts and concerns about general education encroachment are likely to escalate. These trends suggest the need for change in state and federal special education policy.

These changes may become even more necessary, given the increasing public demand for demonstrating education results. School districts across the nation will need to find ways to make better use of financial resources in the provision of services for all students. Although additional state and federal support will undoubtedly be needed, substantial enhancements in funding alone may not lead to the best policy solutions. States reporting the most success in co-ordinating programme and fiscal reform emphasise the need for financial incentives, as well as the provision of a comprehensive system of professional development and ongoing support, to effect desired change.

Conclusion

Although there are important differences in the identification and funding of services for children with disabilities or SEN between the United States and England and Wales, many of the underlying policy concerns appear quite similar. A major difference in the overall identification of students with special needs and the degree of entitlement they are provided is evidenced by the 3 per cent identification rate in England and Wales, as opposed to a 10.6 per cent identification rate for students aged 6 to 17 in the United States (US Department of Education, 1997a, p. A-33). Children with more common disabilities (e.g. students with learning disabilities in the United States) are in school-based 'stages' in England and Wales. While many of these children would be identified for special education and placed on an individualized education program (IEP) in the United States, these children generally do not receive such legal entitlements in England and Wales.

Despite these differences, however, there are many similarities in terms of current issues and the range of policy solutions being considered. These include issues of controlling growth, difficulties in making distinctions between categories of students and the levels of services to which they are entitled, and the need to foster greater trust between service providers and parents. The dilemma of overgrazing, with which this chapter began, is an apt parable for considering some of the most salient special education issues in the United States, as well as in England and Wales. As noted earlier, 'On both sides of the Atlantic, the "commons" of education spending are seen in danger of being overgrazed by those claiming . . . the right to additional resources for particular children or groups of children.' In the United States, concern with over-identification and over-spending special education are major factors causing the federal government as well as a growing number of states to move to census-based funding systems. Under virtually all other special education funding systems in the United States the amount of revenues received is based either directly or indirectly on the numbers of students identified for special education. Thus, there appears to be a clear fiscal incentive to identify special education students to receive these supplemental services and thereby qualify the school district for additional funds. Under census-based systems, the amount of funding received is not based on the number of students identified for special education, but on some overall measure of jurisdiction size, e.g. total student enrolment or total school age population.

Census-based funding systems are seen as one way of limiting the growth of special education funding. An agreeable funding level can be pre-specified by the governing entity with sub-allocations being based on factors independent of local choices or behaviours. However, as noted in the first part of this chapter, this kind of flattening of funding differentials has not been adopted in England and Wales, and appears unlikely for the near future. Where it has been tried in the United States, there is relatively little evidence that this change in fiscal policy alone leads to more creative and flexible ways of serving children with disabilities or serves to curb rates of identification or total expenditure. The state of Massachusetts, for example, adopted a census-based system several years ago and for a number of years prior to this had a virtual freeze on supplemental special education funding for individual school districts. Despite this, Massachusetts continues to identify students for special education at a highest rate of any state. In addition, most states place limits on the percentage of students eligible for special education funding. For example, at the federal level a limit of 12 per cent of all students can be claimed for funding purposes, and under California's old special education system there was a 10 per cent cap. Thus, in this sense, access to the 'commons' has long been limited in the United States. While these policies may have controlled growth in relation to what it would have been, they have failed to stem the long-standing steady growth in special education identification and spending.

Another important similarity as viewed from both sides of the Atlantic is the struggle of how to best differentiate among varying levels of severity in disability. In England and Wales a clear line of demarcation is attempted by placing only the most severe students on Statements (approximately 3 per cent of the population). Only these students have the types of legal guarantees and entitlements afforded all special education children in the United States (10.6 per cent of the population). However, the considerable pressure to place more students on Statements in England and Wales has been noted, with a nearly 60 per cent increase in this count of students over the past five years.

The United States has also struggled with alternative methods for differentiating funding based on the degree of student need. Old funding conventions (e.g. disability category or type of placement) have increasingly been seen as problematic because of fiscal incentives to place students in higher funded categories. States continue to look to factors that are not within district control to serve as proxies for the relative needs of the population served. As described above, California has adopted a system based on prior patterns of more intensive service delivery. Florida is implementing a system based on a typology of student characteristics. At the federal level, the selected severity proxy is the percentage of children living in poverty. England and Wales also use external criteria as bases for allocating special education funds. As noted, 92 per cent of the LEAs use poverty as one criterion. Another commonly used criterion is test results. An interesting approach used in England and Wales, but not in the United States, is for the LEA to perform school-by-school audits of students' special needs. While IEPs are reviewed in the United States through standard monitoring procedures, routine 'audits' of student records to assess over or under identification as a basis for adjusting and monitoring funding is not common.

The use of audits is also not as common in England and Wales as other criteria for adjusting funding (e.g. student poverty). However, selected use of this approach may gain wider appeal in England and Wales, and perhaps even in the United States. Although labour intensive, and therefore costly, it holds the advantage of actually measuring that which we are attempting to adjust (i.e. students' relative need for services). Unlike other measures outside local control (and therefore containing no incentives for certain kinds of local behaviours), it is a direct rather than a proxy measure. For example, a problem with the use of student poverty as a basis for adjusting special education funding, the most common proxy measure used in England and Wales and by the federal government in the United States, is that it is not that well correlated with variations in the degree of special services required by students with disabilities, as described earlier in this chapter.

Because of its high cost, however, student audits may be most useful when used on a 'spot check', or targeted, basis. For example, under California's new severity service adjustment, a relatively small number of districts are singled out for supplemental funding because they have traditionally provided unusually high levels of service to a relatively large number of special needs children. Supplemental funding is awarded on the assumption that these districts have unusually high proportions of students requiring these intensive services. However, it may be that their students are the same as in all other districts and that, in fact, they are just more willing or able to provide higher levels of services. If the former is true (i.e. the conditions they face are different), supplemental funding to compensate for this appears warranted. If they simply choose to provide more, however, and the mix of children they serve is really like that in other districts, the argument for supplemental support is substantially weakened. Once these districts are singled out for supplemental funding, perhaps the only way to tell the difference is the selective use of the type of student audits used in England and Wales.

Another area in which the United States may learn from the experience of England and Wales is in free market solutions to education reform. As described above, England and Wales have increasingly moved toward a system under which schools are funded based on the numbers of pupils they can attract. While this movement appears to be fuelling special education counts in schools because of the relatively higher levels of funding associated with these students, a primary concern in the United States is that under such a system of school choice many schools may opt out of serving children with special needs. Perhaps this depends on the details of how such schools are funded, but the movement toward flat funding for special education students appears largely predicated on the notion of a relatively standard distribution across jurisdictions of students with special needs. Given this, it seems likely that these kinds of flat special education funding systems may conflict with the types of free market schooling models commonly found in England and Wales, and which are spreading in popularity in the United States.

A common theme shared by the two of us, as we collaborated on this chapter, is the importance of finding ways to foster trust between the families of children with disabilities and special education providers, as the basis for more co-operative and collaborative services. This is undoubtedly important to improving the effectiveness and the efficiency of overall education, as well as special education, systems. This will not be easy, and in fact the parable of the commons suggests that some of the reasons for these conflicts are to a large extent inherent to current systems of provision.

All parents want a high-quality education for their children. The most effective way to reduce the demand for special education is to enhance general education. Conversely, the more general education is perceived to be inadequate to meet children's needs, the greater the demand for special education. If this growing demand draws resources from general education, we may be caught in a vicious cycle in which general education will continue to decline and special education demand will continue to grow. This type of cyclical progression appears to be a concern on both sides of the Atlantic. Irrespective of national boundaries and funding systems, an important key appears to be a serious reconsideration of programme effectiveness and efficiency. As previously described, if concepts of 'effective' or 'efficient' use of funds continue to be simply defined in terms of reducing costs, or holding the lid on rising costs, we will continue to fail to gain the efficiencies needed to provide higher-quality education services in a world of finite resources.

To control spiralling costs, it seems imperative that we become more efficient in the use of resources on hand. Attempts to relate effectiveness in education to relative value for money as measured in terms of student outcomes is a relatively new concept in education. Rudimentary attempts at assessing the 'value added' component of interventions have begun in England and Wales. In the United States, a new emphasis on student outcomes is embedded in federal policy under the reauthorised IDEA, and federal and state policy-makers are struggling with the development of new paradigms to encourage shifts in monitoring and programme oversight away from procedural concerns to a new emphasis on student outcomes.

Funding arrangements for special educational needs have to be seen as part of the greater picture. How we define needs and the extent to which they become apparent will be determined by the shape of regular education and the various incentives and disincentives which are offered to parents and schools within that framework. In the United Kingdom context there is little to indicate that the pressure to spend more on special educational needs, whether in mainstream or specialist schools, will abate. Without deep structural change, which seems unlikely, systematic attempts at collaboration between the parties to this complex social dilemma appear to hold out the best prospect of moving forward. As we have seen, research into achieving successful outcomes to such dilemmas suggests that trusts between parties is an important prerequisite of such outcomes. Poor communication, the dismissing of legitimate concerns and an increasing obsession with achieving financial targets may all have a cost and this is ultimately reflected in the funding dilemmas with which local and central government are confronted.

Future challenges on both sides of the Atlantic are formidable – controlling costs while enhancing performance. It seems clear, however, that the similarities in policy issues confronting England, Wales, and the United States have much more in common than not. For the sake of enhanced efficiency, it will be important for us to be aware of what is occurring on both sides of the Atlantic so as to share learning and provide assistance to the greatest possible degree.

Notes

1 Address given to Florida Futures Conference held in Tampa, FL, 16–17 September, 1994. Note that this reference to 'special, categorical' programmes extends beyond special education to include such programmes as compensatory (poverty), limited-English proficient, and gifted education programmes.
2 California Assemble Bill 602, Chapter 854, Statutes of 1997, approved and filed October 10, 1997.

References

Audit Commission (1992) *Getting in on the Act*, London: HMSO.

Bixentine, V.E., Levitt, C.A. and Wilson, K.V. (1966) 'Collaboration among six persons in a prisoner's dilemma game', *Journal of Conflict Resolution*, 10: 488–496.

Bowers, T. (1991) 'Issues in marketing', in T. Bowers (ed.) *Schools, Services and Special Educational Needs: Management Issues in the Wake of LMS*, Cambridge: Perspective Press.

—— (1995) 'Parents, partnership and education officers: a study of attributions', *Child: Care, Health and Development*, 21: 135–148.

—— (1996) 'Is special needs spending out of control?', *Managing Schools Today*, 5,7: 33–36.

—— (1997) 'Co-ordinator or curator?', *Special Children*, 106 (Policy in Practice Supplement): 1–6.

Brann and Foddy (1987) 'Trust and the consumption of the deteriorating common resource', *Journal of Conflict Resolution*, 31,4: 615–630.

Coopers and Lybrand (1996) *The SEN Initiative: Managing Budgets for Pupils with Special Educational Needs*, London: Coopers & Lybrand.

Dempsey, S. and Fuchs, D. (1993) 'Flat' versus 'weighted' reimbursement formulas: a longitudinal analysis of statewide special education funding practices', *Exceptional Children*, 59: 433–443.

Department for Education (DfE) (1994) *Code of Practice on the Identification and Assessment of Special Educational Needs*, London: DfE.

Department of Education and Employment (DfEE) (1997) *Excellence for all Children*, London: Stationery Office.

Fletcher-Campbell, F. (1996) *The Resourcing of Special Educational Needs*, Slough: NFER.

Hardin, G. (1968) 'The tragedy of the commons', *Science*, 162: 1243–1248.

Hartman, W.T. (1992) 'State funding models for special education', *Remedial and Special Education*, 13,6: 47–58.

Lankford, H. and Wyckoff, J. (1995) 'Where has the money gone? An analysis of school district spending in New York', *Educational Evaluation and Policy Analysis*, 17,2: EJ511052.

Lopes, L.L. (1994) 'Psychology and economics: perspectives on risk, cooperation and the marketplace', *Annual Review of Psychology*, 45: 197–227.

Lunt, I. and Evans, J. (1994) 'Dilemmas in special educational needs: some effects of local management of schools', in S. Riddell and S. Brown (eds) *Special Needs Policies in the 1990s*, London: Routledge.

McDonnell, V. (1997) 'SENgate: reality or myth?', *Special Children*, 106: 26–28.

Marsh, A.J. (1995) 'The effects on school budgets of different non-statemented special educational needs indicators within a common funding formula', *British Educational Research Journal*, 21: 99–115.

—— (1997) *Current Practice for Resourcing Additional Educational Needs in Local Education Authorities*, Slough: NFER.

Messick, D.M. and Brewer, M.B. (1983) 'Solving social dilemmas', *Review of Personality and Social Psychology*, 4: 11–44.

Moore, M.T., Strang, E.W., Schwartz, M. and Braddock, M. (1988) *Patterns in Special Education Service Delivery and Cost*, Washington, DC: Decision Resources Corporation.

Parrish, T. (1997) *Special Education Finance*, Washington, DC: Federal Resource Center for Special Education.

Parrish, T., Kaleba, D., Gerber, M. and McLaughlin, M. (1998) *Special Education: Study of Incidence of Disabilities – Final Report*, Palo Alto, CA: American Institutes for Research.

Parrish, T.B., O'Reilly, F.E., Dueñas, I.E. and Wolman, J.M. (1997) *State Special Education Finance Systems, 1994–95*, Palo Alto, CA: American Institutes for Research, Center for Special Education Finance. ED409669.

Poppe, M. and Utens, L. (1986) 'Effects of greed and fear of being gypped in a social dilemma situation with changing pool size', *Journal of Economic Psychology*, 7: 61–73.

Rapoport, A. and Eshed-Levy, D. (1989) 'Provision of step-level public goods: effects of greed and fear of being gypped', *Organizational Behavior and Human Decision Processes*, 44: 325–344.

Rothstein, R. and Miles, K.H. (1995) *Where Has the Money Gone? Changes in the Level and Composition of Education Spending*, Washington, DC: Economic Policy Institute. ED396422.

Shields, P.M., Jay, D.E., Parrish, T. and Padilla, C. (1989) *Alternative Programs and Strategies for Serving Students with Leaning Disabilities and Other Learning Problems – Final Report*, Menlo Park, CA: SRI International.

Smith, A. (1776) *An Inquiry into the Nature and Causes of the Wealth of Nations*, reprinted 1976, Chicago, IL: University of Chicago Press.

Special Educational Needs Tribunal (1997) *Annual Report 1996–7*, London: SEN Tribunal.

—— (1998) *Annual Report 1997–8*, London: SEN Tribunal.

US Department of Education (1997a) *Nineteenth annual report to Congress on the implementation of the Individuals with Disabilities Education Act*, Washington, DC: US Department of Education.

US Department of Education, National Center for Education Statistics (1997b) *Projections of Education Statistics to 2008*, NCES 98–016, by Debra E. Gerald and William J. Hussar. Washington, DC.

Verstegen, D.A. (1998) 'Civil Rights and Disability Policy: A Historical Perspective', in T. Parrish, J. Chambers, and C. Guarino (eds) *Funding Special Education (1998 AEFA Yearbook)*, Thousand Oaks, CA: Corwin Press.

Wright, J. (1997) 'SENgate', *Special Children*, 104: 14–17.

Index